Assessing Needs in Continuing Education

Donna S. Queeney

Assessing Needs in Continuing Education

An Essential Tool for Quality Improvement

Jossey-Bass Publishers • San Francisco

Substantial discounts on bulk quantities of Jossey-Bass books are
available to corporations, professional associations, and other
organizations. For details and discount information, contact the
special sales department at Jossey-Bass Inc., Publishers.
(415) 433–1740; Fax (415) 433–0499.

For sales outside the United States, please contact your local
Paramount Publishing International Office.

TCF Manufactured in the United States of America on Lyons Falls
     Pathfinder Tradebook. This paper is acid-free and 100 percent
totally chlorine-free.

Library of Congress Cataloging-in-Publication Data

Queeney, Donna S., date.
 Assessing needs in continuing education : an essential tool for quality
improvement / Donna S. Queeney. — 1st ed.
 p. cm. — (Jossey-Bass higher and adult education series)
 Includes bibliographical references (p.) and index.
 ISBN 0-7879-0059-1
 1. Continuing education—Evaluation. 2. Needs assessment. I. Title.
II. Series.
LC5219.Q84   1995
374—dc20   94-37102
                                                                CIP

FIRST EDITION
HB Printing   10 9 8 7 6 5 4 3 2 1   Code 9516

The Jossey-Bass Higher and

Adult Education Series

Consulting Editor

Adult and Continuing Education

Alan B. Knox

University of Wisconsin, Madison

Contents

Preface

As continuing educators, we strive to meet the educational needs of our clients—primarily adult students whose needs are not met by the standard programs offered for students of traditional age. Our role is to design, develop, and deliver high-quality educational activities that provide the information these clients need, in ways that make it easy for them to acquire and use it. Because we are motivated by a variety of goals, we define success in different ways, ranging from participants' improved performance to revenue generation. Whatever our purpose, needs assessment can help us achieve it by providing information that enables us to offer programs that meet our definition of success. Whether we are based in institutions of higher education, business or industry, community education or recreation departments, professional associations, social service agencies, or other for-profit or nonprofit organizations, needs assessment is a diagnostic tool that can help us. Because needs assessment can provide information that allows us to tailor educational activities to our clients, it can make the difference between programming that meets minimum standards and excellent programming that delights those we serve.

Assessing Needs in Continuing Education is intended to increase continuing educators' comfort with needs assessment and enable them to venture into it with confidence. The book will not make experts of its readers, but it will give continuing educators the information they require to conduct at least some types of needs assessments. The emphasis is on basic information for continuing educators who, despite considerable experience in the design, development, and delivery of programs, have little or no background in this area. More advanced forms of needs assessment are introduced as well, for those who are ready to move beyond the fundamentals.

Unfortunately, much of continuing education has lacked a coherent, comprehensive process for program development. Needs assessment, a much-promoted and little-practiced activity within continuing education, has often been the missing component. Frequently an educational activity has been offered for no reason other than someone's belief that it is a good idea. Many programs springing from such humble beginnings have been quite successful in meeting continuing educators' goals, but many others have failed. In some cases, the failures have resulted in cancellation of activities, which always has a negative effect on the balance sheet. In other cases, the activities have been delivered, but participants have not benefited from them as anticipated.

As economic constraints have increased during the 1980s and 1990s, continuing educators and those they serve have found their ability and willingness to tolerate such failures waning. Faced with escalating costs and diminishing budgets, they no longer can afford the financial losses that so often accompany program failures. Individual clients, requiring updated or new skills to succeed in a tight and increasingly technical job market, cannot waste limited resources on education that will not give them the knowledge, skills, and performance abilities they need. Employers, professional associations, and other organizational continuing education clients want to spend their education dollars wisely. All these people want some assurance that an educational activity will do what it claims it will. Although needs assessment cannot guarantee the success of any venture, it can provide information that when properly used can greatly increase the likelihood that an educational activity will meet its intended goals.

Yet most continuing educators shy away from needs assessment, perhaps believing that it is an extra step that can be skipped and will scarcely be missed. They may think of it as a luxury they cannot afford, or they may be leery of it because it conjures up images of research and many of them do not have strong research backgrounds or skills. But for the continuing educator who is contemplating large programs or programs to be offered repeatedly, who is expecting to serve a specific audience over time, or who is seeking new audiences or content areas, needs assessment is not a luxury but a necessity. And those committed to continuous quality improvement in continuing education will recognize that needs assessment is an essential component of the planning process, for it helps define the ways in which clients can best be served.

Although it is true that needs assessment can be elaborate and costly, it also can be simplified, conducted in a manner that puts it within the reach of any continuing educator's resources. Perhaps the greatest misconception about needs assessment is that it must be conducted at the most rigorous level to be effective. This simply is not the case. Valuable data can be obtained from the most elementary needs assessments—such as focus groups and supervisor interviews—if they are well planned and carried out with thoroughness, care, and attention to detail. Because a well-executed needs assessment at any level will yield good information, conducting even a simple needs assessment is better than conducting none at all. Any needs assessment can contribute to the ability to make data-based, rather than data-free, programming decisions. The data obtained can assist in identifying a target population, selecting focus and content, choosing appropriate instructional methods and delivery formats, and scheduling activities. There is one requirement, however. If needs assessment is to realize its potential as a useful tool, continuing educators and others associated with the process must be committed to accepting the results even if these results run counter to their individual expectations, beliefs, and prejudices.

Continuing educators are encouraged to recognize that just as they do not develop programs in isolation, whenever possible they should not expect to conduct needs assessments alone. It is strongly recommended that educators form a needs assessment team made up of individuals with experience and expertise that complement their own. Whether formally or loosely structured, this group can provide guidance in planning needs assessment and help gain access to the assistance and resources required to conduct the assessment itself.

Overview of the Contents

In preparing *Assessing Needs in Continuing Education*, I attempted to focus on providing my fellow continuing educators with a systematic yet pragmatic overview of needs assessment as a means of answering the question, Whom should I be serving, and with what continuing education programs? Thus this book has a practical rather than a philosophical or historical orientation. I refer to the conceptual bases of needs assessment when they help strengthen the discussion, but I have not attempted to provide a comprehensive recapitulation of the underlying theory.

The book begins with a definition and description of needs assessment as part of the process of developing a continuing education program. Chapter One describes the role of needs assessment in identifying discrepancies between existing and desired proficiencies and establishes the distinction between needs, wants, and demands. It makes the point that needs assessment does not have to be complex or costly, but it does have to be carefully planned and executed in order to yield useful data. I explain the difference between a single needs assessment exercise and a needs assessment strategy, and the ways in which such a strategy can be planned to incorporate several exercises over a period of time. I also discuss reasons for conducting a needs assessment, the limitations of needs assessments, and differences between needs assessment and competency assessment.

Chapter Two identifies several factors to be considered in planning and conducting a needs assessment, including organizational priorities. It explains that needs are assessed for many different purposes, the most common being to identify target populations and content areas for educational activities. The chapter also sets forth considerations for determining the scope, target population, and level of complexity for an assessment and includes a frank discussion of funding considerations.

Chapters Three and Four focus on choosing the topic of a needs assessment and selecting one or more methods with which to accomplish the assessment. Chapter Three defines knowledge, skills, and performance abilities and describes the types of needs for which assessments can be conducted. The emphasis is on establishing priorities, standards, and content areas. Chapter Four details the benefits and shortcomings of both individual and group assessments and discusses how to identify a target population for the assessment. The chapter provides criteria for selecting specific needs assessment methods and encourages the use of a team approach to needs assessment.

Chapters Five, Six, and Seven describe specific needs assessment methods in some detail. Chapter Five focuses on basic methods that can be implemented with minimal experience, expertise, and resources, including self-reports, focus group and nominal group processes, the Delphi process, the use of key informants, and supervisor evaluations. Surveys, including both questionnaires and interviews, are the subject of Chapter Six; the issues of how to structure questions and how to create a survey methodology are given considerable attention. Chapter Seven, devoted to performance assessment, covers more sophisticated assessment methods. These methods, by and large, demand not only ample resources but also considerable expertise.

Chapter Eight addresses the role in the broader program planning process of needs assessment and the data obtained through it. The chapter includes guidelines for interpreting and reporting needs assessment data, outlines the topics to be covered in a report, and emphasizes the importance of a positive approach to presenting the data. I point out the necessity of translating assessment data into educational objectives, and the potential for using the data to market the resulting continuing education activities.

Evaluating the success of educational activities, a process that begins with identifying educational goals by assessing needs, is the topic of Chapter Nine. The discussion stresses recognizing evaluation as the final step in program development and gives specific suggestions for its use. I explain that many of the needs assessment methods described in the preceding chapters also are appropriate for evaluating program effectiveness, and suggest ways of adapting them for this purpose.

Chapter Ten places needs assessment in the context of the continuing educator's organization. Such an assessment is not an isolated event but should be viewed in light of organizational missions and priorities. Readers will find suggestions for integrating needs assessment in continuing education into the structure of the parent organization to make it an ongoing part of the organization's operations.

Audience

Continuing educators and trainers involved in program design, development, and delivery, regardless of their practice settings or the audiences they serve, are the intended audience for this book. I have assumed some understanding of continuing education but little familiarity with needs assessment.

Whether they provide lifelong education for health care professionals or teachers, enrichment activities for senior citizens, or on-site workforce training, continuing educators can best meet their goals if they routinely incorporate needs assessment into the program development process. Educators who are eager to increase the breadth and depth of current offerings, extend services to new audiences, meet the challenges of new goals, strengthen faltering programs, or shift their missions in new directions will find that needs assessment can help them attain their objectives and, in short, increase the likelihood that educational offerings will satisfy both clients and providers.

Moreover, the needs assessment principles I describe for continuing education differ little from those which might be employed in other areas of postsecondary education. Thus college and university faculty, administrators, and staff members may also find this book useful in planning programs.

Because my own primary area of interest is continuing professional education—and indeed much of continuing education is continuing professional education—many examples are taken from that arena. However, the practices discussed are applicable in any continuing education setting.

Programs to improve professional skills, like those for personal enrichment, are offered in a wide range of settings, all of which can be well served by needs assessment. Within the arena of continuing professional education, the ongoing debate over the value of continuing education in maintaining competence and improving professional practice has increased the emphasis on needs assessment. Coupled with program evaluation, needs assessment has the potential to enable continuing educators to document the effectiveness of continuing professional education.

Continuing educators in all practice settings are being called upon to respond to an expanding variety, complexity, and number of educational needs, and to do so with diminishing resources. Needs assessment can help meet the challenge.

Acknowledgments

A good number of people contributed both directly and indirectly to this book, beginning with the late Floyd Fischer who, in offering me a position at The Pennsylvania State University, provided me with an opportunity to learn about and practice needs assessment from the ground up. Through numerous projects and over two decades, professional colleagues, including Douglas Bray, Samuel Dubin, Morris Keeton, Carrie Lenburg, Carl Lindsay, Philip Nowlen, Benjamin Shimberg, and Wayne Smutz, have expanded my understanding of the topic.

Special thanks are due several people at Jossey-Bass. Lynn Luckow, now president, was the one who initially invited and encouraged me to write this book. Alan Knox, consulting editor, and Gale Erlandson, senior editor of the Jossey-Bass Higher and Adult Education Series, provided invaluable guidance and highly constructive criticism. As editorial assistant, Ann Richardson gave welcome encouragement, support, and friendship during my preparation of the manuscript. Through their detailed and thoughtful comments, the three anonymous reviewers and senior production editor Susan Abel facilitated substantial improvements in the text.

I also am indebted to several Penn State colleagues who provided practical assistance. Deborah Klevans, who reviewed the first draft, and Ellen Campbell, who reviewed the revised version, both supplied valuable insights, suggestions, and support. Without Sandra Rothrock, this book would not have become a reality, for it was she who took full responsibility for putting the manuscript into the format requested by the publisher.

Finally, I am most grateful for the enthusiastic support of my husband, Richard, whose consistent encouragement of my professional endeavors has motivated me not only during the completion of this book but throughout my career.

State College, Pennsylvania   Donna S. Queeney
December 1994

The Author

Donna S. Queeney is director of research and external relations for Continuing and Distance Education and a faculty member in adult education at The Pennsylvania State University. She received her B.A. degree (1963) in liberal arts and her M.S. and Ph.D. degrees (1965 and 1967, respectively) in human development, all from The Pennsylvania State University.

As staff member and then as director of Planning Studies at Penn State, Queeney gained thirteen years' experience assessing the educational needs of a wide variety of populations served by the resident and continuing education programs at Penn State's many campuses. In addition, she was assistant director of the Continuing Professional Education Development Project, sponsored jointly by the W. K. Kellogg Foundation, Penn State, and fourteen state and national professional associations in the 1980s. The project devised and implemented the Practice Audit Model, a needs assessment and program development process for designing, developing, and delivering practice-oriented continuing professional education.

Queeney is the author of numerous book chapters and research articles, primarily on continuing professional education. She served as coordinator of the national consortium of continuing professional education projects in the 1980s (funded by the W. K. Kellogg Foundation), chairing that group's two conferences, A Call to Action and An Agenda for Action, and editing a series of reports that resulted from the latter. She is cofounder and co-director of the Leadership Institute for Continuing Professional Education, jointly sponsored by Penn State and Harvard University, and has served since 1985 as editor of the *Journal of Continuing Higher Education* and since 1982 as a member of the editorial board of the *Continuing Higher Education Review* (formerly *Continuum*). She is a frequent speaker on continuing professional education, needs assessment, and interorganizational collaboration.

Chapter One

What Is Needs Assessment?

A few years ago a university continuing education unit, in collaboration with that institution's nursing department, offered a workshop on patient assessment for nurses providing direct patient care in acute and long-term care facilities. Program participants were enthusiastic about the new documentation method that was introduced, remarking that it would simplify the patient assessment process and permit them to focus on their patients rather than on the paperwork. However, upon returning to their practice settings, most participants found that the institutions where they worked were not receptive to the new method, claiming it was incompatible with other procedures already in place. Thus the workshop resulted in dissatisfied clients. Although the program itself was well received, the participants could not use what they had learned in their daily practice as they had hoped to do. Those who attended the workshop, the employers who paid for their participation, the continuing education unit, and the nursing department were all frustrated. The problem could be traced directly to one factor: in developing the workshop, no attempt had been made to assess potential participants' needs. Had even a simple needs assessment been conducted, program planners could have learned of the limitations imposed by the practice settings in which the program participants worked and developed the content of the workshop to accommodate those limitations rather than introduce information that would be of no use to the people receiving it.

Needs assessment is a decision-making tool for continuing educators' use in identifying the educational activities or programs they should offer to best meet their clients'—and society's—educational needs. Although educational needs assessment, no matter how well conceived and executed, will not guarantee program success, incorporating carefully planned and implemented needs assessment into the program-planning process can substantially reduce uncertainty regarding program appropriateness and viability. As an integral part of the program development and delivery process, a high-quality needs assessment will yield practical data and inform program planning. A comprehensive needs assessment strategy, which incorporates a series of individual assessments over time, can provide a blueprint and serve as "a logical starting point for individual action and program development, as well as a continuing process for keeping activities on track" (Gilmore, Campbell, and Becker, 1989, p. 5).

Needs assessment most often is concerned with educational needs, which are related to program content and the population to be served, rather than with operational needs such as program scheduling, which could be considered a form of market research. It was John Dewey who, in the early twentieth century, first introduced the notion of educational needs. He proposed that identification of educational needs could move education planning beyond a subject-centered approach to one focused on the learner (Atwood and Ellis, 1971). Monette noted, "Labeling a need as educational implies that it is capable of being satisfied by means of a learning experience which can provide appropriate knowledge, skills, or attitudes" (1977, p. 119).

However, both types of needs can be identified through an assessment and addressed by educational programming. Using questions, interviews, observations, and other measures, needs assessments determine the differences between existing and desired knowledge, skills, and performance abilities. From the differences found, educational needs that may be amenable to educational interventions are identified.

Definition of Need

Needs can be described as discrepancies between an actual condition or state and a desired standard (Monette, 1977; Pennington, 1980). Standards used to define needs vary greatly according to the purpose for which needs are being defined, the circumstances, and the person or persons defining them. The standard of need in one situation might be a minimum one, a level that must be attained if an individual is to do no harm, for example. A minimum standard for planning commission members might be that they demonstrate familiarity with zoning ordinances and other local regulations. If the standard for defining need in this case were optimum rather than minimum, however, these same planning commission members might be expected to demonstrate ability to interpret and apply the ordinances and regulations to everyday situations the commission will face. Thus, when viewed within the range of standards that can be applied, need is not a single empirical state but rather, to a large extent, a value judgment supported by those who establish and impose the standard (Pennington, 1980).

Needs differ from *wants* (which imply interest and perhaps motivation but may not reflect a discrepancy of any type) and *demands* (which suggest a willingness to commit resources to obtain education that will address a given situation). Needs, wants, and demands each have a valid place in planning continuing education and training activities, and in fact each can be identified through assessment. Although it is necessary to acknowledge the differences between needs, wants, and demands, needs assessment can provide data that will help relate both wants and demands to the needs that are to be met.

A person may *want* to participate in an educational activity because the content is attractive, the instructor is entertaining, or the setting and facilities have appeal. All are legitimate motivating factors, but they cannot be considered needs. Continuing educators' attention to wants may be well placed, for wants often are indicative of programming opportunities. However, wants alone usually are not sufficient basis for educational programming because they are limited by individuals' perceptions of the scope of potential opportunities available to them. *Demands* may occur when education is sought to correct a problem, prepare for future activities, or provide enrichment or even entertainment, but the education pursued may or may not be appropriate for meeting the underlying needs. Conversely, an educational need may or may not result in a demand for programming, for people may not find the educational activities that they need appealing (Monette, 1977).

Although some needs appear to be educational in nature, upon closer examination it becomes apparent that they cannot be remedied by educational interventions alone. Practice settings, resource limitations, and personal characteristics are among the noneducational factors that may underlie such needs. In the example cited at the start of this chapter, educating the nurses could not alleviate the shortcomings that resulted from the procedures the employing institutions had in place. Similarly, instruction in the use of state-of-the-art technology cannot overcome obsolescence if funds are not available to purchase that technology. In conducting a needs assessment, it is important to differentiate between those needs that can be addressed by education for the designated target population and those that require education of a group other than the one initially identified (in the example, health care administrators rather than direct care nurses) or that require other actions.

It also is important to recognize that different groups have different needs. Although most needs assessment is directed toward identifying learners' needs, continuing educators, instructors, employers, and society also have needs that can be identified and that affect educational programming. Continuing educators' needs usually cluster around fulfillment of their mission, service to identified client groups, and generation of revenue. Instructors may have needs related to disseminating knowledge resulting from recent research or to teaching topics on which they have special expertise.

Employers' needs most often focus on educating employees so that they will be able to perform certain tasks, with the professional development of emerging leaders a second area of emphasis. Public health, safety, and welfare tend to dominate society's needs, along with a related concern for accountability among those who serve the public.

Levels of Needs Assessment

Needs assessment is a process for identifying the gaps, or discrepancies, between what actually is and what ought to be. When broadly conceived, educational needs assessment can reach beyond examination of knowledge, skill, and performance ability deficits into the domain of market research. When this purpose is incorporated into a needs assessment, it may include consideration of appropriate design, delivery, scheduling, and perhaps even promotion of educational activities. On the basis of information obtained through this type of needs assessment, continuing educators can make informed decisions regarding all aspects of programming. However, it is important that the use of needs assessment to provide market research data be closely tied to identifying educational needs. Without consideration of the educational needs of specific populations, continuing educators risk offering the wrong programs, at the wrong times and places, in the wrong formats, and marketing them to the wrong populations. When this happens, neither the continuing education operation nor the population it strives to address is well served.

Valid needs assessments can be conducted at levels ranging from simple to complex. Many types of needs assessment do not require a large project or substantial expertise but can be carried out effectively with minimal preparation and limited resources. The full continuum of needs assessment methods ranges from simply asking people what they consider to be their educational needs to employing sophisticated measurement devices. The key to successful assessment is identifying a method appropriate to the issue and to one's goals and resources, and implementing it well. There must be accurate collecting, recording, analyzing, and interpreting of data. A poorly executed needs assessment, whether simple or complex, can yield data that are incorrect, inaccurate, or misunderstood. Such defective data are potentially worse than no data at all, for they can be taken seriously, used as the basis for planning and developing educational activities, and cause programming disasters.

Exactly that happened when a cursory assessment was conducted to determine judges' needs for programming on ethics. Judges interviewed were asked if they had little, moderate, or considerable knowledge of ethical issues, but they were given no descriptors or definitions of the three response options. As a result, most of those assessed said that they had little knowledge of the topic. Relying on this information, a continuing educator designed a very basic program that was far too elementary for the participants, who expressed their displeasure by vowing not to return to that continuing education provider.

Because educational needs change continually, an ongoing approach to needs assessment is advisable. Although a single needs assessment activity may be employed for a specific purpose, a needs assessment strategy offers an organization or institution a comprehensive means of identifying educational needs over time. A long-term needs assessment strategy may be described as "a planned and purposeful program that combines several methods to collect information about educational requirements" (Fernicola, 1987, p. 71). However, this kind of strategy is not developed overnight. Most successful strategies begin slowly, often starting with a pilot phase consisting of small, single assessment activities that gradually become the building blocks of long-term strategies. Ideally, needs assessment strategies are an integral part of the continuing educator's program development process.

A number of factors merit consideration before the continuing educator embarks on even the most cursory needs assessment.

Examination of each one is essential, regardless of the level of detail and sophistication of the needs assessment effort. Although it is easy to make quick assumptions about the focus of a needs assessment, an objective review of the issues often introduces additional perspectives or ideas. The results of this deliberation should guide the selection and implementation of specific needs assessment methods and procedures. Examining the resources available for assessment and the range of feasible programming possibilities also helps define the purpose, scope, and complexity of the assessment. Sound decisions about the types of data needed to assess educational needs effectively can be made by reviewing priorities, identifying content areas to be assessed, clarifying a focus on knowledge, skills, or performance abilities, and determining what types of needs are most relevant to potential participants or clients and to the continuing educator's mission and goals. Identifying the target population also is important in making procedural decisions. Finally, a needs assessment team—a cadre of people to guide and implement the assessment—is an invaluable asset. Such a team can include representatives of the continuing education or training unit, faculty, client groups, and other interested parties, but the primary criterion for inclusion should be the expectation of active participation in some or all aspects of the needs assessment. A needs assessment team is a working group. As such, it may advise and make policy decisions, or these functions may be left to separate planning or advisory committees (see Chapter Ten).

Role of Needs Assessment in Continuing Education Today

Needs assessment is not a new concept but it is an underutilized one that has the potential to revolutionize the program development process. As Vella suggested, it can be "the key to adult learning. Without it there is no honest defining of learning needs, no dialogue, no listening" (1994, p. 45). Properly utilized, needs assessment will provide solid data on which to base decisions regarding not only program content but also format, delivery mode, and audience, as well as marketing issues such as promotion and scheduling.

The demand for continuing education is substantial, and it is growing. A 1978 report somewhat tentatively observed, "The Learning Society is with us . . . many researchers and educational statesmen posit lifelong learning as an integral part of a postindustrial society" (Arbeiter, Aslanian, Schmerbeck, and Brickell, 1978, p. v). By 1985, survey data indicated that 40 percent of American adults wanted to further their education, and the number was growing (Opinion Research Corporation, 1985). In 1992, the American people elected a new president, Bill Clinton, who cited lifetime learning as essential to the country's economic viability.

Several factors account for the increased interest in lifelong education. Perhaps the most important is the virtual necessity for professionals across disciplines to continue learning throughout their careers (Cervero, 1988; Nowlen, 1988). As Dubin noted, "Recent conditions have catapulted into prominence the issues of professional obsolescence and updating" (1990, p. 9). Forces including rapidly expanding knowledge, technological innovations, and public demands for assurance of professional competence have driven requirements for mandatory continuing education in many professions, and high voluntary participation rates have led other groups to require learning throughout one's career. A second factor contributing to the growth of continuing education is that in the United States as well as in a number of other countries, the level of educational attainment within many segments of the population is rising. People who successfully complete learning experiences are more likely to seek additional education than are those with minimal education or unsatisfactory educational experiences (Wlodkowski, 1985). As the numbers of successful learners increase, the ranks of lifelong learners swell. A third factor generating demand for continuing education is the growing number of people experiencing life transitions, changes in their personal lives and their careers. When people face these transitions, they often look to education to prepare for a move in new directions (Aslanian and Brickell, 1988).

This increased demand for continuing education is good news for those who recognize the value of lifelong learning, and particularly for continuing educators. However, it brings with it a burden of responsibility. Quantitative expansion must be accompanied by attention to quality if the resulting education is to yield positive results. Factors contributing to the quality of continuing education include identification of program content; instructional design; faculty selection; delivery methods; evaluation; and matching of programs with appropriate audiences (Freedman, 1987, p. 148). Ultimately, however, continuing education is successful only if it provides added value by benefiting one or more groups of a diverse clientele. This added value can take many forms, such as improved practice for professionals, more efficient workforce performance for employers, and enrichment for community members.

Continuing education clients include both individuals and the organizations and institutions (for example, employers, government and regulatory agencies, and professional associations) that support and often select education for those they represent. The organizations and institutions are themselves being forced into the role of lifelong learners as they strive to adapt to technology, their own changing clients, and increased regulations and globalization (Aslanian, 1990).

Both individual and organizational clients must be satisfied in two ways. First, each continuing education participant must benefit from participation in the program. Content, method of instruction, instructional materials, readings, and exercises should be relevant and engaging. Second, those who select and pay for the program, whether the individual students or those representing them, should feel that their expectations were met and their investment was a good one. Students should be able to apply what has been learned to their personal or professional lives.

Achievement of these goals was perhaps of less concern, although no less critical, in the 1970s, before demographics, economic and social trends, and technology significantly changed continuing education. Between the 1970s and the 1990s, knowledge expanded exponentially, performance and productivity expectations escalated, and financial pressures increased (Cervero, 1988; Nowlen, 1988). Financial pressures in particular led to increased emphasis on programs that were marketable rather than educational (Nowlen, 1980). This trend had implications for the use of needs assessment as a market research tool rather than one that simply assessed educational needs.

These changes accelerated in the 1990s, and for continuing educators they led to two major shifts: (1) continuing education providers in all settings were faced with less flexibility and a need for greater accountability, and (2) both their clients and the factors motivating their pursuit of education changed. Continuing education institutions became less tolerant of programs that failed to please clients or generate revenue, while their clients became more concerned with the value realized from participation. As a result, continuing educators increasingly found it essential to heed marketplace demands. However, this pattern did not lessen the importance of sound educational practices. Rather they effectively dictated that continuing educators find ways to attract clients as well as to identify and respond to their needs and interests if they were to maintain and enhance viable operations (Freedman, 1987).

The ways in which the practice and environment of continuing education have been altered underscore the importance of assessment in identifying both educational and operational (or marketing) needs. In the past, particularly within colleges and universities, continuing education programs sometimes were offered because faculty members wanted to teach them or because a few potential students requested them. These programs often did not attract enough students to cover costs fully or attracted so little interest that they were cancelled, both results causing disappointment over wasted effort and unrealized expectations, and loss of dollars. Although such practices still take place to some extent, changing conditions have decreased continuing educators' latitude in offering programs with little or no assurance that they will draw an audience. Tighter economic conditions have reduced the ability to sustain such losses, and particularly in the case of distance learning activities, the costs involved have risen substantially (Verduin and Clark, 1991). Also, the continuing education field has become crowded as more trainers, employers, professional associations, for-profit providers, proprietary schools, and others have entered what used to be primarily the domain of higher education (Stern, 1983). The financial and educational successes of these providers have been built on their performance abilities to assess learning needs accurately and to deliver education and training programs directed toward those needs in a timely fashion. In addition, many major companies, including IBM, Aetna, McDonald's, and Xerox, have developed their own education institutes or academies, perhaps as "an indictment of the traditional educational system" (Eurich, 1990, p. 165–166). Similarly, private for-profit providers, which are generally able to respond to trends more quickly than colleges and universities, have been highly successful in the ongoing assessment of individual and corporate needs and the prompt creation of customized programs. As these examples indicate, needs assessment has become an important marketing tool for the successful continuing educator, regardless of organizational setting.

The groups of people seeking continuing education have changed in both composition and purpose. Many individuals used to look to continuing education only to provide enrichment, help them with a hobby, or perhaps serve as a social experience. Frequently they were interested in learning about gourmet cooking, a foreign language, or woodworking, while enjoying an evening out with friends. Although people still enjoy classes for these purposes, the societal trends and economic conditions that have forced many adults to seek new lines of employment and led more women into the workforce have encouraged many others to turn to education to gain the skills and credentials they need. And increasing numbers of employers faced with workers trained before the advent of technology are seeking educational programs to enable those workers to use new technology productively (Eurich, 1990). Employers and employees alike have come to realize that even common career advancements, such as moves from staff to management positions, often no longer can be made successfully without preparatory education. Recent graduates frequently enter the workforce unprepared or underprepared for the positions for which they were hired. As a result of these changes, the goals and purposes of those providing or seeking continuing education have changed dramatically. These new students look to continuing education to help them reach clearly defined goals, often goals on which their professional success, livelihood, or personal satisfaction may depend.

Continuing educators seeking to serve effectively this more focused audience require specific information about the individuals who form it. They need a clear understanding of their potential clients' knowledge, skill, and performance ability discrepancies as related to career preparation, job training and retraining, improved practice, changed behaviors, and integration of new information and technology into their personal and professional lives. Needs assessment can provide this information.

Although all needs assessment requires at least minimal investment of time, money, and skills, extensive resources are not needed. In fact, most needs assessments are fairly modest and they are often informal (Moore, 1980). Needs assessment at some level is possible within the limits of any continuing educator's resources. The thoroughness with which a needs assessment is planned and executed is more critical to its usefulness and value than the size and sophistication of the process employed.

By limiting a needs assessment project to accommodate resource constraints at the outset, the continuing educator is able to keep the scope of the project at a comfortable and appropriate level.

Commitments to choosing sound strategies, insisting on quality implementation of the needs assessment methods selected, asking the right questions, and obtaining the cooperation of potential client groups or organizations are essential but they need not be costly. Indeed, the cost of failure to conduct a needs assessment may be far greater.

Why Conduct a Needs Assessment?

Continuing educators receive many suggestions about programs people believe they need or want or for which they believe a demand exists. This information has value; certainly people are aware of some of their shortcomings and moreover must perceive a need for a program before they will sign up for it. However, one cannot assume that people asking for a program really need, or even want it, or that they will actually participate in it if it is made available to them. Conversely, the content areas left unmentioned often represent areas of greatest need. The wise continuing educator will interpret informal suggestions carefully, viewing them in light of current socioeconomic and technological trends, what is known about the potential audience's participation in educational activities, and other marketing considerations. This process is itself a form of needs assessment.

The shortcomings of self-reported needs became evident during the Continuing Professional Education Development Project conducted at The Pennsylvania State University in the 1980s (Office of Continuing Professional Education, 1985). Representatives of several professions were asked to list the content areas in which they believed they were weak or in which they required further education. They then were subjected to rigorous assessment center exercises simulating actual practice, so that their strengths and weaknesses could be objectively documented. A comparison of the results of the two activities indicated that the areas of greatest discrepancy identified through assessment often were conspicuously absent from the participants' lists of perceived needs. Participants most often believed that their greatest needs were for new knowledge or for refresher courses on aspects of their field with which they seldom worked. But the assessment exercises showed that some of the greatest discrepancies between current and desirable proficiencies were related to functions they performed regularly. For example, although accountants ranked new tax legislation at the top of their needs lists, formal assessment indicated that they were quite weak in interviewing clients to obtain pertinent information, a task many of them performed almost daily. And these accountants are not unusual; most people assume, often erroneously, that they perform their routine activities well (Queeney and Smutz, 1990).

The most fundamental value of needs assessment is in determining which programs should be offered and what content should be included. A program that does not result in the improved knowledge, skills, or performance abilities needed to address a discrepancy disappoints both the students enrolled in the program and those who supported their participation. A program for which no need or market exists fails to attract an audience and results in frustration, wasted resources, and financial loss for the continuing educator. By identifying specific learning needs and related desired outcomes, needs assessment permits the continuing educator to tailor program content to a particular group of potential students and hence increase the likelihood that it will meet its goals for both of these groups. Program design can incorporate information, activities, and experiences that will enable participants to apply the content of the educational activity in work settings, family activities, or other aspects of their daily lives.

When a needs assessment is broadened and exploited to fill a market research function, the data collected can contribute to effective program marketing by examining the target audience and its preferences. Without a clear understanding of the potential audience, the continuing educator may market a program to the wrong population or use an inappropriate marketing strategy to reach the intended group. As a result, people who might have enrolled are unaware of the program and those who are informed of the program may have no interest in it. The continuing educator also can use needs assessment data to focus marketing materials, highlighting program features that have particular appeal to potential participants. For example, the largest print on the brochure for a program jointly sponsored by the Central Pennsylvania Psychological Association and The Pennsylvania State University was reserved for the speaker's name rather than for the program title, because assessment data indicated that clinical psychologists, for whom the program was intended, were eager to hear that person speak.

Use of needs assessment data in this manner does not detract from their primary role—identifying educational needs. However, it does acknowledge the importance of making potential participants aware of educational activities that can contribute to their meaningful education.

Information about potential program participants is always useful in planning programs that will be offered either to the general public or to specific segments of the total population. When the anticipated audience is a general one, needs assessment data can help target marketing to reach the people whose needs and interests are similar to those around which the program will be designed. The data also can provide a focus for the program design, content, and delivery. Continuing educators must depend on data in order to serve specific audiences competently. Managers seeking educational activities for their employees, for example, want assurances that they have minimized the risk of supporting inappropriate programs and that the money spent will bring benefits to their organization. Employees' strengths, weaknesses, skills, educational and occupational experiences, preferred learning styles, and current job requirements—all factors that can be documented through assessment—are important in educational design and delivery. Frequently employees' expectations and attitudes must be weighed against those of their employers. For example, employers may have a short-term view of educational needs, seeking to give employees the education and training they need to meet current job demands, while employees may take a long-range perspective that emphasizes education for career growth. In such cases, assessment data can help identify ways of combining diverse interests in one educational activity or in a series of activities. Needs assessment data can also be used to prepare initial program information that will capture participants' interest and enthusiasm while meeting the requirements of their employers or those who are paying for their participation.

Finally, data acquired through needs assessment can help guide decisions about program scheduling and delivery. Adults' inability to fit continuing education activities into their schedules has been recognized as one, if not the greatest, deterrent to their pursuit of additional education (Knowles, 1980; Apps, 1981; Wlodkowski, 1985; Brookfield, 1986; Daloz, 1986; Queeney, Smutz, and Shuman, 1990). These would-be students often have professional and family responsibilities, and frequently they are limited in the distance they can travel. Without considering these kinds of limitations, continuing educators risk offering programs that people want and need but cannot get to. Needs assessment can answer questions related to most convenient time of year, day, and hours; session frequency and duration; and location preferences, including what distance the people are willing to travel. Desire for college credit, special credit (for example, Continuing Education Units), or non-credit programs can be determined. Preferred delivery modes can be determined, including people's receptivity to delivery via distance education as an alternative to more traditional conferences, workshops, classes, and seminars held at a central location. Independent study by correspondence, teleconferencing, compressed video, satellite, cable television, interactive computer, and other distance learning modes offer a range of possibilities frequently overlooked by continuing educators accustomed to working with centrally located activities (Verduin and Clark, 1991).

An important objective of needs assessment is to provide useful data. However, a frequent by-product of focused needs assessment activities is participants' increased awareness of their strengths and weaknesses. For example, nurses participating in an assessment center for the Continuing Professional Education Development Project cited earlier were asked to develop patient care plans following specified criteria. After the experience, they remarked that they had not realized how much they did not know about integrating their everyday activities into care plans until confronted with these exercises (Staff, 1984). By heightening individuals' awareness of their own abilities, assessment exercises can motivate them to seek educational activities that provide the knowledge, skills, and abilities they need to strengthen their performance. For people who do not themselves participate in the assessment exercises, however, group assessment rarely has this effect. People seldom believe that needs identified for others in their profession are needs that they share (Queeney and Smutz, 1990). For this reason, some professional groups, including dietitians and architects, have begun to explore self-assessment instruments to enable their members to assess their own educational needs (Klevans, Smutz, Shuman, and Bershad, 1992). Because self-assessment is beyond the reach of most groups, one thrust of a marketing strategy may be to help individuals understand that needs identified through group assessment may apply to them, particularly when they share pertinent characteristics with those assessed.

A sound needs assessment supports both continuing education providers and their clients. By producing solid data on which to base decisions, it substantially increases the likelihood that continuing educators will succeed in helping their clients achieve desired learning outcomes and in meeting their own organizational goals. An understanding of specific educational needs enables them to develop and offer programs for which an appropriate audience exists, programs that provide the necessary content, at the right level, in a time, place, and format tailored to their students. Needs assessment serves continuing education clients too, permitting them to invest in educational activities from which they will benefit, thus avoiding expenditures of time and money for programs that are not suited to their needs. Educational activities developed without benefit of identified needs on which to base design, delivery, and marketing decisions can fall short of both continuing educators' and clients' expectations.

What Needs Assessment Can and Cannot Do

Needs assessment is not a precise science. It has limitations. Even the best needs assessment cannot guarantee program success, and problems can arise if expectations are unrealistic. The results of isolated assessments will not form an adequate basis for long-term program planning or dictate all aspects of program development and delivery. A single indicator cannot provide the depth or breadth of information necessary for these purposes, but it can be an important factor in making a range of programming decisions. Needs assessment data are most useful when considered together with other information. For example, needs assessment can readily identify a content area in which people demonstrate a discrepancy between actual and desired proficiencies. This information is critical to program planning, but it may not be sufficient to guide a continuing educator's decision making. Information on existing continuing education activities that address the identified content area can indicate whether additional programming on that topic is warranted. Data obtained from other sources can enable the continuing educator to understand the likelihood that the target audience will perceive a need for such a program and that potential participants, their employers, or some other funding source will support enrollments. Operational data can determine scheduling preferences. A needs assessment strategy incorporating demographic and socioeconomic data can provide all of this information, but a single needs assessment activity usually cannot.

As noted earlier in this chapter, not all discrepancies between actual and desired states identified through needs assessment lend themselves to educational interventions. In some cases, the education must be delivered to someone other than the intended program participant. For example, needs assessment may indicate that a manufacturing company is not using proper procedures for design testing. Further investigation may reveal that the engineers understand the procedures to be followed, but their employer's schedule for projects does not allow time for implementation of the procedures. No amount of continuing education for the engineers will improve the quality of that design testing; only by altering company policy, which could involve economic and perhaps political decisions, will design testing be improved. Thus the continuing education audience in this case may be the company's policy makers.

Usually not one but many needs are identified when a target group is assessed. The continuing educator, often in consultation with representatives of the target population, employers or supervisors, and perhaps faculty members, can select the needs for which continuing education activities could generate the greatest benefit, whether to meet clients' needs or those of an organizational mission. Decisions regarding which needs to address are made in the context of several factors, including intensity of the need, potential participant interest, faculty (and sometimes facility) availability, timing, program design requirements, existing educational activities on the topic, and program costs. This series of considerations most often results in prioritizing programming activities. Some activities are developed and delivered as soon as possible, others are relegated to next year's program planning (sometimes to be eliminated by future needs assessment findings), and yet others are discarded in the belief that educational programming would not yield benefits commensurate with the resources required to develop them.

A standard—or level of mastery—for each area to be assessed usually is defined before the assessment. It serves as the point below which need is defined. For example, clinical psychologists might be expected to demonstrate a series of specific behaviors in interviewing depressed patients. No need is indicated if they meet this standard, but if they do not demonstrate the expected behaviors they will be identified as having a discrepancy, or need, in that area.

Results of needs assessments are neither right nor wrong. They produce data that support or contraindicate further pursuit of specific programming ideas. Both continuing educators and their clients sometimes find it hard to accept data that do not support their interests or plans. Because perfect data do not exist, further assessment may be reasonable if there are serious doubts about the accuracy of the data. However, in conducting a needs assessment, all involved should be prepared to get answers they may not like and should realize that having one's hopes dashed in the initial phases of program consideration is far better than recognizing the folly of offering a program after considerable investment.

Occasionally continuing educators or assessment teams establish specific standards for determining need after, rather than before, the assessment data have been collected. The continuing educator may choose to assess a number of areas, then rank the results and declare those areas in which participants scored lowest to be the areas of weakness. This approach can be useful when the continuing educator has decided, for whatever reason, to develop programming within a broad area but wishes to identify one or more specific topics within that area for program development. Setting standards for determining need also may be delayed when those preparing and conducting the assessment are uncertain of the levels of knowledge, skills, or performance abilities the assessees are likely to demonstrate. In these situations, standards can be set after a review of the full range of levels demonstrated. Frequently the assessment results will cluster in a manner that facilitates such decisions, with levels of knowledge, skills, or performance abilities substantially higher for some topics than for others.

Both individual and organizational continuing education clients may fear that negative findings will be perceived as indicative of failure. For this reason, it is important to emphasize the positive nature of needs assessment: it is intended not to indicate failures but to identify areas in which additional learning can strengthen and enhance existing knowledge, skills, or performance abilities. Needs assessment of competent individuals can be useful in identifying new directions for their learning, which can raise their personal or professional interests to a new level. If properly interpreted and applied, needs assessment data almost always can inspire positive action. The client seeking education to reach a particular goal should be encouraged to view an assessment as an opportunity to identify impediments to that goal and to reduce or eliminate them through educational interventions. Although most clients approach needs assessment in this manner, some require reassurance that an assessment is not an examination and that they will not be judged. A focus on needs assessment as a means to achieving a desired end will reinforce this perspective.

Needs assessment data must be believable. If the data lack face validity, they will be questioned and perhaps not taken seriously. Sometimes data that seem puzzling simply require a bit of explanation. For example, a needs assessment of physicians indicated that family practitioners preferred local continuing medical education programs, whereas specialists preferred to travel to major cities or resorts (Kennedy and Queeney, 1991). No reason for the difference between the two groups was immediately apparent, causing some to wonder if the difference was merely coincidental. But further examination revealed that the family practitioners surveyed tended to be solo practitioners, with no partners or colleagues to handle their practices if they left town, whereas most of the specialists were involved in group practices and had another physician to cover for them. Careful interpretation, explanation, and common sense are helpful in reporting findings.

Finally, only when used properly can the data gleaned from a needs assessment produce satisfactory results. Proper use precludes generalizing from a convenience sample to a total population, for example. Careful interpretation and application of the data are essential to minimize the risks of improper usage. Just as a commit-ment to quality is essential to sound needs assessment, use of assess-ment results to develop educational activities requires faithful attention to the limitations of the data, and a carefully planned and executed program development and delivery process. Directions suggested by the needs assessment data can be incorporated in all facets of this process, including faculty selection; design of instruc-tional programs; marketing; and evaluation. Attention to detail both in integrating needs assessment findings and in program design and instruction is essential to program success.

Often seemingly minor factors make the difference between a successful educational activity and one that fails. For example, a program for bovine veterinarians presented considerable informa-tion on practices to be implemented by dairy farmers, but it failed to provide the veterinarians with tactics for motivating the farmers to adopt the practices. Without this critical skill, the veterinarians found it difficult to carry out the procedures they had been taught.

Differences Between Needs Assessment and Competency Assessment

Properly used, needs assessment is a powerful tool. But if it is improperly used or put into the wrong hands, the forms of needs assessment that examine an individual's knowledge, skills, or per-formance ability discrepancies can be cause for serious concern.

Needs assessment instruments are not devices for determining competency in a trade, occupation, or profession, or for determining mastery of a hobby such as painting or dance. They lack the research, fineness of focus, and depth of measurement that are essential to such evaluations. Because of these limitations, needs assessment exercises are not appropriate for the competency assess-ment portion of any credentialing process. The closest that needs assessment exercises come to supporting credentialing of any type is as a means of identifying areas of weakness to be addressed by mandated educational activities. For some licensed professions, such as clinical dietetics, completion of a needs assessment results in credit toward fulfillment of a continuing education requirement (Klevans, Pollack, Smutz, and Vance, 1991).

Although considerably more rigorous than needs assessment, competency measurements used in credentialing processes themselves have many problems. Many such measurements rely heavily on paper and pencil tests that "tap only a very small part of the richness of human behavior" (Gross, 1984, p. 117). Agreement on critical content areas to be included, issues of consistency and reliability, judges' objectivity, and resource limitations frequently play too strong a role in developing competency measures (Shimberg, 1982). In the absence of clear, objective criteria, decisions regarding what to measure frequently are based on values and social policy (Gross, 1984, p. 123). Although these problems also may be inherent in needs assessment, the differences in use of the resulting data allow much greater latitude. Competency assessment data are used to decide who may perform certain tasks in society; needs assessment data simply suggest additional education, with no implicit or explicit judgment regarding individuals' abilities to perform tasks.

In addition to problems of process and instrumentation, however, there are other issues that needs assessment does not address thoroughly. Chief among them is the question of what defines competency. Is a minimal or entry level of understanding required to declare an individual competent, or does that individual need the more comprehensive knowledge, skills, and performance abilities that come with experience? Are individuals measured against a group norm or standard, or must they earn a particular score or meet specified criteria to be granted approval? Must individuals master all content areas within their professional fields, or, for example, may an attorney be declared competent with no knowledge of patent law but high scores in domestic law? How much breadth of content is relevant for performance of particular tasks? Is competency for new and experienced practitioners defined in the same or different terms? Does mastery of knowledge alone denote competency, or must application of that knowledge be demonstrated?

These questions are tangentially related to needs assessment, but they are more appropriately addressed in the context of competency assessment. Although needs assessment and the resultant continuing education may be directed toward improving competency levels, they should not be confused with determination of competency at any level or in any realm. At best, needs assessment can be viewed as one of several factors contributing to attainment and maintenance of competency.

Summary

Adults' educational needs, whether related to the workplace, leisure activities, or other aspects of their lives, are broad and diverse. Frequently these needs are recognized neither by those who possess them nor by continuing educators who strive to provide educational activities that will enhance knowledge, skills, and performance abilities. Even employers and supervisors with specific goals for employees may not be able to document the educational needs to be addressed in order to meet those goals. Needs assessment can offer a nonthreatening, structured process for identifying those needs and a starting point for addressing them.

Needs assessment offers continuing educators the opportunity to base programming decisions on solid data rather than on instinct, habit, and supposition. Educational activities based on needs assessment data are not guaranteed to alleviate existing discrepancies, but they are more likely than non-assessment-based activities to do so (Safman, 1980). A needs assessment must be implemented thoroughly and rigorously, but it need not be complex or costly. More important than the sophistication of a needs assessment is the selection of assessment exercises that are appropriate to the target audience and topic, and for which the continuing educator has adequate resources. A high-quality needs assessment increases the continuing educator's likelihood of meeting individual and organizational clients' educational needs, resulting in greater client satisfaction than otherwise might be attained. A modest investment in needs assessment before initiating new program development can enable the continuing educator to avoid costly mistakes and often can result in substantial income generation.

Needs assessment requires a commitment on the part of the continuing educator and others whose support and involvement are instrumental in making the process successful. The continuing educator unaccustomed to conducting needs assessments at first may find the process somewhat cumbersome, the identification of needed resources challenging, and the delays annoying. Similarly, clients seeking quick responses to their requests for educational activities may question the importance of first participating in a needs assessment. However, with each subsequent needs assessment these difficulties and doubts will diminish and the value of the process will become more apparent.

Those entering into needs assessment—the continuing educators conducting the assessment and the target audiences—should do so with full understanding that no one fails a needs assessment. Rather, needs assessment offers the opportunity for everyone to emerge a winner.

Chapter Two

Considerations in Developing a Needs Assessment

How does one make the decisions necessary to implement a needs assessment? Certainly a continuing educator's judgment about both topic and process is important, but it is not a sufficient basis on which to proceed (Sleezer, 1992). All stakeholders involved in conducting the needs assessment and utilizing or benefiting from the results should have a common definition of what constitutes a need and agree on the content areas to be explored, the populations whose needs are of interest, and a time frame. They should reach at least general agreement regarding both the type and quality of needs assessment that will be acceptable, and an understanding that the assessment may have to accommodate organizational priorities and constraints. It is essential that those involved in the process, as well as the people who will translate assessed needs into educational activities, be committed to accepting and acting on the assessment outcomes if the needs assessment is to be worthwhile.

Defining and clarifying the objectives of a proposed needs assessment are the first steps in selecting a single needs assessment method or developing a comprehensive needs assessment strategy—one that incorporates a variety of methods. It is not enough to embark on a needs assessment with only the broad goal, for example, of learning what kinds of educational programs senior citizens might find beneficial or identifying the greatest discrepancies in social workers' knowledge, skills, and performance abilities. By specifying objectives that incorporate the needs assessment purpose, the scope of the proposed study, the target population, the resources to be allocated to the endeavor, and the level of complexity, it is possible to bring broad goals into sharper focus. Organizational priorities that guide the planning and management decisions associated with assessing educational needs can help shape these objectives and are critical for a number of reasons.

The priorities of the organization sponsoring the needs assessment (whether it is a corporation, educational institution, professional association, or other entity) will determine the resources —including funds, time, personnel, and support services—that will be allocated to the endeavor. An organization with long-range goals that include providing a full range of educational activities for a specific target population may choose to invest substantial resources in assessing that group's learning needs. In contrast, an institution committed to serving a broad range of audiences with general programming is not likely to commit significant resources to assessing the needs of a specific group but may be willing to make a considerable investment in assessing the educational needs of a more comprehensive population. Identifying educational needs may not be a priority for some organizations, which may choose either to base programming decisions entirely on revenue-generating potential or to offer educational activities only in response to highly specific, discrete, and often recurring needs (for example, a review course to prepare participants to take a licensing examination). Organizations like these, whose priorities are in areas other than defining and meeting educational needs as they arise, are unlikely to make major commitments to identify those needs. They may, however, use needs assessment as a form of market research.

Organizational priorities also may affect or even dictate the content areas to be addressed through educational programming and the types of programming to be offered. Although they can be viewed as constraints, these priorities also help focus the areas a needs assessment will examine. For example, a professional association may limit its educational offerings to technical topics, or a university may wish to build on its strengths in a particular academic field. Continuing education providers may choose to emphasize credit or noncredit courses, one-day workshops or weekly programs. An institution in which engineering and science are the academic areas of greatest strength may wish to emphasize programming in those content areas, for example, and their regulations may limit continuing education to offering only noncredit programs. Organizations may pride themselves on flexible scheduling or adhere to a rigid format, or they may have special capabilities or facilities that enable them to deliver unique educational activities or reach distance learners.

All organizational priorities merit consideration when establishing needs assessment objectives, because it is counterproductive to assess needs without a strong likelihood of addressing them. For example, it makes little sense to solicit information on a target population's needs for variable scheduling or specific subject matter if responsive programming would not be compatible with the organization's priorities. Such exploration can raise false expectations and negative feelings when assessment participants realize that the programming for which they indicated a need will not be forthcoming.

Purpose of a Needs Assessment

Needs assessments have one or more purposes. Broadly described, those purposes may range from strict identification of educational needs to market research, from (1) focusing the content of an educational activity to (2) identifying potential audiences to (3) determining whether a program idea merits further consideration. The more specific the purpose, the more useful it is for developing a sound, efficient assessment. Examples of more specific purposes might be (1) to clarify the material to be covered in a program on historic preservation of nineteenth-century farmhouses, (2) to determine the career stages, practice settings, and current positions of educators likely to attend a seminar on portfolio evaluation or (3) to decide whether sufficient need and interest exist to pursue development of a workshop on parent-teenager relationships.

One reason for conducting a needs assessment is to gain new information. Either a single needs assessment exercise or a comprehensive strategy can put "in perspective problems confronting a target population, services available to it, and actions that might be taken" (McKillip, 1987, p. 29). The purpose of a needs assessment will be guided, if not governed, by institutional and organizational politics, mission, goals, strengths, and priorities. The continuing education unit's past successes, disappointments, and failures also will be strong factors, as will the current socioeconomic and educational climate. Within that context of opportunities and constraints, a statement of purpose, citing one or more reasons for conducting a needs assessment and tailored to the individual assessment being contemplated, will help focus the assessment. Specifying purpose forces the continuing educator to make decisions about one or more issues on which information will be sought, including content areas, level of education, underserved populations, target populations, delivery mode, and scheduling. Some of these issues are directly related to educational needs, others to operational needs. Among the latter one may find considerable emphasis on the needs of the continuing education provider rather than on those of the learner. The use of needs assessment as a market research tool also is valid.

Content Areas of Educational Need

Identifying the discrepancies between existing and desired conditions for translation into program content is the primary purpose of much if not most needs assessment. This is needs assessment in its purest form: identification of educational needs.

The continuing educator may seek information on the educational needs of a particular target population or of a general, less defined population. A target population may be a large group sharing common characteristics, such as local elected officials or social workers, or it may be more specific, such as middle managers at the local manufacturing company. In seeking to identify educational needs for more general populations, the continuing educator might look to community groups or, if ambitious, the total population of the service area. In any case, if the needs assessment purpose includes identifying the content areas of educational need, the statement of purpose will specify the groups for which needs are to be identified.

A needs assessment focused on content often will identify and examine in some detail the topics about which target group members need better knowledge, skills, or performance abilities. Another approach may be to identify topics that are outside of the target group's expertise but are relevant to their performance or practice. For example, programming in psychology or philosophy would not address the content for which physicians are responsible, but such programming might help them deal with ethical issues.

The following are examples of purposes that address educational need content:

- Identify the areas of practice in which social workers' knowledge, skills, and performance abilities are weakest, and determine which of these areas are amenable to educational intervention.
- Determine the greatest needs of people approaching retirement and learn whether these needs are in the area of money management, trusts, and wills, in health care options and services, in productive use of leisure time, or in travel programs.
- Learn about the educational needs of people becoming parents for the first time.

Level of Education Needed

Educational activities can be designed to address most topics, or content areas, at any one of several levels of complexity, from quite simple to highly sophisticated. Similarly, different populations may need education at significantly different levels, ranging from that of a basic introduction through intermediate and advanced approaches. People having little or no education or experience in a given topic understandably will best be served by an educational activity that assumes no prior knowledge. They will be frustrated by programming that is based on the erroneous assumption that they have certain information, and may get little or no benefit from such a program. Conversely, individuals who have some facility with a topic but need to enhance and update their knowledge or skills will lose interest in an educational activity that begins at an elementary level. Because educational activities are most effective when they are structured at a level that is appropriate to the participants, identification of potential students' levels of need can be an important purpose of a needs assessment.

The following are examples of purposes related to level of education needed:

- Identify local businessmen's level of understanding of the basic principles and tools of total quality management.
- Learn the extent to which clerical personnel understand and feel competent to use disk operating systems.
- Determine real estate agents' level of familiarity with qualifications to be met for various types of mortgages.

Educational Needs of Underserved Populations

Through needs assessment a continuing educator can discover groups for whom the content of the existing program does not meet educational needs or for whom programming is beyond reach because of location, scheduling, costs, or other factors. Identifying underserved populations is useful for continuing educators who want to expand services to new audiences or replace previously served audiences that no longer participate in their programs. Educationally underserved groups may not always have lacked educational opportunity, and those groups for which appropriate education is available during one period may find themselves with severely limited opportunities only a short time later. As portions of the population change their activities and their ways of doing things, their educational needs also change. New audiences emerge as societal interests, socioeconomic trends, and professional and occupational practices change.

The following are examples of purposes related to educational needs of underserved populations:

- Identify specific professional groups that are required to participate in continuing education as a condition of licensure or certification but lack a sufficient range of educational activities to choose from.
- Learn what factors are deterring hazardous waste material workers from updating their knowledge, skills, and performance abilities.
- Determine the characteristics common to community members who are former continuing education participants but have not recently enrolled in any activities.

Target Populations for Specific Educational Activities

An educational provider may have unique expertise in certain content areas or access to faculty members who are widely recognized for their research, teaching, or practice. Needs assessment can enable providers whose organizations have recognized subject matter expertise, cutting-edge research, unique facilities, or outstanding faculty to capitalize on those capabilities by providing a method of identifying target audiences who can benefit from them. Some creative thinking or brainstorming may be needed to look beyond traditional audiences for particular topics, for often the most receptive audiences are not those who automatically come to mind. For example, a university wanted to develop a continuing education program featuring an engineering faculty member with expertise in the fracture and fatigue of metals. They knew that manufacturers of metal products would be interested in the topic, but upon reflection they realized, quite accurately, that lawyers dealing with product liability and personal injury cases also needed knowledge in this area.

The following are examples of purposes related to target populations for specific educational activities:

- Identify a range of potential audiences for dissemination of research findings regarding the effects of chocolate consumption.
- Ascertain whether physicians, increasingly concerned about ethics, would be receptive to a literary approach to that topic.
- Learn which professions or other groups would benefit from workshops on servant leadership.

Preferences About Delivery Mode

Different types of program delivery suit different audiences. Many continuing education students are location-bound, face scheduling constraints, or for other reasons require flexibility beyond that afforded by traditional site-specific seminars, workshops, conferences, and classes. Many professionals who wish to pursue continuing education cannot afford time away from the work site because it means lost income, another expense to be added to the obvious ones of registration, travel, and so forth. In contrast, other adult students, having experienced only standard lecture formats in the course of their learning, may be most amenable to education delivered by a teacher in a classroom. Clearly, not all topics lend themselves to all delivery modes; educational activities involving laboratory work or interaction among participants are most easily handled when all participants meet together at a single site, for example. However, various modes of distance education are being used quite successfully for increasing numbers of programs, and they offer both educational and logistical advantages. Because of the amount of planning they require, programs delivered this way frequently are better conceived and more carefully executed than programs on the same topics presented to a standard classroom audience (Verduin and Clark, 1991). Continuing education delivered "at your place and at your pace" is enabling large numbers of adults to participate in educational activities that once were beyond their reach.

Because of the range of possibilities, understanding an audience's delivery mode preferences is an important factor in continuing educators' success in transforming potential clients into enrolled program participants.

The following are examples of purposes that address delivery mode preferences:

- Learn if architects are receptive to independent learning activities incorporating print, audio, and video components.
- Use the demographic characteristics of target audience members to determine which delivery modes would be most appropriate for them.
- Determine whether target audience members have access to computer links for student/student and student/instructor conferencing.

Preferences About Scheduling

All site-specific continuing education programs and many activities offered through distance education are subject to scheduling decisions. Although scheduling at the convenience of the faculty, facilities, and continuing educator may be tempting, the needs of potential participants should be the primary consideration in determining seasons, days of the week, times of the day, hours, and locations. An assessment of operational needs can determine if members of the intended program audience find it feasible to participate in educational activities at only certain times of day, week, or year; are within reasonable distance of particular locations; or prefer certain program lengths and frequencies (for example, one four-hour session per week rather than two two-hour sessions).

Appropriate scheduling can make the difference between the success and failure of an educational activity. Identifying participants' scheduling requirements can often be a secondary purpose in needs assessments that have some other, primary purpose.

The following are some examples of purposes related to scheduling preferences:

- Identify the times of year when housing sales are slowest, freeing real estate salespeople to enroll in continuing education activities.
- Find out whether psychiatrists prefer to learn new therapy techniques in a series of one-day workshops in a metropolitan area or in a single weeklong program offered in a vacation spot.
- Determine how the time for brief continuing education modules could be integrated into nurses' work schedules.

Thus, although the primary purpose of most needs assessments is to provide data on educational needs, information on the other topics described here also can serve as a starting point in the program planning process. Additional purposes may be served as well. Needs assessment activities can substantiate a program planner's educated guesses or generate information for marketing purposes.

Continuing educators can quote facts and figures relating specific, documented educational needs of a particular group in publications and advertisements to inform potential participants that a program was developed to respond to clearly identified needs. They can use information on a target group's preferences and expectations to develop a marketing plan that highlights those factors in promotional materials. For skeptical administrators, needs assessment data can provide documentation that justifies allocation of resources for programs.

Needs assessment is not rigorous scientific research and, despite the use of solid research methodology, should not be perceived as such. For this reason, a needs assessment cannot be expected to provide data guaranteed to lead to successful programming decisions. A more realistic expectation is for a meaningful database that will guide the program design, development, and delivery process, enabling providers to use their resources productively and participants to be well served. A strategy that incorporates ongoing or repeated assessment of a specific audience over time can document changing needs. Ideally, continuous assessment will provide the information needed to keep program planning current.

Scope of a Needs Assessment

What can the continuing educator realistically hope to accomplish in a single needs assessment, or even in an entire needs assessment strategy? Is it feasible to consider the needs of all clinical psychologists, for example, or is it more reasonable to look at only those clinical psychologists who work with children? Should a continuing educator investigate the full range of potential educational needs, or should he or she limit the content to be explored to use of new therapies?

The scope of a needs assessment—including the magnitude and characteristics of the population under consideration and the breadth and depth of the content areas to be examined—has important ramifications for the assessment's methodology and design. Defining these characteristics is a critical step in the needs assessment process.

Population

Determining the size and diversity of the population to be assessed (for whom educational programming is anticipated) is a key factor in defining the scope of any needs assessment. An understanding of the potential participants' educational needs is essential to the program planning process, and the ease or complexity of reaching different audiences for assessment varies greatly. This variation is an important factor in defining needs assessment scope and determining the effort needed to reach those whose participation in the assessment is required. The educational needs of a small, homogeneous group often can be assessed in a simple, straightforward manner on a relatively modest scale. For example, members of a metropolitan area's art alliance or nurses employed by the local hospital often can have their needs identified by an assessment that is quite limited in scope. But as the group to be examined increases in number and heterogeneity, the size of the effort required also increases.

The target population can be described in many ways: by geographical area, organizational setting, profession or occupation, or one or more other demographic characteristics. A target audience can be stratified and a sample drawn using these characteristics—an approach with particular merit if the intent is to develop programs for the total population. However, if these areas prove too broad and programming for subgroups is a possibility, the target population can be further segmented. For example, focusing on a single specialty area within a profession, employees at a particular career stage within an organization, residents of one region of a state, or persons within a specified age range can define a manageable target population for an initial needs assessment activity. Sometimes the expertise available to a continuing educator limits or defines the target population. Initial needs assessments results, coupled with the continuing educator's increased experience and expertise, programming successes, and consequent decisions to commit more resources, may result in expansion of these populations for future steps in the needs assessment strategy.

Content

The effect of content on the scope of a needs assessment is not as dependent on the size or variety of the content area as much as on the character of the content. Assessment of discrepancies between actual and desired information usually is far simpler than measurement of performance discrepancies. The former requires only determining whether members of a target population possess certain knowledge, but the latter involves determining their abilities to apply that knowledge.

Assessing the full range of educational needs of even a narrowly defined target population usually is feasible only as part of a long-term commitment to provide comprehensive continuing education programming for that group over an extended time period. For an initial or short-term project, continuing educators should direct their attention toward a discrete content area, just as they are advised to focus on a carefully delimited target population. They may base selection of the content area to be considered on one or more factors relevant to the target population. The content area selected may (1) represent a perceived need, (2) be considered an area of considerable importance to the group (for example, a critical component in professional practice or an essential concept), or (3) represent knowledge, skills, or performance abilities that members of the group use frequently. Continuing educators also may select a topic because (4) the educational provider has strengths in that area, (5) the topic is expected to generate substantial demand, (6) little continuing education programming currently exists in that

area, or (7) the individual or organization paying to send participants to the program believes that the topic merits consideration.
Identification of content areas is discussed further in Chapter Three.

Other Factors

Other factors affect the scope of a needs assessment to a lesser
degree. The time period for which programming will be planned
may at least partially dictate both the breadth and depth of the
assessment. A professional association seeking to develop educational activities for several years will be concerned with a wider
range of needs than one wishing to identify a topic for the next
annual meeting, for example. The type of programming to be
offered is another contributing factor. For example, an educational
institution striving to expand college credit offerings to new audiences, an ambitious and potentially costly objective, will need fairly
extensive information regarding potential students' educational
needs for the proposed courses, the likelihood of attracting participants to credit programs, and the content areas in which needs and
interest are greatest. By comparison, a provider of one-day workshops may require only some general information on content area
needs and preferences.

The scope of any needs assessment should be appropriate to the
type and scope of information the continuing educator requires and
to the expectations or requirements of those for whom the needs
assessment is being conducted, if they represent yet another group.
For example, the continuing education provider who agrees to conduct a needs assessment for an employer may require certain types of
information on which to base decisions about educational programming, while the employer may have some other, or different,
expectations for information about the employees. Aslanian (1985a,
pp. 52–53) suggests that needs assessments may be conducted for
any of five groups interested in adult learning:

1. People who provide adult learning
2. People who supply information and counseling to adults
3. People who make public policy for adult learning
4. Adults who are learning or who should be learning
5. Scholars who study adult learning

Each group's mission, goals, sphere of operation or influence, and, perhaps, political considerations will affect the scope of a needs assessment differently. Educational providers will seek practical data that enable them to design and deliver programs to meet the target population's needs and their own institutional goals, such as revenue generation, public service, or transfer of faculty research results to people who can apply them. Adult counselors may want knowledge about potential students' educational backgrounds and experiences, while those engaged in making public policy for adults will find data on factors facilitating or inhibiting educational participation noteworthy. One would hope that enrolled or potential students would want straightforward information on their learning needs, and they also may want to know how their knowledge, skills, and performance abilities compare with those of other adults. Scholars of adult education may benefit from additional information about any aspects of the adult learning process.

A healthy dose of realism is essential in determining the scope one reasonably can expect to address within the considerations and constraints already noted and those related to resources, discussed later in this chapter. Setting boundaries for potential target populations and content areas is an important step in defining the scope of any needs assessment. The continuing educator developing a comprehensive needs assessment strategy may be reluctant (and rightly so, perhaps) to impose the limitations of such boundaries but will find it helpful, if not essential, to do so at each phase of the needs assessment strategy.

Initial needs assessment measures may be undertaken with the realization that they are limited in comparison with long-range programming goals but represent a valuable first step. Often a total needs assessment strategy will begin on a small scale but include plans to expand the scope of the assessment if early measures prove fruitful. For example, the continuing educator wishing to offer a series of programs regionally or nationally might begin by assessing needs for one local program, a far simpler step than assessing the total population's need for multiple programs. If the local needs assessment for a limited content area yields useful data, the continuing educator can conduct additional assessments incorporating more content areas and populations representing broader geographic areas.

The scope of a needs assessment may be reduced by predetermined constraints. As noted earlier, needs assessments can include collection of information on scheduling, location, delivery preferences, and other procedural issues. However, if decisions regarding these factors have been made or imposed before the needs assessment, such data collection would be both unnecessary and counterproductive. Soliciting information on any topic implies that the responses given will affect decisions made regarding it, and it carries with it the continuing educator's obligation to consider that information in the decision-making process. If participants in a needs assessment realize that even a small portion of the information they are asked to provide will have no impact, they will understandably lose confidence in the continuing education unit or other organization or individual responsible for the assessment. For example, if an employer or educational provider has decided that programming will adhere to a specified time frame or delivery mode, or if the proposed program content dictates that the program be held in a laboratory available only on a college campus, or if the delivery mode has been predetermined, then the target population's preferences for scheduling are irrelevant. The scope of the needs assessment can be reduced by eliminating consideration of these factors.

All of these factors affect the scope of a needs assessment.

Therefore, before any decisions can be made about specific activities to be incorporated in a needs assessment strategy, the continuing educator has to make several decisions that help define the scope of the project.

Target Population

The target population (the group that is the subject of the assessment) is the population for which educational needs are to be identified. As discussed in Chapter Four, a needs assessment can focus on either the needs of the total group or those of individual group members. In either case, the nature of the population is another consideration in planning a successful needs assessment. Some populations tend to respond well to interactive assessments, while others are more accepting of written or visual exercises. For many groups, an assessment must be brief if participants are to remain attentive and active. Some populations respond differently according to the environment in which an assessment is conducted and the degree of formality imposed. For each target group, the continuing educator can find ways of making participants comfortable with the notion of being assessed and help them recognize that needs assessment is not pass-fail testing—they will not be judged. Similarly, because reluctant participants do not provide optimum data, continuing educators can encourage a target group's willing cooperation by knowing enough about the group to help participants recognize that their involvement is valuable. Several aspects of a target group, including their characteristics, accessibility, related data sources, motivation to identify needs, and ability to respond, are relevant in developing a needs assessment.

Characteristics of Group Members

Members of a group often share certain traits. Although it may be unwise to assume that all of those in a group are similar, most members of a given group often do have a number of characteristics in common. A high concentration of certain characteristics within a group may make that population more or less receptive to particular needs assessment methods or may cause some strategies or methods to be either particularly suitable or totally impractical. Some groups are more likely than others to be tolerant of a group of needs assessment activities requiring complicated and extensive responses. For example, nurses and accountants, who must deal with detail daily, may be receptive to fairly exhaustive assessment requiring substantial written detail but might feel self-conscious participating in role playing or videotaped exercises. Other groups may be amenable to only limited participation or may cooperate most fully in those activities that do not require detailed written responses. Clinical psychologists are experienced listeners and also tend to be comfortable speaking out in small groups, so they might respond well to assessment exercises dependent on these behaviors. Population groups differ in their educational level, pragmatic and theoretical leanings, degree of introspectiveness, and simply their amenability to assessment. Knowledge of all of these characteristics is helpful in planning a needs assessment and particularly in selecting the specific needs assessment methods and activities to be used.

Motivation to Identify Educational Needs

Some groups are eager to define their educational needs, often because they recognize the value of lifelong learning or face a mandatory continuing education requirement and would like to make their required learning a worthwhile experience. Obtaining the participation of such highly motivated group members generally is not difficult, and they may be receptive to complex needs assessment strategies requiring considerable effort on their part. For example, clinical dietitians, who are required to complete continuing education to remain registered, may be sufficiently interested in their educational needs to participate in an assessment requiring considerable initiative and involvement. When working with groups less concerned with their educational needs, the continuing educator may have to develop strategies to make needs assessment participation attractive. As an example, manufacturing plant workers forced to learn a new, radically different process may resist this change. An attractive needs assessment process that offers a positive social experience and requires little or no initiative on their part may be the key to obtaining their cooperation. Use of short, simple needs assessment strategies also can help earn the participation and cooperation of less enthusiastic groups.

Accessibility of Group Members

Some groups, such as employees within a given company or members of an organized community group (for example, a church group or a local Lions club) are easily accessible. Furthermore, frequently their participation in needs assessment activities is encouraged or even required by supervisors or organization leaders. For example, a school district establishing a wellness program for employees can easily schedule assessment exercises with expectations of reaching most members of the target population. Other groups may be widely scattered or not clearly defined, so that obtaining their participation is difficult, costly, or even impossible. (If it is truly impossible to reach them, the continuing educator may go to other sources to collect data with which to identify their needs.) Accessing hard-to-reach groups can be time consuming and expensive, but it is often possible to identify a means of reaching a similar group or a representative sample whose assessment can yield comparable data.

For example, in assessing need for an extended degree program in a metropolitan area it is impractical, if not impossible, to contact a representative sample of potential program participants. Therefore, the assessment may rely on information gathered from employees of one or more local firms who have characteristics similar to those attributed to potential enrollees. Although the data collected in this way cannot be generalized to the larger population, they can indicate whether the critical mass required for programming exists within the group assessed.

Related Data Sources

As already noted, members of some target populations may be so difficult to reach that it would be impractical to use them as participants in a needs assessment, and other data sources must be used instead. However, data sources other than the target population are usually used because the target population may not have sufficient understanding or control of the context in which it operates, or is engaged in providing services to others who may have additional, valuable perceptions of discrepancies in the target group's proficiencies. In assessing the needs of some populations, obtaining data from the target group alone may not be sufficient. Supplemental data sources can include census data, local or state planning reports, and a wide range of commercially and government maintained databases. For example, the unemployed often are a target population but they may have little understanding of the skills needed to qualify them for available employment. An occupational outlook database forecasting future employment opportunities may be the best source of information to indicate the types of knowledge, skills, and performance abilities that might make those individuals employable. Related data sources might include people whose roles are relevant to the target population's work or activities, such as peers, supervisors, clients, and colleagues. Nursing supervisors, who must handle nursing care problems that arise in health care institutions, can be an excellent source of information on the areas of practice in which floor nurses have educational needs.

Ability to Respond

Members of some target groups may lack the skills or physical capabilities required to engage in certain types of assessment. Additionally, some may have negative attitudes toward needs assessment or proposed educational programming, or they may simply lack the motivation to complete the assessment exercises. Ensuring that target group members will be able to participate as expected is an important consideration often overlooked because of assumptions that all people are physically and mentally capable and able to communicate easily.

Individuals may have physical handicaps, language barriers, learning disabilities, phobias, or educational deficits that prevent them from fully understanding and responding to assessment exercises. Continuing educators cannot assume literacy when working with target groups that do not have high school diplomas, for example. Thus, they might choose needs assessment methods incorporating direct observation, simulation, or oral (rather than written) methods to improve the likelihood of obtaining accurate responses from members of these groups. Participants who are unable to handle assessment exercises easily are forced to pay too much attention to the mechanics of the assessment; this focus on process will be at the expense of their consideration of the assessment substance, causing results that do not adequately reflect their knowledge, skills, or performance abilities. Older adults who have physical limitations, such as poor vision or hearing, or decreased manual dexterity, may have difficulty participating in some written exercises or group activities or using certain materials. Continuing educators can plan assessment strategies for these audiences that minimize activities requiring acute sight, hearing, or dexterity.

Attention to these variables is important. A needs assessment must be suited to the target population identified, because a technically excellent needs assessment can fail miserably if it is not. Inclusion of representatives of the target population in the needs assessment planning process is the best way of ensuring the process's appropriateness to the audience. Ongoing consultation is another way to gain insights into the group.

Resources

It is essential to come to a realistic determination early in the planning process of what funds, personnel with relevant expertise and experience, support personnel and services, facilities and equipment, and other assets are available to design, conduct, and evaluate the needs assessment. Attempting to stretch insufficient resources is imprudent, for resource scarcity can cause the continuing educator to compromise on the quality with which the assessment is conducted. A needs assessment conducted without adequate resources can be expected to produce poor results. Fortunately, it is possible to gain valuable information from needs assessments carried out with only limited resources, but it also is possible to develop a needs assessment strategy dependent on a substantial infusion of resources. The critical issue in conducting a high-quality needs assessment is not level of resources; it is selecting a strategy within the reach of one's resources, and then designing and implementing it in the most comprehensive, accurate, and thorough manner.

When available resources do not match those required for the desired needs assessment, plans can be revised to accommodate the resource limitations. Most often this means scaling down the assessment plans, but sometimes creative solutions can be found without sacrificing the original intent. For example, the cost of data collection, frequently an expensive step in needs assessment, can be reduced by taking advantage of others' investments to reach the target population. Fernicola addressed this possibility in writing about professional associations, noting, "The trick for associations with limited budgets is to find existing opportunities, such as meetings convened for other purposes or conference registration forms, to collect information related to specific questions about the educational needs of their members" (1987, p. 71). Often secondary information sources (for example, publications, commercial information services, research reports, U.S. Census data, county planning offices, *Statistical Abstracts of the United States*) can provide some of the information required, so that not all the data for the needs assessment must be collected from scratch. These sources are particularly useful for demographic, socioeconomic, and other data on population characteristics. Furthermore, by including a few such items in a needs assessment, continuing educators can compare their data to the normative information available, and perhaps identify subpopulations in addition to the originally targeted population.

A thorough evaluation of available resources before making any decisions about the complexity of a needs assessment helps the continuing educator avoid raising false expectations or devoting time to planning a needs assessment that is beyond the organization's resource capabilities.

Funding

Often funding is the first resource considered. By approximating available funding early in the planning process, those responsible can narrow the focus to appropriate options, particularly when they view their resources in the context of broad cost estimates for potential assessment methods. Presumably, an organization for which an assessment is to be conducted has committed some funds to the project. In addition, funds may be available from other sources.

Identification of funding opportunities most often must be initiated by the continuing educator, and it usually involves some development effort, if only on a small scale. Organizations with a vested interest, such as employers of target group members, those who insure them, or professional associations, may be amenable to providing financial support. Continuing educators also can seek funds through proposals to funding agencies. Other groups with similar data needs may be willing to contribute funds to a joint assessment, with the understanding that either the assessment will be conducted collaboratively or the data collected will be made available to the second group. (Collaborative relationships are not to be entered into casually. In the case of collaborative ventures, a number of additional factors must be considered, including the loss of autonomy that accompanies shared decision making.) Confirmation of all funding before adoption of a needs assessment strategy is critical, for embarking on a needs assessment without a total funding commitment can result in an abortive effort.

Expertise

Depending on the needs assessment method selected, people with competence in general research methodology, population sampling, group process, survey research, instrument design, design of simulation exercises, data analysis, statistics, and communications can be useful or even essential. Just as the range of available funding should be a factor in initial discussions, available expertise should be inventoried for consideration early on. Continuing educators can decide whether they have access to the necessary resources by comparing available expertise to the capabilities needed by specific assessment methods. If the assessment methods they are considering require expertise that is not readily available, they must address the practicality and cost of obtaining that expertise. Conversely, the continuing educator with ready access to certain areas of expertise can use it as a selection factor, giving special consideration to needs assessment methods for which that expertise would be an asset. The continuing educator who lacks access to the expertise required for a particular assessment method and has no plan for obtaining that expertise may have to consider alternative approaches.

Relevant Practical Experience

Practical experience with needs assessment differs from the expertise just discussed. In fact, it may have little to do with that type of expertise. Experience in designing, implementing, analyzing, and evaluating a needs assessment provides practical qualifications that are directly related to the needs assessment process. Examples of the experiences that may be desirable are involvement in enlisting participation, creating a positive environment, ensuring that all details of the assessment are handled properly, and anticipating and handling questions and problems that might arise. Familiarity with the organizations involved in the needs assessment and knowledge of the target population may also represent useful experience. All of these types of experience are helpful in ensuring that the assessment proceeds smoothly.

People bringing expertise but not relevant experience to the needs assessment process may benefit from the opportunity to work with one or more individuals having needs assessment experience. Because they lack understanding of the needs assessment process, people with expertise may have difficulty applying it to educational needs assessment. For example, the emphasis on needs assessment as a diagnostic tool, rather than as a test exercise with the potential of failure, may be a concept with which inexperienced people lack familiarity. Difficulty gaining participation and encouraging a constructive attitude toward the assessment could be the result.

Support Personnel

Those people with expertise and experience to define and guide the needs assessment process require staff support to carry out specific tasks. They direct or supervise support staff members, whose functions cover a range of activities including such things as scheduling appointments and facilities, conducting interviews, facilitating focus groups, and computerizing data analysis. For example, a demographer might determine how a sample of participants will be selected and provide instruction to the support personnel who actually draw the sample. Support personnel hired to conduct interviews would then be trained by someone knowledgeable about interviewing practices and procedures. Although support personnel need not always have special skills, it is important to know to what extent people with pertinent capabilities and characteristics are available to assist with the needs assessment. The roles of clerical and data entry personnel should not be underestimated.

Support Services

Many needs assessment methods rely on specialized services for their implementation or for analysis of the data they provide. Videotaping capabilities may be necessary (to prepare assessment materials or record activities such as role playing, for example), and computerized scoring of questionnaires can facilitate data analysis of large group surveys. When an institution or organization has access to such services, they often are available for a fee. Recognition of the support services that are available and the costs associated with using them can be helpful both in selecting a needs assessment method that takes advantage of those services and in determining that use of some methods would be ill-advised.

Facilities and Equipment

Some types of assessment exercises require large rooms, others are better performed in a series of small rooms, and still others may call for specialized space such as hospital rooms to provide the proper setting. Microphones, one-way mirrors for observation, multiple telephones for interviewing, and recording devices are among the equipment types that may be needed. Although it is difficult to inventory all available facilities in advance of planning a needs assessment, it is important to consider the special requirements of particular methods as they are discussed. Similarly, some types of data collection and analysis have facilities requirements quite apart from those needed to conduct the assessment exercises themselves. Computer hardware and software to support data entry and analysis are critical to many types of assessment. A telephone survey laboratory that includes computers for direct data entry eliminates the need for separate data entry steps when conducting telephone interviews. Other capabilities, such as photocopying and mailing services, also may be important.

Other Considerations

Resource limitations put constraints on the needs assessment process, but availability of plentiful resources need not dictate their use. It is not necessary to consume all funds available or to use state-of-the-art facilities if these resources are not essential to successful completion of the project. The purpose of identifying available resources is to put parameters on the selection of methods and to suggest methods that might build on the use of strengths; it is not to determine how extensive the needs assessment may become. Expansion or elaboration of an adequate needs assessment simply to use available resources is wasteful and can lead to escalation of a modest project into one that goes far beyond the effort required to obtain the data sought. Resource limitations can be frustrating, but they are best confronted early in the needs assessment development process, and they must be taken seriously. A successful needs assessment makes optimum use of those available resources that are appropriate to the project.

Level of Complexity of a Needs Assessment

The complexity of a needs assessment strategy can be determined by the number and intricacy of the methods used, the detail of the data they yield, and the ways in which the assessment is designed to collect, interpret, and use data. Needs assessments range from very basic (such as asking individuals what they believe their educational needs to be) to sophisticated endeavors. In planning an in-service program for school district personnel, the director of staff development used a basic form of needs assessment: she asked teachers to list five content areas in which they felt they needed more skills. A more complex assessment occurred when bank employees were videotaped as they interacted with clients, and their recorded behaviors and the paperwork they generated were rated using a predetermined scoring scheme.

A comprehensive needs assessment strategy may use a variety of assessment methods, ranging from simple to complex, over an extended time period. Although some individual needs assessment methods are associated primarily with basic, intermediate, or sophisticated degrees of complexity, a direct correspondence is not consistently found between the degree of complexity of a needs assessment and the specific needs assessment method used; most needs assessment methods can be applied with varying degrees of complexity. Interviews or mail questionnaires, for example, can be appropriate for the most basic or the most complex needs assessment strategy.

Assumptions about the complexity of specific needs assessment methods should not be made lightly or generalized. For example, Klevans (1987, p. 15) noted that "the assumption that paper-and-pencil tests do not tap complex performance-related skills has been challenged." She reports that when a variety of formats, including multiple choice, were used, they were found to be of comparable validity in assessing some aspects of competence. However, she also notes that whenever possible the assessment methods employed should be comparable to what is being measured, saying, "If behaviors are what is meant by competence, for example, then one should evoke behaviors in measuring it" (1987, p. 6). The complexity of a needs assessment plan and the detail of the data it produces, not the specific methods employed, determine the degree of complexity of a needs assessment.

Degree of complexity is not to be confused with scope. As Figure 2.1 indicates, needs assessments ranging from those which are quite narrow in scope to those of the broadest scope can be conducted with any degree of complexity. The simplest, most basic assessment strategy that can accomplish the stated purpose within the scope delineated is the best choice. Unnecessary complexity adds nothing to the final product, and it usually results in excessive expenditure of resources. Indeed, if the people conducting the assessment have limited experience and expertise in needs assessment, they actually may reduce the likelihood of producing high-quality data by conducting a more sophisticated needs assessment. Regardless of the degree of complexity of a needs assessment, the most frequent reason for poor data is that those responsible do not have the resources necessary to use the chosen methods correctly.

Figure 2.1. Relationship Between Complexity and Scope.

C	SCOPE	
O		
M	Narrow scope	Broad scope
P	Low complexity	Low complexity
L		
E		
X	Narrow scope	Broad scope
I	High complexity	High complexity
T		
Y		

The degree of complexity suitable for accomplishing the task can be determined once the purpose and scope of the needs assessment are determined. Appropriateness to the group being assessed and the availability of resources with which to implement the assessment are other considerations that enter into this decision. If the complexity of a proposed needs assessment would be incompatible with either the target population or the resources allocated to the project, the purpose or scope of the needs assessment most likely will require modification. Setting the degree of complexity for an assessment below that suggested by its purpose and scope is likely to result in a needs assessment that does not accomplish the intended objectives.

Most often, assessments can be accomplished in a simple, straightforward process when the purpose is to measure unidimensional educational needs and the scope is fairly narrow. Examples of unidimensional educational and operational needs are information gaps in the target population's knowledge, the availability of educational activities in a particular content area, the scheduling preferences of a target population, and the identification of underserved populations. Assessment of multidimensional needs may require more complicated assessments. Ability to apply skills across a spectrum of activities and development of a full continuing education curriculum for a given population are examples of purposes for which a continuing educator must assess multidimensional needs. Assessments that are broad in scope may require more complex needs assessments because of the number and diversity of objectives generally found in them. Table 2.1 illustrates the degrees of complexity appropriate to a range of purposes and scopes.

Sometimes the desired degree of complexity goes beyond what can be measured practically. In such cases, it is important to be realistic about the limitations of needs assessment and to balance the value of the information to be obtained against the cost of obtaining it. Often the continuing educator finds that beyond a certain point the value of anticipated needs assessment results cannot justify the time and money required for the complexity desired. For example, Argyris and Schön (1974) talk about theories of action that set behavioral norms that are important in identifying discrepancies between actual and desired proficiencies that indicate educational needs. However, it is difficult to assess people's performance in relation to these norms, because in addition to requiring sophisticated measurement devices and labor-intensive procedures, such assessment requires evaluation over time and in a variety of settings. The resources necessary for this type of assessment may be justified in some situations, but most often they will be too extensive for a continuing educator's consideration.

Table 2.1. Continuum of Needs Assessment Complexity
with Examples.

Degree of Complexity	Purpose Examples	Scope Examples
Least Complex	To determine optimum scheduling for management programs	Middle managers at local manufacturing firm, for winter seminar series
	To identify information deficits about tax laws among accountants	Local accountants' knowledge of tax laws new this year
	To learn which program delivery methods are best suited to senior citizens	Regional senior citizens' receptivity to a variety of classroom and distance education methods
Intermediate	To identify target audiences for dissemination of findings from educational research	National groups concerned with collaborative learning methods
	To measure lawyers' communication discrepancies	National legal professional association members' use of communications skills in the courtroom
Most Complex	To assess teachers' language arts teaching discrepancies in the classroom	Public school teachers' success nationally in teaching language arts in grades one through six

Summary

Continuing educators must consider several factors before they begin to plan a needs assessment. First, they must determine the purpose and scope of the assessment, its appropriateness to the target population, the resources available to implement it, and the degree of complexity with which it will be conducted. Then they must proceed with more specific decisions about content areas, audiences, and other topics to be assessed (preferences about scheduling, for example), and the methods they will use. Thorough examination of these factors represents a big step toward ensuring that the needs assessment, when developed, addresses the defined objectives in a satisfactory manner.   The continuing educator who does not take the time to evaluate these factors risks finding midway through the assessment that the needs assessment as it is being executed will not produce the data anticipated or that the support needed to complete all phases of the assessment (from conception and data collection through analysis and reporting) is not there.

A needs assessment can be designed to meet a wide range of purposes. The scope can be narrow or broad, and of any degree of complexity. However, it cannot be successful unless it is relevant to the target population, for irrelevance quickly leads to diminished participation and inaccurate data.

Perhaps most important, a needs assessment can be conducted at little or great expense. The size of the resource commitment does not determine success; rather, the congruence between the resources needed and the resources available does. For this reason, a realistic, comprehensive comparison of the resources available with those needed for the proposed assessment is critical. Many needs assessments fail because during the process the continuing educator finds that the cost is greater than anticipated. Corners are cut in an attempt to operate within the confines of existing resources, destroying the quality of the assessment and resulting in poor, incomplete, or inaccurate data. It is far better to design and execute a modest needs assessment that is well within the continuing educator's means than to embark on an assessment that stretches resources to the point that any unanticipated expense will leave the project without sufficient funding for completion.

When addressed before embarking on a needs assessment, these considerations provide a framework and guidelines that describe the parameters of the needs assessment and enable those responsible for it to focus on what to assess and how to assess it.

Chapter Three

Deciding What to Assess

Observing the opportunities to provide programming for professionals in midcareer, a small university established a continuing professional education department. Starting with a broad mission statement, the new unit set out to define its role and its niche as an educational provider. One of the first tasks the small staff faced was establishing goals and objectives for the populations they would serve and the ways in which they would serve them. Staff members recognized that needs assessment was a key to defining their goals but they struggled with decisions regarding what to assess. Should they begin by exploring the educational needs of specific groups or should they identify underserved populations first? Should they look for audiences that would serve as outlets for dissemination of faculty members' research results or ways of capitalizing on their partnerships with other institutions?

Few continuing educators find themselves in the enviable position of building a new operation like this one. However, frequently they do face similar decisions regarding use of needs assessment. The reasons for conducting an educational needs assessment may be varied and multiple, and they may relate to any aspect of program design, development, and delivery. As indicated in earlier chapters, needs assessments can provide information related to the content, structure, audience, scheduling, marketing, and presentation of educational activities. Despite this range of opportunities, the primary focus of needs assessment often is on identification and clarification of educational needs. Continuing educators use the information obtained from such assessments to define program content that will enable them to serve their clients effectively while meeting their organization's goals and objectives. Identification of target populations for an educational activity is another likely focus for needs assessments, frequently enabling a continuing educator to expand the audience for a particular program or take advantage of a faculty member's expertise. Operational information that will guide selection of delivery methods, scheduling, and marketing can be an important result of a needs assessment, but rarely do such market research topics constitute the primary focus.

In continuing education, assessment of educational needs most often is associated with continuing professional education (Nowlen, 1980, 1988; McKillip, 1987), defined here in the broadest sense as education for the workplace, with no concern over what constitutes a "profession" as opposed to an "occupation" (Queeney, 1992). Whether measuring individuals or groups, needs assessment for continuing professional education emphasizes identification of both strengths and discrepancies between actual and desired knowledge, skills, and performance abilities in the workplace. Recognizing strengths allows educators to help practitioners build on them and also highlights content areas in which additional education may not be needed. Recognizing discrepancies often helps identify areas that can be addressed by educational programming, although education cannot be expected to address all types of discrepancies. For example, failure to meet some standards may stem from characteristics of the practice setting and may not be amenable to educational intervention. However, for the majority of discrepancies identified, education can lead to improvement and continuing educators can develop programming with the goal of improving workers' performance (Klevans, 1987).

Although continuing professional education may be the most frequent focus of needs assessment in continuing education, it is far from the only appropriate one. Needs assessment can be used to develop programs to further personal enrichment or leisure interests or to promote the public interest. Successful continuing educators recognize that needs assessment can enhance their programming in all areas and then review their rosters of activities and clients in that context. For example, when data revealed that older Americans' driving skills were not as sharp as they might be and that such drivers presented a potential danger to society, driver refresher programs for senior citizens were developed, generating large enrollments and positive evaluations.

Establishing Priorities

As discussed in Chapter Two, continuing educators usually conduct a needs assessment for one or more specific purposes, some of which have higher priority than others. Continuing educators' priorities in conducting an assessment most often are an outgrowth of their organizational priorities, established as part of goal setting, strategic planning, and related organizational activities. Forthright acknowledgment of these priorities is important to ensure that the needs assessment will achieve its intended purpose. It is easy to assume that the continuing educator's sole reason for assessing needs is to gather data on which to base program development and delivery and to look no further. However, such an assumption ignores the fact that the continuing educator may be responding to other priorities as well. One or more of the following priorities may drive a continuing educator to conduct a needs assessment:

- To further the educational mission of the institution
- To generate revenue
- To serve a particular professional group, segment of the community, or other target audience
- To increase use of available academic resources
- To build relationships within the institution (for example, with academic departments)

- To build external relationships (for example, with influential citizens or groups)
- To generate favorable publicity
- To develop a research agenda
- To identify new audiences
- To utilize new or unique delivery systems
- To meet programming quotas
- To provide education of the highest quality
- To protect the public interest by providing continuing education for professionals

The procedure for establishing priorities varies. Those organizations and institutions with a strong strategic plan may need only refer to it for guidance in translating mission statement, goals, and objectives into needs assessment priorities. For example, a continuing education unit striving to generate revenue might devise a needs assessment to identify high-demand programs, whereas the organization emphasizing building faculty relationships might want to identify groups that would be interested in the content areas represented by key faculty members. Particularly those continuing educators who do not have a strong plan may find it helpful to involve a needs assessment team, as discussed in Chapter Four, to select priorities for a needs assessment. Such a team, composed of unit and institutional representatives, individual and organizational clients, and faculty members from relevant academic departments, functions most effectively if given some criteria for the establishment of priorities. Factors that can affect the likelihood that needs assessment findings will be translated into successful educational activities often are among the most important criteria. The strengths and weaknesses of both the continuing education unit and the institution that houses it, commonly recognized areas of need, competing continuing education programs, and organizational politics are examples of such criteria. If the continuing educator or needs assessment team identifies more priorities than reasonably can be addressed by the projected needs assessment, additional criteria may further refine the list.

At first glance several priorities may appear reasonably compatible, but upon closer consideration it may be seen that they present potential conflicts. The course of action necessary to respond to one priority may be in direct opposition to that indicated to address another. For example, a continuing educator may recognize that serving a professional association, utilizing available academic resources, and generating revenue are equally important. A conflict occurs when the data collected indicate that the professional association members need updating in content areas for which the continuing educator has no academic resources and that potential program participants have so little interest in the topic that they are unlikely to enroll in such educational activities. Thus such educational programming would not use available academic resources, and generating even enough revenue to cover expenses would be difficult. Often the continuing educator is forced to make hard choices and to respond to only one of several competing priorities. Sometimes it is possible, through creative program design, marketing, or other strategies, to respond at least in part to two or more apparently incompatible priorities. Occasionally the continuing educator may find that certain priorities cannot be adequately addressed by the educational programming under consideration. There may be political or policy issues beyond the reach of educational programming. Or the type of educational programming required may be so costly that the program would have to operate at a financial loss, be exorbitantly priced, or gain external funding.

Although continuing educators may not be eager to acknowledge that their first priority is to generate revenue or that they want to offer only educational activities that build on faculty expertise, doing so frankly at the outset forms the basis for constructing a sound needs assessment. If such priorities are not acknowledged in initial discussion, they are not incorporated in the needs assessment and the assessment data will be of limited value. In addition, participants in the assessment may develop false expectations based on the assumption that topics covered in the assessment reflect genuine possibilities for specific types of educational activities when in fact they do not. A needs assessment should cover only those areas that are consistent with the priorities of the continuing educator and any other groups or individuals included in the process. For example, continuing educators should not assess interpersonal skills if priorities dictate that they will be unable to deliver the type of labor- and time-intensive programs required to teach this topic.

Identifying Content Areas

In some cases, the priorities selected define the content areas to be considered in a needs assessment. For example, if providing an outstanding researcher with a forum in which to present her research results is the highest priority, the content of the program will be the researcher's field. The needs assessment would identify a target audience that needs education in that content area. The assessment also might address the audience's level of understanding, requirements for background information, and possible opportunities for application of the material presented.

Frequently, however, a needs assessment is conducted at least in part to identify specific strengths and discrepancies within particular content areas, with the intent of offering educational activities to address the discrepancies. For needs assessments of this type, identification of the broad content areas to be considered is an important step. A single needs assessment activity can effectively address only a limited content area; a comprehensive needs assessment strategy can consider a number of areas, up to and including the entire range of content areas representing the potential educational needs of a specific target population. But regardless of the scope, unless limiting factors have been imposed, continuing educators are well advised to approach identification of content areas from a broad perspective. For example, whether a narrowly focused, discrete needs assessment activity or an extensive needs assessment strategy is the goal, continuing educators can begin by looking at an overview of all areas included in the practice of a profession, or all activities a particular clientele group engages in. From this broad view they can identify the content area for their needs assessment. In addition to providing an essential framework for a total needs assessment strategy, this approach can facilitate informed decisions regarding the content focus of individual assessment activities. It also creates a context in which continuing educators can incorporate otherwise isolated needs assessment activities into comprehensive needs assessment strategies at a later date, and it helps ensure that they do not overlook pertinent content areas or unintentionally eliminate them from consideration.

For a professional group, a practice description can serve as the framework for identifying potential content areas. A practice description outlines the scope of practice of a given profession, listing at several levels of specificity the things practitioners do in the daily execution of their job responsibilities. The scope of practice includes all broad areas, or domains, of practice within the profession. Within each domain are a number of more narrowly defined responsibilities, or categories of duties, and each responsibility includes a number of specific tasks that make up the daily practice of members of that profession. Although each practitioner may not do everything contained in the practice description, the profession assumes responsibility for performance of all of the tasks (Queeney and Smutz, 1990). Using nursing as an example, domains included in the practice description range from providing direct patient care to conducting research. Most nurses do the former at some stage of their careers, but relatively few become involved in research. In the domain of providing direct patient care, responsibilities include assessing the patient's condition, performing medical procedures as directed by a physician, and attending to the patient's personal hygiene needs. Tasks incorporated in the responsibility of assessing the patient's condition include interviewing the patient, examining the patient, and reviewing patient records. (Staff, 1984)

In a number of professions, including clinical dietetics, accounting, speech/language pathology, and architecture, fairly sophisticated practice descriptions delineating domains, responsibilities, and tasks as described here have been developed. A practice description of this detail certainly is not necessary to provide a basis for selecting the content areas of a needs assessment, but it can be used if it is available. A far simpler outline of the broad domains of practice also can provide an adequate starting point. In a similar manner, the continuing educator who wants to serve target groups other than professionals can approach identification of content areas by outlining the full range of the things the groups do that are relevant to potential programming. A functional outline of this type can be developed for any target group by brainstorming, using a Delphi technique, or in many cases by reviewing available literature.

Ideally, an ongoing assessment to identify a group's range of continuing education needs eventually would cover all areas included in a practice description or outline of topics, although it is neither practical nor feasible to attempt to assess the entire scope of content areas at one time. The data resulting from such an effort would be overwhelming, so that by the time all data were analyzed and interpreted they would be out of date and perhaps no longer relevant for program planning.

Whether the goal is to select the content area for the first step in a needs assessment strategy or for a single activity, several criteria can help continuing educators evaluate the range of possibilities and select the ones for which they will assess needs. Educational criteria for selecting the content areas for a needs assessment are perception of need, importance to the target population and to those supporting participation, and frequency of use. Operational criteria necessary to ensure program viability are the provider's strengths, likelihood of demand, and existing programming. Taken individually, some of these criteria may not point to selection of a particular content area, but they can serve as filters to determine program feasibility.

Perception of Need

Often representatives of a target group, their supervisors, or their colleagues have perceptions of group members' educational needs or areas with which they have difficulty. For example, new managers may feel that they need to learn about dealing with problem employees, or recreational joggers may believe that they need to learn about stretching exercises. On the assumption that members of the target population have valid perspectives and would welcome assistance with the knowledge, skills, and performance abilities they find most challenging, a continuing educator may choose this criterion to identify the focus of a needs assessment activity. Potential participants' perceptions that they have an educational need also can be powerful factors in motivating them to enroll in a continuing education activity. As Monette observed, "Some educators believe that a need is a need only when it is recognized by the potential learner as a need, thereby providing motivation to close the gap" (1977, p. 121). Selecting content areas in which potential participants believe they have a need offers an advantage: it enables continuing educators to market the programs that were developed on the basis of the needs assessment data. Assessment of an area of perceived need also may help target group members realize that they are not weak in an area in which they felt they were. More often, however, assessment of areas of perceived need will identify specific discrepancies that, once addressed, might be eliminated and thus ease participants' difficulty with activities based in that content area.

Importance to the Target Population and to Those Supporting Participation

Some activities and the content areas they represent are of considerable significance to a target population or to those supporting their educational participation; others are less important. Importance may be relative to an individual's life or career stage or to an organization's priorities. For unemployed or underemployed individuals, programs that enhance professional credentials or improve job skills can be expected to take priority over those providing personal enrichment, for example. Within a given profession, some areas are considered more important to satisfactory performance than others. Librarians, for instance, may regard application of new technology as more important than cataloguing. Importance also may be related to the criticality of knowledge, skills, or performance abilities to actual behaviors. As an example, hospital administrators may consider hospital safety procedures more important than housekeeping efficiencies because the former are more likely to affect patients. Similarly, employers or others paying for the continuing education may consider some content areas very important but may be reluctant to support education on other topics that they believe have little or no importance. The relative importance of content areas and the tasks or activities they represent offer valid criteria for determining the content focus of a needs assessment.

Frequency of Use

Members of any target population have the greatest need for proficiency in content areas that relate to the things they do most often. For example, news reporters must have strong interviewing skills. Although people often believe that their strengths are greatest in the areas with which they have greatest familiarity and experience—their daily activities—research shows that this frequently is not the case (Office of Continuing Professional Education, 1985).

Often people are complacent about routine tasks, becoming lax or failing to recognize and implement new and better ways of performing them. Thus, emphasis on assessment of content related to regularly performed activities can be meaningful, because when discrepancies are discovered, continuing education has the potential to have a positive impact on the practices that make up a substantial portion of people's daily activity.

Provider's Strengths

Continuing educators' organizations or institutions may have some areas of particular expertise represented by a well-known faculty member, a leading undergraduate or graduate program, or outstanding research. Such strengths offer continuing educators opportunities to develop unique programming and a particular market niche. For example, continuing educators at a large state university developed a series of workshops around an engineering faculty member with an international reputation in fracture and fatigue of metals. Identifying audiences that have a need for educational activities that take advantage of these types of strengths enables continuing educators to build positive relationships with individual faculty members or academic units. Recognized personnel and programs can be useful in attracting program participants, and their contact with new audiences can enhance the institutional or organizational image.

Likelihood of Generating Demand

Regardless of how intent continuing educators are on meeting educational needs, none want to offer programs in which the target audience has little or no interest. They can avoid this by collecting information that indicates potential demand for educational activities on particular topics or for programs taught by particular instructors during a needs assessment conducted primarily to determine educational needs. For example, in assessing landscape architects' educational needs, one continuing educator also collected information indicating that members of this group were likely to enroll in programs on marketing their services but that they were not eager to participate in activities related to plant identification. Market research to determine demand alone can be conducted using needs assessment principles, procedures, and methods. Even if the content area is not one for which substantial need exists, the continuing educator may decide to develop and deliver programming for other reasons (to respond to a demand, for instance, or to generate revenue).

Existing Continuing Education Programming

A study of the environment can tell the continuing educator which existing programs might compete with a proposed educational activity and can provide information on their focus, quality, and success in attracting participants. Regardless of the amount of educational need, if a number of good continuing education activities are available on a particular topic, it might not be a productive one for further consideration. For this reason, the continuing educator may choose to focus on content areas for which programming is scarce. However, lack of available continuing education alone is not sufficient reason to focus on a content area. There may be a dearth of programming because the topic does not warrant the programming; a sufficient audience may not exist or the topic may be one that cannot attract an audience, for example. Thus, continuing educators should use this criterion in combination with one or more of those already discussed.

Other Considerations

In order to consider fully all possibilities, continuing educators are well advised to base their initial identification of potential content areas to be assessed on their priorities and the factors discussed in Chapter Two. At this early stage, they should not eliminate topics because of perceived difficulties in assessing them. They can select several content areas even though assessment of some of them may prove infeasible or impractical. To eliminate them from initial consideration would be to risk ignoring potentially critical and fertile areas. Once a content area has been identified as appropriate and the details of its assessment considered, the continuing educator may find that it is more feasible than originally thought.

Knowledge, Skills, and Performance Abilities

Knowledge, skills, and the performance abilities to apply them are required at all levels of professional performance and personal activity, and all represent potential areas for assessment. Knowledge is the most basic area. Without knowledge, even basic performance of skills and abilities is not possible. For this reason, and because it is least difficult to measure and to address, knowledge is the focus of most educational needs assessment. However, continuing education, which generally strives to build on previous learning, often has as its objective not only imparting knowledge but also enabling participants to improve their performance through enhancement of existing skills and abilities or acquisition of new ones. If continuing education participation is expected to improve the quality of what people do, a needs assessment must include examination of practice-oriented skills and performance abilities, those applications of knowledge to daily activities that define practice or behaviors. The information gathered can point to areas in which individuals exhibit discrepancies that could be addressed by educational interventions, leading to improved performance.

When continuing educators have as their long-range goal the provision of education that will lead to improved performance, they must examine knowledge and skills, finally getting as close as possible to assessing performance abilities, or proficiencies. If educators do not consider knowledge and skills separately, they may find themselves unable to determine the locus of the need—that is, whether the need relates to knowledge, to skills, or to performance abilities. For example, an assessment of accountants' auditing performance may indicate that they are producing inaccurate audits. In order to identify their specific needs, the continuing educator first has to find out whether they lack adequate knowledge to conduct audits. If the knowledge appears adequate, the next step is to determine whether their skills are sufficient to allow them to apply the knowledge to the task of conducting an audit. If their skills are at an acceptable level, the final question is whether they have the performance abilities, including the judgment, to use the knowledge and skills in a practice setting.

Knowledge

A base of knowledge is not sufficient to ensure that individuals perform well in their personal, family, community, and professional lives, but it is necessary. Knowledge was recognized as key to professional practice as far back as 1915, when Flexner, perhaps the first person to write about the professions, stated that professionals "derive their raw material from science and learning" (1915, p. 904). Houle (1980) observed that possession of a unique body of knowledge is one of the key traits of a profession. Professions can be described in part by "a basic body of specialized knowledge and methodologies which, if properly applied, provide the solutions to well defined and recurrent problems" (Elman and Lynton, 1985).

For needs assessment purposes, this description goes well beyond the professions. Everyone requires knowledge to function effectively in all facets of daily living, ranging from family management to pursuit of leisure activities to community participation, and hence it is a key component of educational needs assessment.

Three types of knowledge needs can be described as *existing knowledge, presumed knowledge,* and *new knowledge.*

Existing Knowledge. Existing knowledge is knowledge that is available but not new; it is information to which people have had access for some time. Individuals' needs for existing knowledge frequently are underestimated. It is often assumed that if information exists, it is in the hands of those who have a call for it. In reality, these people may need a focused, systematic review of the knowledge that underlies tasks and activities that they perform routinely.

Individuals' receptivity to knowledge changes over time. People frequently have not thoroughly assimilated available, relevant information, even if they have been exposed to it. They may have considered it uninteresting or irrelevant and hence failed to acquire it, but the importance of that information may become apparent in a different context or professional or personal life stage. The engineer with no knowledge of public speaking techniques whose new position requires that she speak before large audiences and the citizen appointed to the local planning commission who lacks knowledge of zoning regulations are examples of people who have developed new needs for existing information. Some people, although generally familiar with a content area, do not realize that a particular knowledge base exists and thus are unaware of their need for that information. Even more frequently, people assume that they have a comprehensive base of knowledge related to their routine activities when in fact their knowledge is incomplete or outdated. For these reasons, knowledge assessment that goes beyond self-identification of needs is critical.

Presumed Knowledge. Knowledge presumably already acquired through education and experience may in fact be lacking; this represents a potential need worthy of investigation, and one that often is overlooked. People do not like to admit that they lack knowledge others presume they have or that they are operating without the solid base of information they should have. Knowledge gleaned some time ago but not used recently may be outdated or forgotten, or it may have different implications when considered from the perspective of a new life or career stage. For example, the high school science teacher who has taught chemistry for many years and is assigned to teach biology during the coming year may need to review the biology that presumably was learned earlier. Often assumptions are made that certain knowledge was gained in the course of one's education and experience when such is not the case. Sometimes people actually misunderstand information, so that the knowledge they believe they have is inaccurate. Needs assessment can uncover these knowledge deficits.

New Knowledge. Because new knowledge constantly is being created, it is more easily recognized as a need. Continuing educators usually do not have to conduct formal assessments to determine that recently developed knowledge represents areas of need for those target groups working with or affected by it. The continuing educator seeking to serve specific target groups may be able to identify this type of need simply by keeping up with research findings, trends, laws, policies, procedures, and practices related to those groups, a task that advisory groups or representatives of individual professions can assist with. Identifying needs for new knowledge also can be approached from the perspective of content areas. Environmental scanning, or systematic review of appropriate publications and other information sources, can reveal new knowledge in a variety of content areas that may be appropriate for educational programming. A market research–oriented needs assessment can identify potential users of that knowledge for whom educational activities might be designed. For example, knowledge of the disabled students' rights specified in recently passed legislation may be of interest not only to those students and their educators but also to the parents of such students, advocacy groups, and social service agencies. The continuing educator's challenge, to be addressed by further needs assessment, may be identifying target audiences and their specific knowledge deficits for educational programming on this topic.

Because knowledge is an essential component of both skills and performance abilities, the continuing educator should have some assurance of adequate knowledge before assessing related skills or performance abilities. Without documentation of knowledge, it is difficult if not impossible to distinguish between identified discrepancies caused by the absence of skills or performance abilities and those which are the result of a knowledge deficit. An alternative approach to assessing knowledge first is to begin by assessing performance abilities or skills, and then back up to assess skills or knowledge, respectively, if discrepancies are identified. This approach is recommended when indications of a sound knowledge base or strong skills are present.

Skills

Elman and Lynton's (1985) notion that professional knowledge includes three components can be used to describe the relationship between knowledge and skills as a continuum. The first component they describe is the *basic knowledge* inherent in any content area. This body of information underlies a profession, practice, or content area, distinguishes it from other areas, and provides the base from which it is developed. For architects, design elements are an example of basic knowledge. *Applied knowledge,* the second point on the continuum, represents the integration of isolated facts and pieces of information into procedures and processes. At this point, individuals' comprehension of the basic knowledge allows them to see ways in which various components are related and can be combined. An element of diagnosis or judgment may be involved. Again using architecture as an example, aggregating understanding of individual design elements into a process to be used in designing structures represents applied knowledge. The last point on Elman and Lynton's continuum is *skills*, which they define as building on basic and applied knowledge to carry out specified activities. Skills represent practical application of theoretical information—the ability to use knowledge to produce results. Referring once again to architecture, designing structures using accumulated knowledge about design elements and the design process represents a skill.

As this metaphor implies, skills involve application of knowledge and usually require integration of a number of facts and concepts in a coherent, productive manner. Skills are essentially technical in nature (Cervero, 1988). They reflect substantive learning, content knowledge, and facility with advanced cognitive processes. Because they are tools that individuals use in all aspects of their lives, skills are critical to accomplishing personal and professional tasks. Without the ability to convert knowledge into the skills required for daily living, work, and recreation, people cannot perform even simple tasks effectively.

Assessment of skills represents the next, substantially closer, step toward identifying discrepancies between actual and desired performance or practice. Skills assessment determines whether individuals can apply specific knowledge in accomplishing tasks and solving problems. In assessing skills, it is possible to determine that individuals can design a building, extract a tooth, balance a checkbook, or diagnose a case of depression. It is possible to learn that although people have adequate knowledge, their skills in applying it are limited in certain ways. This type of assessment data is useful in pinpointing educational needs. However, in collecting and interpreting such data, it is important to recognize that assessment of skills alone lacks context. Individuals may have the skills necessary to perform a task or procedure but not the judgment required for successful application of those skills. Architects with good design skills may not apply them appropriately, for example, because they fail to consider their clients' financial constraints, site topography, zoning restrictions, or other factors. Like knowledge, skills are a necessary, but not sufficient, component of performance.

As the continuing educator seeks to serve a specific target population over time, assessment of that group's skills can be significant in providing meaningful, practice-oriented educational programming. Improved performance may be the ultimate goal, but discrepancies in performance cannot be confirmed without first ascertaining mastery of relevant skills.

Performance Abilities

The term *performance abilities* refers to the application of a series of skills to specific situations. It represents the integration of those skills, with their underlying knowledge base, into daily activities and practice (Smutz and Queeney, 1990). Performance abilities include an attitudinal component (Schein, 1973) that enables individuals to carry discrete skills into a practice context, often applying them in combination with other skills.

Decisions regarding what to do, when to do it, and whether to act at all represent the contextual component of actual performance. Individuals' consideration of timing; alternative strategies; physical, sociological, economic, or psychological conditions; and long-range implications are among the contextual factors that comprise performance abilities. People who can perform isolated skills properly are not always able to incorporate them satisfactorily in their routine practices. Consideration of context requires conceptual and critical thinking. It relies heavily on judgment to make decisions about the appropriateness of using particular knowledge and skills in specific situations. As societal conditions change, individuals increasingly are forced to cope with competing priorities and values, uncertainty and ambiguity, and ever-increasing complexity.

These changes have implications for the continuing educator, particularly in the area of continuing professional education. Effective workplace education recognizes that professional practice no longer requires only that individuals be able to apply a specified body of knowledge or set of skills to a standardized problem. The emphasis appears to be shifting "from solving problems to defining them, from answering questions to deciding which is the right question to ask" (Elman and Lynton, 1985). Professionals must define and analyze the problems they face and then derive an appropriate plan of action from their storehouse of knowledge and skills. Assessment of performance abilities thus becomes an examination of individuals' strengths and weaknesses in applying their own education, experience, and values to specific situations in the context of societal values (Elman and Lynton, 1985).

In assessing performance abilities, emphasis is on defining and solving problems. Both the processes used and the outcomes achieved are valid components of performance abilities assessment. If the correct process was used but the outcome was poor, even though external factors may have been involved, it is possible that sound knowledge and skills were not applied with sound judgment, perhaps signaling a role for continuing education. It is difficult to assess judgment and even more difficult to teach it, but it cannot be ignored. Regardless of the outcome, if the process was incorrect one also must consider whether knowledge and skills were applied incorrectly. If so, this may reveal discrepancies in ability that result in poor performance and indicate an educational need.

Ideally, performance abilities are assessed directly in the actual practice context. Strict observation and evaluation of daily activities or practice in personal or work settings offers the opportunity to obtain a clear picture of strengths and discrepancies, and hence of areas that need educational intervention. Unfortunately, such assessment is costly, frequently inconvenient or even disruptive in the situation under observation, and therefore out of reach for most if not all organizations seeking to identify continuing education needs. Fortunately, as discussed in Chapters Five, Six, and Seven, more practical alternatives are available.

A needs assessment strategy intended to guide continuing education for a specific target audience over an extended period of time often includes a combination of knowledge, skills, and performance abilities measures. This comprehensive approach has particular merit for development of continuing professional education, which most often has improvement of practice as its primary goal and emphasizes competent execution of duties and responsibilities (Queeney and Smutz, 1990). However, even for some areas within continuing professional education, assessment of knowledge may be all that is required. If knowledge needs are substantial, they must be addressed before application of knowledge to skills or performance abilities can be considered. In other cases continuing educators may recognize that they lack the capabilities to teach skills or performance abilities; in such cases assessment of needs directly related to performance or practice would be of little use or even unnecessary.

Types of Needs

As discussed in Chapter One, needs are different from either wants or demands. Needs describe discrepancies between current and desired states; they may or may not reflect wants or demands. However, educational needs assessment frequently spills over into areas of wants and demands. For example, assessment of operational needs may seek information regarding potential participants' scheduling preferences or willingness to pay for educational activities. For the continuing educator, incorporating such factors in a needs assessment may be a matter of practicality. The opportunity to collect what might be termed marketing information cannot and should not be ignored. Broadly defining needs assessment to include factors related to wants and demands reinforces the appropriateness of their inclusion. The only caution to be issued here is one of balance. Unless the continuing educator's primary purpose is market research, the primary emphasis of a needs assessment should be to identify educational needs. Solicitation of other information should be an unobtrusive component of the overall exercise. Participants in a needs assessment may feel deceived if they are asked to identify strengths and weaknesses but find themselves instead providing information about program delivery.

Needs can be classified in a number of different ways. Bradshaw (1974) described social needs as normative, comparative, felt, and expressed. Monette categorized "basic human needs, felt and expressed needs, normative needs, and comparative needs" (1977, p. 117). Others writing on the topic have used different organizational schemes, all of them valid (Argyris and Schön, 1974; Boyle, 1981; Klevans, 1987; Sleezer, 1992).

Building on the variety of classifications available, for purposes of educational needs assessment it is useful to consider needs in terms of several characteristics, all describing valid subjects for assessment. These characteristics can best be explained by a series of mutually exclusive pairs: *perceived versus assessed needs, felt versus expressed needs, normative versus comparative needs, discrepancy versus maintenance needs,* and *current versus anticipated needs.* Within each pair of descriptors, a need can be of one type or the other but not both. A need may also have one characteristic from several or even all of the pairs. Clarification of type of need helps continuing educators understand the kinds of needs they are dealing with, and the limitations and implications of those needs. This focus increases the likelihood that a needs assessment will generate data that will enable continuing educators to make sound program planning decisions.

Perceived Versus Assessed Needs

Perceived needs are those needs that individuals believe they have; assessed needs are identified through a structured assessment process. This pair of needs is the most important to the concept of needs assessment, for if no difference existed between needs individuals perceive they have and those identified through assessment, the role of needs assessment would be limited to asking individuals to identify the discrepancies between their current levels of knowledge, skills, or performance abilities and those they wish to attain. However, most often individuals' perceived needs have been found to differ substantially from needs identified through continuing educators' assessment (Office of Continuing Professional Education, 1985). People generally cite as their areas of weakness "those procedures and knowledge they use infrequently but might perceive as necessary for a higher-level position (such as management skills), or those that are new . . . (such as new tax laws for accountants)" (Queeney and Smutz, 1990, p. 180). They usually report few or no educational needs regarding things they do regularly, yet upon assessment are found to have some of their greatest needs in these areas. This is not to say that only assessed needs are of importance. Perceived needs also are of considerable value because people who believe that their knowledge, skills, or performance abilities are weak in certain areas may lack the confidence to perform well in those areas. Individuals' perceptions that they have specific needs may motivate them to participate in continuing education. This motivation may be lacking when needs they do not recognize are identified through assessment but not convincingly communicated to them. Thus, whether perceived needs are real or imagined, they represent opportunities for continuing educators.

Felt Versus Expressed Needs

This pair of characteristics describes a person's ability to acknowledge educational needs. Felt needs are those individuals are somewhat conscious of but do not discuss. Felt needs exist when people are reluctant to recognize their educational needs. Part of the assessment process might include examination of felt needs to determine their validity (Monette, 1977). When people go beyond awareness of needs to articulating them, they become expressed needs. People usually are willing to spend time and money to address expressed needs.

Sometimes needs are felt rather than expressed simply because people have not actively considered or acknowledged them. At other times, people feel threatened by the notion that either individually or as part of a group they have certain identifiable needs. Some discrepancies may be more threatening or embarrassing to acknowledge than others. For example, people may be more reluctant to reveal limitations of their knowledge regarding procedures that have been in place for some time than to admit they are unaware of a new research finding. People having felt needs often view needs assessment as a test with the potential for failure, perhaps fearing that the needs they have been suppressing will become apparent. Those with expressed needs are more likely to view assessment as a tool to confirm what they already know, and to assist in the structuring of educational programs from which they can benefit. The continuing educator will find data on both felt and expressed needs useful in program planning, particularly in developing marketing strategies for the resulting educational activities.

Normative Versus Comparative Needs

In any needs assessment, continuing educators must define standards for acceptable levels of knowledge, skills, or performance abilities, levels below which they will consider an individual or group to have discrepancies. Needs exist when an assessment reveals discrepancies between the acceptable levels and the knowledge, skills, or performance abilities demonstrated.

Normative needs involve experts' establishment of specific standards of knowledge, skills, or performance abilities to be met regardless of other people's performances in the assessment or in other contexts. Normative needs describe deficiencies between those standards and assessed levels. For example, the standard for volunteer firefighters' performance on a knowledge test was set at 75 percent, meaning that firefighters who scored below 75 percent were considered to have a knowledge discrepancy or a normative need. This standard was used regardless of the number of firefighters who scored below 75 percent, and those assessed were not compared with each other or any other groups of firefighters.

Comparative needs transpire when certain individuals or groups do not attain the levels of other individuals or groups. An existing measure (such as the average performance of past assessees) or the performance of those scoring highest on the assessment (for instance the top 20 percent) can become the standard for defining comparative need. Frequently the individuals who do not demonstrate need or the members of the group used to set the standard have had the advantage of education on the topic, while those demonstrating the comparative need have not. Using the previous example to illustrate comparative need, individual firefighters' scores could have been compared with the average score earned by the total group assessed with the average score used as the standard.

People who are knowledgeable about the content area being assessed have a perspective that is valuable in deciding whether normative or comparative needs are more appropriate. It is extremely important to identify either normative or comparative standards in a needs assessment. Educational needs cannot be identified without clear standards that define areas of weakness. Setting standards is discussed in some detail in the next section of this chapter.

Discrepancy Versus Maintenance Needs

Whether normative or comparative needs are being assessed, discrepancies found between standards that have been established and the actual performance reflect the difference between what is and what should be, discrepancies that point to areas of educational need. But other needs are for maintenance of existing levels of knowledge, skills, and performance abilities. The periodic retraining of people certified to administer cardiopulmonary resuscitation is an example of education directed toward maintenance of an existing level of ability.

Discrepancy needs are more easily identified through needs assessment than are maintenance needs. Because people rarely question capabilities about routine practices, maintenance needs often are not discovered until they have deteriorated into discrepancy needs. Yet seldom-used knowledge, skills, and performance abilities may become dull or forgotten. Therefore, review of them can lead to identification of maintenance needs.

Current Versus Anticipated Needs

Many people turn to continuing education to help them handle current responsibilities more effectively. They are concerned with needs related to their ongoing activities. At other times, however, continuing education can contribute to people's success in shifting from one role to another, expanding the scope of their responsibilities, or adapting to a changing environment. The nurse seeking to move into supervision, the citizen striving to become an effective school board member, and the senior citizen wanting to purchase and use a computer are examples of people with anticipated needs.

Anticipated needs tend to be of particular importance during times of financial hardship, when people pursue education to prepare for career or lifestyle changes. People in life transitions (for example, recently divorced or widowed people, those whose children have just left home, and those who have lost their jobs) also have more anticipated needs than people for whom life is more stable (Aslanian and Brickell, 1988). In planning on the basis of anticipated needs, continuing educators should be aware that people's plans often change, and with them, so do their anticipated educational needs. For this reason, employment projections, trend data, and other information are valuable additions to data on anticipated needs.

Setting Standards

Need has no meaning without a defining standard, a level below which an individual or group is considered to fall short (Queeney, 1992). The standard defining need can be compared with the more commonly understood concept of the point at which an individual is considered to have passed rather than failed an exam. The danger in using this comparison is that it may create the misperception that needs assessment is indeed a pass/fail exercise rather than a diagnostic tool. A needs assessment participant who demonstrates knowledge, skills, or performance abilities below the defined standard has not failed; rather, the assessment has succeeded in revealing an area of potential educational need for that person.

Setting standards to be used to identify need is a critical step in any needs assessment. Without a clear definition of such standards the determination of need is often reduced to a value judgment that is open to interpretation, misunderstanding, and potential disagreement. The standards against which needs are measured vary, but most often they are described in the following terms: *deviations from standards, at-risk indicators,* and *maintenance requirements* (McKillip, 1987, p. 11).

Deviations from Standards

Gaps or differences may exist between an individual's or a group's assessed level and either the ideal level, the basic level, or the level of a comparison group. Standards are necessary to define each of these levels for use in an assessment. The ideal level represents the optimum attainment of knowledge, skills, or performance abilities for those being assessed, the mastery to which people with professional, personal, or other interests in the content area should aspire. The basic level represents the minimum knowledge, skills, or performance abilities necessary for people to function with reasonable effectiveness in the area being assessed, often described as the entry level for professionals. The comparison group level involves using another group's attainment as the standard for the assessment; assessment participants whose knowledge, skills, or performance abilities fall below those of the comparison group are considered to have needs.

At-Risk Indicators

Some individuals or groups may be in danger of providing substandard services, developing poor outcomes, or otherwise performing poorly. For these people, considered to be at risk, a needs assessment can identify the specific knowledge, skills, and performance abilities in which they have discrepancies that could be addressed through further education. Standards are set to identify the levels below which negative or undesirable results are likely to occur. These needs assessment standards cannot be mistaken for certification standards, however. Certification connotes successful completion of certain educational, practice, or examination requirements and attainment of a specified level of proficiency. Because of the legal, ethical, and socioeconomic ramifications of certification, rigorous standards and procedures must be employed in establishing and implementing certification programs. Although assessment standards can help identify at-risk individuals' specific discrepancies and corresponding areas of educational need, meeting these standards does not imply competence or ability to meet certification standards.

Maintenance Requirements

In many professional fields and personal interest areas, periodic updating is necessary for individuals or groups to maintain an acknowledged level of performance or service. The updating may be introduction of new information, reinforcement and review of previously learned knowledge, skills, and performance abilities, or a combination of the two. Standards can be set to define the acceptable maintenance level, stipulating the extent to which assessment participants must demonstrate familiarity with or mastery of new information and retention of old material.

For a given assessment, standards of any of these three types can range from the absence of potentially harmful misinformation to excellence. Standards defining need should reflect conscious decisions regarding the levels required to enable individuals to go about their work, family, community, or leisure activities and tasks properly. For some assessments, acceptable levels may be defined according to age, experience, role, or the context in which an individual works and lives. For example, the standard for recently licensed real estate agents might be mastery at a basic level, whereas the standard for an agent with considerable experience might be far higher. Particular topics may suggest acceptable levels at which standards should be set. Firefighters' understanding of emergency rescue procedures could be expected to be at the highest level, for example, whereas their reporting skills could be tolerated at a much lower level.

The following three factors merit consideration in setting assessment standards:

Role of the target population. The significance of the target population's activities to society can be relevant to the level of knowledge, skills, and performance abilities that can or should be expected. For example, a target population dealing with issues of public health, safety, and welfare might be required to meet higher standards than one whose role does not involve such life-or-death matters.

Characteristics of individuals within the target population. The people being assessed may have demographic or other characteristics that imply certain expectations for their levels of performance. People with extensive experience can more reasonably be expected to meet standards of excellence than those new to a subject area or field of practice, for example.

Importance of the knowledge, skills, and performance abilities being assessed. In any content area, some knowledge, skills, and performance abilities are more important than others. They may be used more frequently, or their use may be more critical to overall practice or activities. Higher standards might be set for areas that are key to the individual's or group's daily practice than for those of less importance.

Integrating the standards selected into a needs assessment involves defining each knowledge, skill, or performance ability level according to the specific measurable items that describe that level. Examples of the particular information commensurate with the standard selected provide this definition for knowledge assessment. In skills assessment, a comprehensive listing of the components of the specified skill performed to the designated level is important, and a performance abilities assessment requires recognition of the hallmarks that distinguish performance at or above the level of need. The extent to which the individual's or group's actual assessed knowledge, skills, or performance abilities fall below the standard represents the extent of deficit or need. (Queeney, 1992)

In addition to these factors, continuing educators should consider the levels that can be attained by proposed educational activities, because different standards have implications for the content level of the programs developed. A standard of excellence suggests that the educational activity be developed at a fairly high level, for example. If continuing educators set assessment standards at levels they cannot address through programming, they will not serve the target population.

Examination of the ways in which individuals and groups fall short of meeting the standards set can provide additional information for use in developing program content. Those areas in which the greatest discrepancies are found offer the greatest opportunities for continuing education programming. In some cases, needs assessment reveals that knowledge, skill, or performance ability levels exceed the standards that have been established. Although they do not point to a current educational need, such findings may have implications for the level of future programs on related topics.

Summary

At first glance deciding on the topic of an assessment appears to be a straightforward and simple process. The continuing educator wants to find out what people need to know. In fact, deciding what to assess need not be a complicated process, but it does merit consideration and some conscious decisions. It is easy to make assumptions about the subject of a needs assessment without considering the factors described in this chapter. If continuing educators overlook them, it may not be until they are well into the assessment, or even at the data analysis stage, that problems occur and they recognize the omission. Without consciously establishing priorities, identifying content areas to be considered, deciding whether the assessment should be of knowledge, skills, or performance abilities, and determining the types and levels of needs to be defined, the continuing educator most often either discovers during the course of the needs assessment that the pieces are not fitting together or finds at its conclusion that the data gathered are of limited use, if not meaningless.

Continuing educators should not choose needs assessment topics in a vacuum. Their perspectives, as well as those of potential participants, employers, faculty, and other interested parties, such as professional associations, may all be useful. When assembled, representatives of these groups can provide a wealth of information with which to make the decision regarding what to assess.

Decisions can be of two types, those related to an immediate assessment activity and those involving a more long-term, comprehensive strategy. Finally, decisions about what to assess should not be inflexible but should be seen as guidelines for an assessment, to be altered if desirable as the needs assessment process unfolds.

Chapter Four

Deciding How to Assess

A properly designed, constructed, implemented, and interpreted needs assessment is the first step in developing educational activities that will both serve a target population and enable continuing educators to meet their goals. A number of models can assess educational needs, each characterized by a step-by-step process that operationalizes one or more methods. These models are of two basic types: those which address unidentified educational needs and those which focus on identified educational needs (Sleezer, 1992, p. 41).

Models of the first type are the most common. They focus on a specific audience or are used as a broad environmental scanning effort to identify problems that can be addressed by education. Needs assessments based on this model begin by surveying the targeted environment or culture to see where problems exist. They then identify the content areas in which educational activities are needed. These assessments are more subjective than objective, more general than specific. They include gathering information from involved or knowledgeable parties and then piecing it together to identify issues, trends, and societal needs toward which education should be directed (Sleezer and Swanson, 1992). A review of patient outcomes to identify discrepancies between actual and acceptable proficiencies in neonatal intensive care physicians and nurses is an example of a needs assessment based on this type of model. From this assessment, a continuing educator was able to define specific educational needs for both physicians and nurses.

Models of the second type—those which assume that an educational need has been identified—are designed to determine the context in which the need exists and should be addressed. The continuing educator uses data collected in such assessments to clarify and focus the needs. Such assessments usually are more objective and specific than the first type. They may deal with operational needs. They often deal with issues such as identification of an audience for a proposed educational activity, of the level of education needed, and of optimum ways of delivering it. For example, the continuing educator who surveyed front-line supervisors in a large manufacturing company knew that they needed management development programming. The survey provided information on the supervisors' existing levels of knowledge and familiarity with the topic as well as their scheduling preferences.

Regardless of the type of needs assessment conducted, to be of value it must result in a final product—information—to guide the program planning process. Viewed another way, data that document specific needs are obtained through needs assessments and then interpreted carefully to identify the educational interventions necessary to respond to the needs. It is this "identification of a solution" (Sleezer, 1992, p. 41) that makes a needs assessment valuable to the continuing educator. Lampe (1986), writing about workforce training, identified several types of information that can be derived from needs assessment to guide programming. To a large extent, the information will guide decisions regarding how to assess because the assessment will be designed to yield that type of information. Thus decisions regarding the desired final product—the type of information—to be produced by a needs assessment must be made early in the process. The broad categories of information identified by Lampe with relevance to continuing education are the following:

- Purposes of an educational activity

- Objectives of an educational activity

- Content of an educational activity

- Activities performed by target group members
- Responsibilities of target group members
- Factors affecting performance of the organization, system, or other environment in which group members operate
- Undocumented policies and procedures affecting target group members
- Issues of importance to those served by or interacting with target group members
- Target group members' self-assessment regarding their knowledge and skills
- Key concepts inherent in necessary skills and performance
- Target group members' preferred ways of learning
- Strengths and limitations of educational opportunities currently available to target group members
- Current knowledge, skill, and performance levels of target group members

A clear understanding of the type of information sought from a needs assessment enables the continuing educator to make good decisions regarding how to assess. But defining expectations about the type of information desired is very different from having preconceived ideas about the findings of a needs assessment. Many times it is possible to design a needs assessment exercise that will produce exactly the findings a continuing educator wants. However, to conduct a needs assessment only to produce predetermined findings is to engage in a meaningless activity that will not yield valid information; it is not an attempt to derive sound data but an attempt to create data that will support an agenda or serve other political purposes. Continuing educators who want to conduct an objective needs assessment to confirm a hunch or justify an activity can do so if they are open-minded and design the assessment to be objective. If needs assessment is to be truly useful in guiding program planning, continuing educators have to be prepared to accept the findings, whether they support their viewpoints or not.

Group Versus Individual Assessment

Clinical dietitians who have participated in the American Dietetic Association's Self-Assessment Series (Klevans, Pollack, Smutz, and Vance, 1991) have engaged in an individual needs assessment. The exercises they have completed in their homes or offices have provided information on their own perceptions of their gaps in content areas related to dietetic practice. From the information included in the individualized reports of their performance on the assessments, they have been able to identify their specific educational needs and presumably enroll in educational activities that could address those needs.

In contrast, members of a regional chapter of a professional association for clinical psychologists participated in an assessment of group needs when they completed questionnaires that asked about their perceptions of discrepancies between existing and acceptable proficiencies in their profession. Individual respondents were not identified and data from the questionnaires were aggregated. The survey results said nothing about the needs of the individual participants, but they did summarize information on the needs of the group.

It is possible to assess the needs either of individuals or of an entire group, and the two need not be mutually exclusive. Although some needs assessment methods lend themselves only to use with groups, many can be used for either individual or group assessments. The same knowledge, skills, and performance abilities can be assessed for both. When data are collected to provide information on the needs of individuals in a discrete group or in a group whose members share common characteristics, the data can be used for both individual and group purposes.

Group assessment frequently is easier to accomplish than individual assessment because it is often easier to access groups of people than to obtain individuals' participation. In addition, people may be more willing to participate in a group assessment, where their responses are anonymous, than in an assessment that looks at them individually. The information obtained from group assessments generally is of greater use to continuing educators, because it is far more feasible to tailor educational activities to meet the needs of groups. However, people who might believe that the needs identified for the group are not relevant to them as individuals cannot as easily deny needs identified through individualized assessment. Thus, both group and individual assessment have merit. Each also has its drawbacks.

Individual Assessment

Members of a group are likely to share some needs. These may be the result, for example, of similar educational backgrounds or professional experiences; development of theories, knowledge, and regulations that are new to everyone; or expanded technology. However, other educational needs are more personal. Some, such as those related to special experiences, previous training, and work setting, are not difficult to recognize and document. Needs that derive from personal characteristics are more amorphous and not as easily determined. Individuals all approach education and life experiences with different degrees of thought and reflection. The extent to which they have performed tasks as isolated events, handling them automatically rather than viewing them within a broader context, is another factor that distinguishes people. Because the effect of individual factors on educational needs is substantial, each person's unique needs cannot be ignored.

Individual assessment of needs can discern these differences, which are likely to be lost in group data. Perhaps more important, individual assessments—during which participants receive feedback—also give them information on their educational needs that is specifically meaningful to them. Applying adult learning theory (Knowles, 1980; Brookfield, 1986; Knox, 1986; Freedman, 1987), continuing educators increasingly encourage individuals to assume responsibility for their own learning and to make informed choices about educational activities. In order to do this, adult learners need information. Although group data can be helpful, they lack specificity. Even when identified group needs have a clear relevance for all group members, individuals may be reluctant to believe it. Individualized assessment removes much of the doubt.

In individual assessment even more than in group assessment, continuing educators should take steps to ensure that participants do not feel threatened by the process. They may need help understanding that an assessment is not a test but a measurement device to identify educational strategies. Whether individual or group assessment is used, participants should be encouraged to view the assessment as a part of a process they can use to develop an educational plan or strategy that will guide their selection of educational activities.

It is critical that an individual assessment remain confidential. People usually do not want others to know of their shortcomings. Anonymity is maintained best when individual assessment results are reported to others only in aggregated form (that is, as group data) and the individual results are accessible only by the individual being assessed. This may mean, for example, that an employer who contracts for an assessment of employees' needs agrees to waive any rights to see individual reports and to rely on anonymous group data in order to make decisions.

Individual assessment often is considered more costly than group assessment because of both the logistics involved and the assessment methods employed. The tendency is to think of individual needs assessment as more detailed, more in-depth, and more extensive. However, this need not be the case. The same logistical strategies and assessment methods can be used for both kinds of assessment. Individual assessments can be conducted in group settings, eliminating the need to contact individuals or to schedule individual appointments, and they can be as basic or as detailed as any group assessment. If individual assessments are of the same degree of complexity as comparable group assessments, then their cost need not be substantially greater, and the only additional expense may occur in providing the individual feedback. For example, a continuing educator who frequently provides management development programming to large firms developed a generic needs assessment questionnaire that he tailors to each client as necessary. All employees who will be eligible to participate in the educational activities are asked to complete the questionnaire. For some firms, data from the questionnaires are analyzed and reported only as group data. For others, however, the continuing educator provides individual feedback to each employee so that an educational program can be designed for each person. The continuing educator uses the same questionnaire for both individual and group assessments.

Whereas the results of group assessment can be compiled and presented in a single report, individual assessment demands that a separate report be given to each participant. Without this there is no value to an individual needs assessment. Depending on the number of people assessed and the complexity of the information provided, the continuing educator can use individual conferences, computer-generated reports, or simple letters to provide results. By including information on educational activities appropriate to the participants' identified needs, the feedback report can help individuals adopt a positive attitude toward the results and encourage them to take action to address discrepancies.

Two self-assessment projects, conducted at The Pennsylvania State University for the American Institute of Architects and the Commission on Dietetic Registration of the American Dietetic Association (Klevans, Smutz, Shuman, and Bershad, 1992; Klevans, Pollack, Smutz, and Vance, 1991), offer information about available educational activities that would meet participants' individual needs as an incentive for them to pursue educational activities.

They also contain computerized feedback reports on the participants' scores, their scores compared with those of other participants,
the specific content areas in which they responded incorrectly, and
for dietitians, explanations of why certain responses were correct or
incorrect.

The feedback report used for the *Self-Assessment Series for Dietetics Professionals* (Staff, 1992, p. I–1) includes four sections, summarized here:

An Overview of the Self-Assessment Process

Guidelines for interpreting the report

Self-Assessment Results

Individual participants' scores, peer comparisons, an analysis of participants' responses to the module items, and experts' reasons for
selecting certain responses as best

Planning Ahead

Suggestions and tools for implementing a personalized professional
development action plan

Supplemental Answer Key

Why experts scored some responses as incorrect or less appropriate
than others

The information provided in this report helps participants
understand the ways in which their knowledge, skills, and performance abilities could use improvement and enables them to
become self-directed learners.

In sum, although most continuing education needs assessment
is group assessment, it is important not to lose sight of the value of
individual assessment. It can offer the continuing educator all the
benefits of group assessment while also providing individuals with

information that may motivate their educational participation and enable them to develop their own learning plans.

Group Assessment

Continuing educators can aggregate individual assessment results, without any identification of participants, for use as group data to guide program planning. Aggregated data from individual assessments are useful in informing employers and other interested parties about the strengths and weaknesses of a group, perhaps pointing to desirable educational and noneducational interventions. When individual assessment data are available, it makes sense to use them in these ways, for the resources necessary to aggregate the data are usually minimal and the value is likely to be great.

However, most information on group needs is derived though group assessment. Because continuing educators' primary concern is to provide educational programming that serves certain target populations, pursuit of group assessment is logical. Group assessments provide information on areas of educational need for broad populations, so they are potentially more useful than individual assessment for program planning purposes. The continuing educator seeking any of the types of information described by Lampe, noted earlier in this chapter, can obtain it through group assessment.

Group assessment may or may not mean that all members of the group participate. If the target group is small in size and discrete, assessment of the total population may be quite feasible. Employees of a bank, clerical employees in a school district, or members of the local American Association of University Women chapter are examples of groups for which such a goal might be reasonable. For larger, more dispersed, or less easily identified groups, assessment of the total population may be impractical if not impossible. In some cases, continuing educators can obtain an accurate random or purposively drawn sample, accept it as representative of the population, and make generalizations to the total group. In other cases, it may be either impractical or impossible to draw a random sample. The continuing educator wishing to identify educational needs of residents in a metropolitan area may be able to obtain a random sample with considerable expenditure of effort and resources but may rightly believe that the results would not justify the investment. Similarly, obtaining a random sample of all senior citizens nationwide would be virtually impossible. In situations like these, assessment of another type of sample certainly can suffice. It is important to interpret the data according to the group assessed, however, with special attention to the manner in which the group was identified. Generalizations based on nonrandom samples are likely to be unreliable, a fact taken into account in this type of data interpretation.

Group assessment data based on nonrandom samples can be used to determine whether there are enough potential participants with given needs to justify an initial offering of a program. Program development can proceed with the expectation that early enrollments will come from the assessed group and that additional participants will be attracted through marketing. However, any generalizations from assessment of this group to a larger population will not be valid because the group does not represent a random sample.

Choosing the Population to Be Assessed

Identification of the target population for an educational activity obviously must precede identification of the group from whom the assessment data will be collected. The two populations are often the same, although the characteristics sought in a target audience differ from those required of needs assessment participants. Needs assessment participants must be willing to take an active role in the assessment process and respond fully to the exercises presented. Unlike members of the target audience for an educational activity, they need not be likely candidates for program enrollment. Potential program participants should demonstrate some likelihood that they will commit the necessary time and other resources to participate in an educational activity. Indicators of likely participation can include reasons for participation, including a need to learn new skills or to qualify for recertification. Past participation in educational activities also is a good predictor of future participation (Aslanian, 1985a, 1985b). Because of the different characteristics needed for potential program participants and for needs assessment participants, continuing educators use a separate decision-making process in selecting each group, considering different factors for each.

Potential Program Participants

As noted in Chapter Three, marketing considerations, faculty interest and expertise, and institutional strengths are among the factors that contribute to the decision to provide an educational activity in a particular content area. Once continuing educators have evaluated these factors and defined programmatic areas, their next step is to identify specific audiences toward whom they might direct the related educational activities. Often the potential participant pool may appear obvious. Journalists are a logical target audience for a program on ethics in reporting, for example, and social service organization employees come to mind for a program on fundraising practices. Although promoting educational activities to these readily apparent audiences may be quite sufficient, assessing other groups to see if they, too, might be appropriate participants may allow continuing educators to expand their reach. In addition to the audiences cited in the preceding examples, ethics in reporting could be of interest to some citizen groups or local government bodies, and a program on fundraising practices may be just what community volunteers need to initiate or enhance their projects.

Continuing educators can begin to identify the field of potential participants by broadly defining target groups for whom they might develop educational activities. Either informal or structured environmental scanning will reveal groups, such as those working in a failing or overcrowded industry or business, who need education or retraining to get on with their lives. A needs assessment can confirm that such groups actually do have educational needs and then identify them. For marketing purposes the assessment also can seek information on group members' likelihood to enroll in appropriate programs. Colleges and universities increasingly emphasize service to alumni, in an effort to become their graduates' lifelong learning home. In striving to identify new audiences, continuing educators will find it helpful to seek groups known to include active learners; unless prompted to engage in further learning activities by a significant life change or transition, or by an employer, people who have not engaged in learning activities for the past two years are not likely to do so (Aslanian, 1985a). A target audience can be limited to a given geographical area; organization, institution, or business; occupation or profession; or demographic group with whom the continuing educator has or seeks to build a strong relationship.

Once the target population for educational programming has been identified, needs assessment can provide the continuing educator with the information necessary to focus the educational content, and to develop and deliver educational activities appropriate to that group. Needs assessment data that pinpoint certain characteristics also can be useful in further targeting potential participants, distinguishing those who have needs in the content area under consideration from those who do not.

Needs Assessment Participants

After choosing a target population, continuing educators can turn their attention to choosing the population (or population sample) they can best assess to identify the target population's educational needs. Members of the target population itself, secondary populations of people with whom they work or interact, clients they serve, or people who oversee them in relevant activities may be suitable. Records and other forms of documentation also can be sources of valuable needs assessment data. For example, review of physicians' prescriptions for patients having certain clinical conditions has been used successfully to determine whether the physicians were following currently accepted practices (Manning, Lee, Denson, and Gilman, 1980).

Often it is appropriate to collect data concerning the target population's needs from other people, a secondary population. Sometimes data obtained from this secondary population are used to supplement data gathered from the target population; at other times they are used as an alternative. Continuing educators most often seek needs assessment data from sources other than anticipated program participants when they expect a secondary population to have different or clearer perspectives on the target population's performance, or when the target audience is dependent on others for financial support or permission to participate in educational activities. Employers' perceptions may be essential to determining what their employees need to know, for example, and experts in local government may be key sources of information regarding the educational needs of local elected officials.

No matter which population is used for the assessment, continuing educators can focus data collection on all members of the group or limit it to specific subgroups within that population. Use of a subgroup may be advised if the total population is too large to access readily; if use of the knowledge, skills, or performance abilities to be covered in the assessment is limited to only a special segment of the total population; or if the subgroup represents enough individuals to make programming feasible. For example, if police officers' interpersonal and communications skills were to be assessed, the assessment could be limited to police officers within a city's boundaries, those with ten or more years of experience, or officers handling only investigations.

A *total population, random sample,* or *convenience sample* can be drawn from the group of needs assessment participants. Any one of these groups can provide useful data. However, in reporting and interpreting needs assessments, it is important to differentiate between the data obtained from each.

Assessment of the total population is exactly what it appears to be: all members of a target population are asked to participate in the needs assessment.

Random samples are drawn using a random-numbers table to identify people from a list of the total target population. They can also be selected by taking every nth person from a population list (for example, every fifth person would be chosen to participate in the assessment). In either case, the list used should include the total population and should be arranged in a consistent, objective manner, such as in alphabetical or postal zip code order. Random samples can be stratified, with the entire target population being subdivided into smaller groups on the basis of certain characteristics. A population of clinical psychologists might be stratified into subgroups according to the age group of their clients (for example, young children, teenagers, the elderly). When a stratified random sample is used, a sample is drawn from each subpopulation in the manner described. Stratified random samples must include a population of sufficient size to yield meaningful numbers of respondents in each stratification category. It is imprudent to make generalizations based on very small numbers of respondents in any category, because a sample that is too small may not be representative of the population.

Using convenience samples—groups of people who are readily accessible and are members of the larger group for whom the proposed educational activity would be designed—frequently can reduce needs assessment costs. Using a convenience sample can help continuing educators avoid the expense of identifying a sample, and often can minimize or even eliminate the travel, telephone, and postage costs associated with assessing a geographically dispersed group. Continuing educators can often collect assessment data from a convenience sample in conjunction with another activity. For example, people assembled for a meeting, conference, or other purpose may be available to participate in a needs assessment. Convenience sample data can provide information on absolute numbers of people with particular needs or characteristics. However, because a convenience sample is not a random sample, it cannot be considered representative of a total population. Similarly, when assessments of total populations or random samples yield low response rates, continuing educators cannot assume that the data collected are indicative of the total population.

Selecting Needs Assessment Methods

The educational needs of different populations range over many content areas and levels, the needs of specific groups vary over time, organizational and institutional priorities change, resource availability fluctuates. All of these factors affect methodology decisions, making it impossible to identify a single needs assessment method that is uniformly appropriate (Gilmore, Campbell, and Becker, 1989). Each of the needs assessment methods described in this book has particular strengths and shortcomings, making it more useful in some assessment situations than in others. Some methods are best for identification of discrepancies in knowledge, others address discrepancies in skills or performance abilities. Some methods are for use in group assessment, others are more suitable for assessment of individuals, and still others have applications for both types of assessment. All require the continuing educator to translate the discrepancies identified into educational needs and then into educational programs that respond to those needs.

The goals of the continuing educator, of the target population, and if applicable, of the employer or other individual or organization for whom the needs assessment is being conducted are the most important factors in selecting assessment methods. Because certain needs assessment methods are best for ferreting out particular types of information, continuing educators can select a method based on its strengths in collecting information compatible with those goals and objectives. Available resources are a second key consideration in the decision on how to assess, just as they can be a factor in deciding what to assess. Trying to stretch inadequate resources almost always results in an unsatisfactory assessment that provides data of little or no use. By selecting a needs assessment method that is well within the reach of available funds, facilities, equipment, and human resources, the continuing educator will not be hampered in carrying out the assessment. Third, a continuing educator may select some methods because they serve a particular purpose beyond data collection, or have dual purposes. For example, continuing educators who wish to use needs assessment to increase public awareness of educational opportunities as well as to learn of potential participants' needs probably will not select an impersonal mail survey. They will recognize that most people are not fond of surveys and that one does not build any bridges by surveying people (Aslanian, 1985a). Instead they may choose a personal interview, focus group, or other method that allows them to provide information and build relationships with potential participants. The climate for assessment within the target population, organization, or secondary population from whom data will be collected is a fourth important factor. Some individuals and groups are eager to participate in needs assessment as a first step in obtaining relevant education, whereas others resent spending time on assessment. It may be important to use a needs assessment method that entertains, as well as collects data, for the latter. For example, focus groups that allow time for informal conversation over refreshments can provide a social component that makes needs assessment attractive to otherwise reluctant participants.

It is tempting to think of assessment in only objective terms, for this type of assessment can be simple, straightforward, and easily accomplished. It can yield a wealth of information, most of it on the cognitive aspects of needs or in the form of loosely connected or unrelated facts and figures. Underlying the standardized short-answer tests usually used for this purpose is the assumption that an individual's strengths, weaknesses, and other characteristics can be described by isolated pieces of information. However, most testing experts do not agree (Simon, Dippo, and Schenke, 1991), recognizing that objective data do not present the total picture. Unless they are balanced with qualitative, or narrative, data that explain and clarify the information derived, they often oversimplify the situation. "A narrative format can capture variations and exceptions, and portray the needs as completely as possible" (Gilmore, Campbell, and Becker, 1989, p. 6). By collecting some subjective data along with objective information, the continuing educator may be able to report needs assessment data within a context.

Chapters Five, Six, and Seven describe a number of needs assessment methods, outlining their strengths and weaknesses and offering guidelines for their use. These and other means of assessing needs are derivatives of the following approaches:

Task Forces and Committees

Task forces and committees are particularly useful for preassessment guidance, assisting the continuing educator in deciding what and how to assess. The groups formed should represent the proposed target population and be guided by a clear mission.

Consultation and Interviews

Consultation and interviews—oral data-gathering techniques—can be simple, inexpensive ways of learning about a population. Their success depends on both careful selection of respondents and wise framing of the questions asked or topics discussed. Unless these precautions are observed, methods based on this approach may reflect the needs of only the respondents and not of the groups they are intended to represent.

Surveys

If well designed and executed, surveys are consistent and relatively inexpensive ways of collecting needs assessment data. They can reach large numbers of people regardless of location, and they allow for confidential responses. Considerable time and expertise are required in order to develop valid, reliable questions and to analyze and interpret the data.

Consensus-Rendering Techniques

Consensus-rendering techniques range from nominal group processes and leaderless discussions to Delphi techniques. Some are most effective when led by a skilled facilitator. Considerable time may be required to allow the group to achieve consensus.

Work Samples, Records, and Documents

Analysis of work samples, records, and other documents can help identify specific discrepancies. These documents can be particularly useful in pointing to needs that target group members do not realize they have, tasks they have been executing in the same manner, and perhaps incorrectly, for some time.

Self-Evaluation Measures

Measures based on self-reporting can introduce bias, but they can also be constructed and used in a manner that avoids this pitfall. Because they force individuals and groups to reflect on their strengths and weaknesses, they can encourage self-directed learning.

Observation of Performance

Observation can provide immediate data. The potential for lack of reliability is a disadvantage that can be overcome by training observers to look for specific actions and types of behavior, and providing them with a rating scale for recording what they see in an objective fashion. Costs for this approach can rise quickly if videotaping, complex scoring systems, or other techniques are used.

Simulations

Simulations allow for observation of performance in a controlled setting. Although they may be expensive to develop, implement, and score, they can provide highly reliable data that, unlike data from direct observation, are comparable across assessees.

Secondary Data

Data collected for other purposes (for example, test scores) frequently are best used to provide supplemental information. Because they are not collected primarily for needs assessment, they may bring a different focus or bias.

Building Needs Assessment Teams

In discussing the individuals and teams that contribute to needs assessment, it is easy to confuse those who provide guidance and advice to the assessment effort, including planning and advisory committees (discussed in Chapter Ten), with the individuals and teams who actually design and carry out the needs assessment activities. Both groups are important, but their roles are very different. Planning and advisory committee members usually are not involved in actually conducting the assessment, although they may contribute to its conceptualization from development and design through interpretation and application of the data collected. These people have a variety of perspectives that differ from the viewpoints of those who are directly involved in conducting the needs assessment.

Ideally, a continuing educator will have access to other staff members or consultants with whom to plan and conduct the assessment. But for some continuing educators who work alone assessment is not a group, but an individual, activity. When possible, however, including an assessment team can provide a variety of skills and perspectives that facilitate and enhance the project. An assessment team should be "comprised of the professionals directly involved in the planning, coordinating, or facilitating of the needs assessment" (Gilmore, Campbell, and Becker, 1989, p. 7) as well as those responsible for actual data collection, analysis, and reporting. This is not to say that only individuals with assessment expertise should be included in assessment teams. In assessing needs of professional practitioners or employees, for example, design of assessment exercises almost always can be enhanced by including members of the target population as well. "They have firsthand knowledge of what competencies are required to do the job" (Elman and Lynton, 1985) and understand the content area and its application—useful in any assessment and particularly important in evaluating actual practice or designing simulation exercises.

These perspectives on the topic under consideration are useful, but they are not sufficient. Adequate technical expertise also is essential. Attempting an assessment without it is to doom that assessment to failure. Because the technical competence needed for an individual assessment team is highly dependent on the assessment methods selected, the continuing educator cannot form a full needs assessment team until some initial planning has occurred.

Before building an assessment team, the continuing educator might meet with one or more individuals who have broad, general knowledge of needs assessment methods and others who have knowledge of the content area and its application. Working with an advisory committee's recommendations and any other background information, this group has as its task the identification of one or more appropriate needs assessment methods. Following their selection of the methods to be used, the continuing educator can either add to the existing group or begin anew to form an assessment team that includes individuals with the specific expertise needed.

An assessment team relies on one or more people with expertise to guide development and implementation of the assessment, coordinate the work of other team members and support personnel, train team members who require additional skills, and ensure the quality of the needs assessment. The size of an assessment team will vary according to the size and complexity of the undertaking. From its inception, the assessment team should include individuals responsible for all aspects of the assessment. Far too often, for example, needs assessment data are collected before the individual who is to be responsible for data analysis is fully informed of the activity. To ensure smooth data analysis and interpretation, that individual needs the chance to make suggestions as the process unfolds.

Some needs assessment expertise, such as population sampling and simulation development, involves skills acquired through extensive education, training, and experience. Other competencies, such as data reporting and interpretation, can be developed with a little formal preparation, enabling competent, interested people with sound judgment but few strong technical skills to be contributing team members. In still other cases, people may have technical expertise in areas such as survey design or data analysis but little experience in applying their expertise to the needs assessment process. These people may require special assistance or support.

Some individuals lack technical expertise but for one of several reasons have a strong interest in the assessment and wish to be involved. Useful roles can be found for them. For example, individuals who are knowledgeable about the content area to be assessed may require little preparation to become competent in performance observation within their field, or an organization conducting a needs assessment can train staff members and volunteer leaders to facilitate discussions (Fernicola, 1987). These people may be full members of an assessment team, involved in ongoing operation and decisions, but they are more likely to have secondary support roles.

Ideally, a needs assessment team includes members with the expertise to assume primary responsibility for several functions. The design of the assessment procedure and instruments is critical, no matter which methods are used. It is necessary to identify, contact, and enlist the cooperation of the population or sample to be assessed. Data gathering requires careful planning and attention to detail, and for some methods, such as those requiring interviewing or group facilitation, it also depends on considerable expertise. Data analysis may be computerized, and it also can involve coding of information collected. Data interpretation provides the continuing educator with an understanding of how the discrepancies identified can be translated into educational activities. Finally, a report on the data and its implications can be an important marketing tool both within an organization or institution and for external clients.

Although each needs assessment team member may have special responsibilities, only by meeting and working together can they ensure a smooth process from start to finish.

Summary

After deciding upon the group to be assessed, determining the factors that will affect the choice of assessment methods to be used, and convening the people who will be a part of the needs assessment process, the continuing educator is ready to embark on the needs assessment itself.

If the continuing educator has paid adequate attention to the topics discussed in this and the preceding chapters, determining which needs assessment method or methods to use will be an informed decision. Several possibilities will have been eliminated because they will not have met some of the criteria established. They may be inappropriate for the target group or the content area or not lend themselves to assessing the knowledge, skills, or performance abilities that are to be the focus of the assessment, or they may be too costly or complex. Having narrowed the field of possible needs assessment methods in this way, the continuing educator is likely to find the choice of assessment methods straightforward.

Guidelines for implementation of the methods also will be clear for the continuing educator who is committed to a quality needs assessment. The importance of thoroughness and attention to detail cannot be overstated.

Chapter Five

Methods for Beginners

Continuing educators entering the needs assessment arena are well advised to begin simply, develop an ongoing strategy, and expand their repertoire of needs assessment capabilities as resources permit. Perhaps the greatest fallacy about needs assessment is that only the most sophisticated procedures yield useful data, and that those data must be perfect. In reality, delaying action until resources are available to employ the ideal methodology is a luxury no continuing educator can afford. Sound data can be obtained fairly simply. However, regardless of the level of sophistication of a needs assessment, reliance on a single indicator—one study or question—to provide all answers over time is folly.

The needs assessment methods described in this chapter include self-reports, focus groups, nominal group process, Delphi method, key informants, and supervisor evaluations. These methods can be somewhat informal and low to moderate in cost. They require limited expertise and relatively few resources to implement. However, like all needs assessment methods, they will produce useful data only if they are carefully planned and executed, and if their limitations are recognized. Used properly, they will provide valuable information to help guide continuing education program planning.

Self-Reports

Self-reports of educational needs may be initiated by the potential program participant or generated in response to requests from supervisors, continuing educators, or others soliciting their perceptions of their needs. Expressions of educational needs initiated by potential participants themselves arrive unsolicited when, for example, people contact a continuing education office and state that they "need" education on a particular topic. This information, random in nature, does not constitute a needs assessment, and by itself it is not a sufficient base on which to build an educational program. Such requests frequently reflect a passing interest and cannot be taken as a commitment to participate in a program once it is offered. However, self-initiated reports may merit attention, because they do indicate some level of interest in a given content area. If several such reports are received on one topic, that topic may warrant further consideration through one of the types of needs assessment described in this book.

In contrast, self-reports that are used in needs assessment are responses to inquiries regarding individuals' perceptions of their learning needs. Self-reports are particularly appropriate as a first step in identifying needs for a major programming initiative, or when a continuing educator seeks only broad, general perceptions of needs. Several of the guidelines governing other types of needs assessment, such as those concerning what and how to assess, apply to self-reports of educational needs. However, self-reports are not as highly structured as many other needs assessment methods. More sophisticated interviews and questionnaires also may seek individuals' perceptions of their educational needs. These methods go beyond basic self-reporting, usually collecting a range of both objective, or quantifiable, data and data that are more subjective, or perception-based, from which to draw conclusions about educational needs.

Asking individuals to identify their own learning needs is the simplest form of needs assessment. It involves potential learners in the planning process. Because they identify the needs, they are likely to believe that they could benefit from educational programs developed to address those needs and to be motivated to enroll in them. The primary disadvantage of self-reports is that they are the product of individuals' limited awareness and understanding of their own needs. In considering their educational needs, people are prone to cite areas of new knowledge. As Nowlen's (1988) Update Model suggests, people are comfortable reporting that their knowledge and skills may need updating but usually are less comfortable admitting that discrepancies between their behavior and that which is desirable exist in areas related to their past learning or to regularly performed activities. In fact, they may be unaware of such discrepancies, for people tend to assume that what they do daily, they do well. For example, journalists asked to describe their educational needs would be more likely to identify recent developments in computer technology (new information) than interviewing skills (needed for regularly performed activities). People also tend to identify educational needs in content areas they are interested in. Although interests are important, can motivate educational participation, and can result in good programs, they cannot be considered synonymous with needs.

Continuing educators can overcome the shortcomings of self-reports to some extent if they carefully word the questions to elicit individuals' real perception of their needs. Instead of one or more broad questions, a number of specific questions can guide respondents to consider relevant factors rather than simply offer quick answers without much thought. Often, unless particular areas are pointed out to them, people simply do not think of them. Specific questions lead them to consider those areas and elicit responses that are closely related to discrepancies in respondents' proficiencies and to their educational needs. The following example contrasts a broad question with a series of specific questions to focus responses. If the continuing educator had asked only the broad question of hospital volunteers serving in the emergency room, the respondents might not have considered the various facets of the issue and identification of their educational needs might have been difficult.

Broad question

- What types of information and skills do you need to communicate with Emergency Room patients and their families?

Specific questions

- Are the Emergency Room intake forms clear to you?
- Do you have any trouble obtaining the patient information needed to complete the Emergency Room intake forms?
- Do you feel comfortable explaining our Emergency Room policies and procedures to patients and their families?
- Do you know your way around the hospital well enough to have confidence directing or escorting patients to other locations within the facility?
- Do you find it awkward to talk with patients when escorting them to hospital locations beyond the Emergency Room?
- Do you fully understand the rules governing confidentiality of patient information?
- Do you feel you could do a better job of handling impatient, angry, or difficult patients and patient families?

Use of specific questions can make the difference between obtaining a list of casual interests and a list of perceived needs. The continuing educator can phrase the questions in a nonthreatening manner, so that respondents recognize that the purpose of the inquiry is to help, not evaluate, them. Words that convey failure or inadequacy are best avoided. By taking care to phrase questions and comments in ways that do not lead respondents toward particular answers, the continuing educator also helps ensure responses that reflect participants' thoughts and not the answers they believe they are expected to provide.

The continuing educator can follow several steps to lead respondents to differentiate between interests and needs, and then identify their educational needs as they perceive them. These steps include setting the context for the assessment, defining what is meant by interests, defining what is meant by needs, and finally framing the specific questions to which the participant will respond.

An example of a series of statements and questions that could be used to solicit a self-report of school board members' educational needs follows.

Set the Context. It is important to us that we provide educational programming that meets the needs of people in our state. For example, we want to serve you and your fellow school board members by helping you acquire the capabilities you need to do this important job well. As a school board member and a potential student, you can help us identify areas that we should address in our programming for school board members.

Define Interests. Sometimes people enroll in continuing education programs to pursue interests or enrich their lives. For example, a contemporary American literature course may attract participants who simply want to learn more about American literature. One aspect of our mission is to serve people pursuing such interests, and we always welcome suggestions for programs that will help us do so.

Define Needs. At other times, people need education to help them become better professionals, citizens, or family members, or to improve their performance of certain tasks or jobs. These educational activities may not be the same as those in which people have a personal interest, but they may be necessary for their competence or improved performance.

Frame the Specific Questions. Today we want to gather information that will help us learn what educational activities are needed to enable school board members to maximize their effectiveness in that role. We are asking you to help us by answering the following questions.

- On what topics do you need additional information?
- A variety of skills are necessary for you to perform effectively as a school board member. Which skills do you need to improve your abilities?
- What new information and skills do you need?

- School board members routinely perform many tasks. Which of those do you perform least well?

Self-reports can be solicited either orally or in written form, and they can be used to identify either individual or group needs. Oral self-reports are effective and efficient for collecting data from a limited number of respondents to describe their needs individually or to be aggregated into a profile of group needs. This process does not constitute full-fledged interviewing but it does require that someone talk with potential students and record their responses. Informal conversations can be held with individuals at convenient times and locations. A structured interview is not necessary, but it is important to have some questions in mind, such as those used in the preceding example.

In collecting self-reports orally the interviewer can probe for information in a positive, nonthreatening manner, leading individuals to think about their educational needs rather than simply give quick responses. Reflective listening techniques are appropriate to indicate understanding of an individual's responses, but judgmental replies are not acceptable. Thus, "I understand you to say that you would like to improve your interviewing skills," which simply rephrases the respondent's remark, is a good comment, whereas comments such as "Interviewing skills aren't very important for municipal managers" or "Yes, judges need to improve their interviewing skills," which offer an opinion, are inappropriate.

Written self-reports eliminate the opportunities that oral self-reports offer to probe for further thoughts or additional information. People's general reluctance to write more than a few words is another deterrent to use of a written format. However, written self-reports are advantageous when working with a substantial number of respondents (that is, more than twenty-five), particularly to identify group needs. By eliminating the need for individual conversations they allow an economy of effort, making data collection less time consuming and ensuring that responses are recorded. Except in those cases where interview data are entered directly into a computer, written reports also facilitate compilation of the information collected in a computerized database, which may be critical for the data analysis necessary to transform individual data into group profiles.

Breaking down written information requests into a few questions that each require only a short answer encourages respondents to realize that writing about their educational needs is not a difficult chore. Short-answer questions can require simple yes or no responses, can call for responses of just a few words like those required in the hospital volunteers example cited earlier in this chapter ("What do you find most difficult about your work in the Emergency Room?"), or can ask respondents to produce a list of items (for example, "What types of additional information do you need to be more effective in your role as a hospital volunteer?"). Oversimplification of response options can jeopardize the breadth and depth of the data gathered. For example, offering response options requiring only a check mark may encourage people to respond but also may limit the range of responses received. A good response rate is important, but it should not be pursued at the expense of the quality of the information collected. Continuing educators should strive for a balance between questions that facilitate participant response and those that allow for detailed information. Soliciting self-reports at a meeting or other gathering and then collecting the completed reports before adjournment can result in good response rates for written self-reports.

Continuing educators can use data obtained from self-reports to help individuals structure their own lifelong learning plans, or they can aggregate them to guide program planning decisions. Because of the limitations of self-reporting, however, data obtained in this manner should be integrated with data from other sources to inform any important decisions regarding long-term continuing education programming.

Focus Groups

Elman and Lynton (1985) noted that "small group interactions provide abundant opportunities for assessment. It is well known from organizational theory that small group dynamics offer unique insights into understanding individual behavior. This lends itself well to assessment."

Focus groups are one type of small group interaction. Focus groups offer a relatively easily arranged and implemented way to gather primarily subjective data from a cross section of people. They bring between six and twelve participants together with a facilitator for a structured yet informal discussion. Although a discussion outline directs discussion to the topic at hand, openness and brainstorming are encouraged. Focus groups are particularly useful as an initial step in identifying broad areas of interest; learning about a potential target population; obtaining reactions to new ideas; and generating ideas for program topics, presenters, marketing, and scheduling. The qualitative nature of the data collected (requiring that it be interpreted carefully) and the fact that results cannot always be generalized with confidence are among the weaknesses of focus groups (Gilmore, Campbell, and Becker, 1989, p. 70).

Although a particular focus group may meet more than once, most often a focus group meets only one time to discuss a specific topic. Several separate focus groups may be convened to discuss a single topic, with new groups being created until no new ideas are generated. Focus group meetings generally are about ninety minutes in length. A shorter period does not allow sufficient time for the participants to get comfortable sharing their ideas with one another so that they can have a full discussion. Interest and attention wane if a focus group session extends much beyond this time frame. However, the time participants spend interacting informally—perhaps over refreshments—before beginning the structured discussion is not considered part of the meeting time. Focus group discussions generally are recorded. The continuing educator can choose to capture highlights in written notes, to audiotape and transcribe the entire session so that no details are lost, or to do both.

Once a continuing educator has decided to convene a focus group to address a specific topic, it is advisable to develop an outline, which includes a limited number of targeted topics stated in simple terms, to guide the discussion. Successful focus groups usually address only five or six general questions. This may seem like a meager agenda for a ninety-minute discussion, and indeed it would be if a single individual were being interviewed. However, group participation substantially broadens and prolongs discussion. An emphasis on concepts, rather than specific details, helps the group avoid getting bogged down on one topic. In a good outline, questions are carefully formulated and sequenced, and any terms that may be unfamiliar or misconstrued are defined. Open-ended questions, rather than those requiring a yes or no answer, generate the best discussions. If the first question asked is one that all participants can relate to, it may help initiate conversation easily and involve all group members.

Some topics lend themselves to focus group exploration more readily than others. For example, a continuing educator may recognize that the chief executive officers of several small firms in the area have become familiar with total quality management and are striving to implement it in their companies. They will require some employee education to do so. To begin to understand the type of education that will be needed, the continuing educator might convene several of the chief executive officers for a focus group and ask questions like the following:

- What is your employees' understanding of the concepts of total quality and continuous improvement? How much of an introduction to the topic is needed?
- How receptive will your employees be to the notion of total quality? How can their receptivity be increased?

- What skills, such as team building and conflict resolution, do your employees need to begin implementation of total quality practices?

- How can educational programming most conveniently be scheduled?

Responses to these questions would give the continuing educator considerable information about employee readiness for education in total quality, topics to be covered, and preferred scheduling formats. However, the level at which topics should be addressed might remain unclear; should team building, for example, be taught at a beginning or an advanced level? If questions such as this one cannot be satisfactorily answered in a focus group, it may be necessary to follow up with a survey of potential program participants to determine what, if any, knowledge of the topic they would bring to the program.

Because the facilitator is critical to the success of the focus group, the continuing educator will want to select this person early in the focus group preparations so that he or she can be involved in the planning and can offer suggestions for improving the discussion outline. Leading a focus group may appear to be a simple task, but it is not. The facilitator is not a participant in the group and does not contribute to the discussion or indicate agreement or disagreement with comments made, although he or she may use reflective listening techniques (for example, repeating or rephrasing what has been said) to summarize. A capable facilitator unobtrusively controls the conversation to ensure that all participants are heard, keeps the conversation flowing in a productive and comfortable fashion, and guides transitions into new topics. Appropriate timing is important. Interrupting valuable comments can result in loss of important information, yet discussion cannot be allowed to stall on one aspect of the topic and the group's interest must be maintained. The facilitator should be experienced with group process techniques, have strong interpersonal skills, and be a good listener. This person's ability to establish rapport with the participants is enhanced if he or she shares some characteristics or experiences with them, such as knowledge of the field being discussed or educational background (Krueger, 1988). The facilitator also should be totally familiar with the discussion outline, committing it to memory so that notes are not needed. He or she will determine approximately how much time will be devoted to each question so that the group can move through all questions in the time allotted.

Careful selection of focus group participants also is critical to the procedure's success. A continuing educator usually chooses participants because they have some knowledge, understanding, opinions, or interest in the topic to be discussed. Extreme care must be taken to ensure that participants are either similar to the population to be served in experience, education, and demographics or are knowledgeable about and familiar with these aspects of the target population. However, including individuals with a range of viewpoints and perspectives on the assessment topic will provide a breadth of ideas. For example, a continuing educator wishing to identify programming needs of middle-level managers in a large corporation might convene one focus group of these managers' supervisors (who are similar in general characteristics), selecting individuals from different departments across the operation (who offer a range of viewpoints and perspectives). He or she might also hold a second focus group that includes the middle managers themselves, also from a variety of units within the company. Focus groups function best when participants are not well known to each other, and when grouping of close friends or colleagues is avoided (Krueger, 1988). When talking with acquaintances, not only do people speak about needs less freely, but also they are more likely to allow the conversation to deteriorate into discussion of specific incidents known only to them, or to unrelated chatter. Inclusion of people at different levels of authority within an organization, and particularly of those involved in direct supervisory relationships with one another, can have a detrimental effect on the openness of the discussion and is to be avoided. Some individuals may be concerned that their ideas will be perceived as worthless or naive by group members holding higher positions than theirs, for example.

Focus group participants need some time to become acquainted, perhaps informally over light refreshments before the session begins. In any case, after convening the session, the facilitator should initiate group introductions, perhaps suggesting that participants briefly share some information regarding their interest in the topic to be discussed. After introductions have been completed, the facilitator clarifies both the topic and the process. At this time the tone of the meeting is set. The facilitator strives to achieve a balance between the formality imposed by ground rules (necessary to ensure an orderly discussion) and a more relaxed, comfortable, atmosphere. He or she also explains that open, frank discussion is the goal, and that there are no right or wrong answers. Following these opening remarks, the facilitator asks the first question and then proceeds to guide the group through the outline. If discussion lags or questions are not being addressed thoroughly, the facilitator may need to probe for additional information. Requests for participants to "say more about" a statement or give an example are probing techniques that can be used effectively.

Part of the facilitator's job is to involve all participants in the discussion, directing questions to those who have not spoken or who have demonstrated some reluctance to contribute to the conversation. The facilitator can encourage participants who dominate the conversation to retreat a bit by avoiding eye contact with them or by directing a question to another participant when a dominant person pauses. With a nod of the head, the facilitator indicates interest in comments being made. As the time to conclude the session approaches, the facilitator may announce that time remains for only two or three additional comments. He or she may summarize the discussion or simply thank focus group members for their participation. Throughout the meeting the facilitator must be free to devote full attention to guiding the focus group and should have no competing responsibilities such as tape-recording or note taking.

Soon after the focus group, the facilitator should meet with the continuing educator, and perhaps the rest of the needs assessment team, to offer general impressions of participants' viewpoints, suggestions, and comments. However, it is not the facilitator's role to provide definitive summary statements about the data collected. Transcription, analysis, and interpretation of the session tape and any notes that were taken will provide a detailed report of the ideas that emerged from the discussion. Because of the subjective nature of focus group discussions, quantification of the resulting data usually is inappropriate.

Nominal Group Process

Nominal groups are a suitable needs assessment method for the continuing educator who has access to a number of individuals who are well informed about the topic being examined. In this process, groups of between five and nine knowledgeable participants are convened by a facilitator and asked to respond to a specific question by jotting down their answers. Participants are asked, one by one, to share their written responses, and group members vote to rank or rate all responses. Through this voting process, nominal groups, unlike focus groups, generate data with a quantitative component. Several nominal groups often are conducted simultaneously, with the results generated by all groups aggregated into a single broad definition of need. Thus the nominal group process is a logical assessment choice for the continuing educator working with a large group of, for example, conference participants. The total group of attendees can be divided into a number of small groups, often within the same large room, for this assessment exercise.

Among the advantages of the nominal group process is its highly ordered structure, which avoids some problems inherent in group dynamics, such as discouragement of participation by judgmental comments or domination by one or two participants (McKillip, 1987, p. 88). All participants have equal opportunity for input, and everyone's ideas receive equal consideration (Gilmore, Campbell, and Becker, 1989, p. 62). The continuing educator is able to involve the people most likely to be affected by the decisions in the decision-making process. Requiring participants to put their ideas in writing encourages presentation of considered comments rather than random thoughts. Disadvantages of this process include the generally subjective nature of the data and the time commitment required of participants. Inclusion of nominal group participants in further program planning is advantageous, because they may develop a sense of ownership of the program, make further suggestions about it, and informally market it.

As with focus groups, nominal group process requires early definition of the question to be posed. Usually only one question is used, and it is a broad one, such as "What is the greatest educational need faced by you and your colleagues in the solo practice of law?" or "In what ways can continuing education best serve professional engineers?" Questions are stated clearly and simply and present a problem to be solved. In developing the question, pilot testing or use of a planning committee can help to ensure that the question will be easily understood and elicit a range of responses.

The criteria for facilitator selection discussed in the section on focus groups also are appropriate for facilitator selection for nominal groups. If a number of nominal groups are to be conducted simultaneously, each group will require a facilitator.

As with focus groups, the facilitator's role is to guide the group without influencing the outcome. Before convening the groups, the continuing educator can hold a brief training period to provide all facilitators with the same understanding of their tasks and purpose, and prepare them to approach their role in a consistent manner. Conducting a trial run, with facilitators acting as participants, is an effective means of preparing them (Gilmore, Campbell, and Becker, 1989, p. 63).

Participants in nominal groups should be representative of the target audience and may even be the target audience. For example, nominal groups could be conducted at an association's annual conference to determine topics for the following year's meeting. A sample must be large enough to allow for representation of all major components of the audience, with those included possessing the range of characteristics present in the total population. Relevant characteristics include education, experience, interests, type of employment or practice setting, specialty, and demographic data. As with focus groups, nominal groups are most successful if the people within each group are of relatively equal status. An opening statement, to introduce participants to the nominal group process and the specific issue, sets the tone for what follows. If several nominal groups are to operate simultaneously, it makes sense to address opening remarks to all of them together. The convener explains the importance of the task at hand and of each participant's contributions, the purpose of the exercise, and the process to be followed (Moore, 1987). Members of each group are seated together, with each group at a separate table, for example. Each participant is given paper and pencil. The facilitators assume responsibility for their groups, introducing themselves and inviting participants to do the same.

After the introductions, each facilitator states the question, which also may be written on a flip chart or chalkboard or on the paper provided for participants. Respondents are given sufficient time to write their responses and encouraged to work independently. Conversation is discouraged during this process. The amount of time appropriate for writing responses will vary somewhat depending on the question, but fifteen minutes is usually sufficient (Gilmore, Campbell, and Becker, 1989, p. 64). After this time period the facilitator leads group members in sharing their responses one by one in round-robin fashion and writes the responses on a flip chart or chalkboard, numbering each. This process continues until all participants have had an opportunity to report all of their responses. The facilitator encourages participants to clarify their responses as necessary, making sure that the discussion does not digress into a debate over the merits of the ideas presented. The facilitator then asks participants to rank-order a specific number of responses they consider most important on a separate card. For example, if thirty responses have been listed, participants may be asked to select the six they consider most important and rank them in priority order. Using the flip chart or chalkboard, the facilitator tallies the votes, identifying the responses deemed most important. He or she then may ask participants to rank-order the top responses, or to rate the importance of each of the top responses on a specified scale (for example, one to eight, with one being least important and eight the most important). In this way, the response considered most important is identified. When several nominal groups are operating simultaneously, the last step in the process is the integration of the results from all of the groups into a final statement of need. This can be accomplished through another round of voting, or by statistically combining the data from all groups.

Delphi Method

The RAND Corporation introduced the Delphi method in the 1960s for use in business forecasting, and it quickly gained wide acceptance (Merriam and Simpson, 1989, p. 121). When used for needs assessment, this method relies on a panel to identify and achieve consensus on educational needs. Data are collected by soliciting panel members' responses to a series of questionnaires, each derived from responses to the preceding questionnaire. The first questionnaire is quite general in scope, and subsequent questionnaires narrow the focus. Like the information gathered from self-reports and focus groups, needs identified through use of the Delphi method are based on opinion rather than fact. The Delphi method may be a good choice for a needs assessment when a variety of perspectives are desired and resources are somewhat limited. A continuing educator might use the Delphi method to answer questions such as "What content should be included in an introductory art history program for teenagers?" or "What are the greatest educational needs of workers being promoted to management positions?" Delbecq, Van de Ven, and Gustafson (1975) present a detailed discussion of the history and application of the Delphi method.

In selecting a Delphi panel, the continuing educator seeks people with expertise on the target population, the content area, or other factors pertinent to the needs assessment topic. Often members of a particular group or committee, such as the continuing education section of a national professional association, are asked to serve as a Delphi panel. Since the Delphi method relies on written communication that can be mailed, panel members can be selected without concern for their geographic location. Continuing educators should consider the members' levels of expertise and the breadth of the topic to be covered in determining the panel size. If panel members are highly knowledgeable and competent, or if the scope of the needs assessment is narrow, a small panel of under twenty-five people can be quite satisfactory. Although there is no generally prescribed number, a sufficient number of members are needed to provide enough responses to result in meaningful data. Because the per-person costs encountered are limited to those for duplication, postage, and individualization of follow-up questionnaires, additional panel members can provide valuable information at moderate expense.

The continuing educator's initial contact with potential participants is through a letter explaining the purpose of the Delphi project and inviting them to serve on the panel. A statement regarding the time required, including the number of questionnaires that will be included in the process, will enable potential participants to understand the extent of the commitment they are being asked to make. The continuing educator can provide a form for the potential participants' response to the invitation or can let them know that they will be called within a few days. In either case, the continuing educator should obtain their agreement to participate before beginning the process.

As already mentioned, the first questionnaire presents broad areas for the panelists' consideration. It may, for example, ask their perceptions regarding a target population's educational needs in a number of content areas. Participants are presented with a list of topics, often based on information obtained either informally or through prior structured group discussions, program evaluations, or other input. The questionnaire follows standard questionnaire design methods and recommended procedures (see Chapter Six), and the mailing includes a cover letter and a postage-paid return envelope. Construction of individual questions so that all have numeric responses facilitates data analysis and design of the next questionnaire in the series. The questionnaire is sent out with a response deadline indicated. The distribution of responses, or the number of panel members selecting each available answer to each question, is the focus of the data analysis.

A second questionnaire is developed based on the information obtained from the first. The same questions are repeated, and for each question, each panel member receives two pieces of information: (1) the distribution of all responses to that item on the first questionnaire, and (2) that panel member's original response. Panel members are asked to decide if they wish to alter their responses and to explain any of their responses that deviate significantly from the median. The information provided again is analyzed, a new distribution of responses is prepared, and rationales for deviant responses are compiled. At this point, some trends in responses begin to emerge. For example, in a needs assessment seeking to identify program content, some areas will be cited frequently as topics of substantial need and others will receive few, if any, strong endorsements.

The third questionnaire is an updated version of the second, again presenting response distributions and each panel member's current response to each question. In addition, the information includes panel members' rationales for responses above or below the norm. Panel members once again may change their responses, and they also are invited to provide additional information explaining their deviant responses. The information provided is analyzed in the same manner as the second questionnaire. The process may end at this point, or it may continue until either the panel members cease to change their responses or the person directing the process is satisfied that the information provided is sufficiently conclusive to provide the needs assessment data sought. When the areas that panel members consider to be those of greatest educational need become clear, for example, the Delphi process can be considered completed.

In a less traditional adaptation of the Delphi method, the first questionnaire presents panel members with open-ended rather than multiple-choice questions. Panel members may be asked, for example, to list topics they believe should be addressed by continuing education activities. As these questionnaires are returned, the data analyst groups similar responses to produce a comprehensive list for the second questionnaire. In this second instrument, panel members are asked for numeric responses to each of the items listed, and the process continues in the same manner described. This variation on the Delphi method is useful when continuing educators are not convinced that they are aware of all possible responses, or when they are eager to obtain new ideas.

Key Informants

Key informants are leaders within a field, organization, or community who have valuable perceptions and insights regarding the educational needs of a particular group. In many cases, data from key informants may not be sufficient to prompt program planning but can yield ideas to be further explored through a more formal needs assessment process. Usually key informants are not members of the group they are discussing but are knowledgeable about it and occupy an influential position in relation to it. They may be elder statesmen, community or religious leaders, government officials, respected professionals, or teachers. They are selected because they can be expected to have a unique perspective on the group, but they should not be assumed to speak for the group. Continuing educators or assessment teams may ask key informants to participate in a formal interview process or respond to a written questionnaire (see Chapter Six), or they may simply ask them to provide informal comments about the group's educational needs. Needs assessors may solicit key informants' perceptions orally or in writing.

Selection of Key Informants

If key informants are easily identified and available, continuing educators can access their observations quickly and at little cost. If those selected have considerable knowledge about and understanding of the group in question, their perceptions may be extremely valuable. And if the key informants are respected by the target population, their association with an educational activity's needs assessment may be helpful in marketing the activity. Disadvantages to the use of key informants include the concern that their own perspectives or biases may be reflected in their observations. Also, a key informant's belief that members of a group have a strong educational need in no way implies that group members recognize that need or would welcome an opportunity to participate in educational activities that address it.

Careful selection of appropriate key informants is critical to the success of this needs assessment method. A group (often including between ten and fifteen people) of key informants should be selected to represent the full range of relevant backgrounds, opinions (Hagedorn, 1977), and where pertinent, practice settings. For example, a continuing educator seeking to develop programming for hospital nurses in a variety of practice settings might select physicians, directors of nursing, and hospital administrators as key informants. By nature of their professions, the individuals identified will have different backgrounds and perspectives on nursing. In this example, representation of large and small, rural and urban, and teaching and non–teaching hospitals also would be desirable. Because those selected as key informants usually are busy people, it is wise to request their participation in the needs assessment either by telephone or if convenient, in person. A written confirmation, containing details such as location, can follow.

Questions Key Informants Can Address

The questions posed can be broad or specific, and they can cover topics related to content, audience, and delivery of proposed educational activities (Gilmore, Campbell, and Becker, 1989). Keeping questions focused on issues that can be addressed by educational intervention is critical. Asking key informants to provide factual data that can be obtained (often more reliably) elsewhere is a waste of the limited time they are devoting to the needs assessment. For example, asking key informants the turnover rate of critical care nurses or the number of child support suits settled out of court annually is not the best use of their time. Key informants usually are well qualified, and hence best used, to answer questions relating to the educational programming potential suggested by broad trends and topics. Key informants can be particularly helpful about topics such as those illustrated in the following examples.

Current Concerns Within a Field.   Unlike newly developed knowledge, which is somewhat discrete in nature, current concerns deal with more comprehensive, important issues and their implications for a particular field. A shortage of radioactive waste disposal sites for health care facilities and physicians' growing concern with medical ethics are examples of current concerns.

Discrepancies Within a Field.   Many practitioners may require help in improving their skills to be on a par with others in their field. Discrepancies often can be addressed through continuing education. Trial lawyers who frequently come to court without adequate case preparation and architects whose cost estimates are consistently below project bids exhibit discrepancies in their fields, for example.

Societal Trends.   Socioeconomic changes may have ramifications for educational programming. With the number of senior citizens increasing, for example, greater demands are placed on the field of gerontology, and there are more opportunities to provide programming about productive activities for the older population.

Community Issues.   Often factors within the community affect the roles, duties, and requirements of certain segments of the population. For example, the proximity of a new interstate highway may increase the local crime rate, giving additional responsibilities to local law enforcement officials.

Application of New or Revived Theories, Practices, and Technology.   New ways of doing things emerge with some regularity, and older methods often are resurrected. People need help applying practices that are unfamiliar to them or that they have not used in some time. The reintroduction of cooperative learning in many school districts is an example of a revived practice.

In sum, key informants can provide information on the relevance of these types of topics to the target populations they are knowledgeable about. Continuing educators can expect them to have sound ideas about the content and level of programming needed to address the issues, and the specific populations to whom the education should be directed. Continuing educators should encourage them to interpret questions broadly and offer additional perceptions, for they may have valuable ideas that go beyond the scope of the specific questions asked. Documenting information on the informants, such as their profession, organizational affiliations, and relation to the target group being addressed, can help the continuing educator understand their perspectives.

Supervisor Evaluations

Supervisor evaluations most often are used to ascertain educational needs related to the work setting, but they may also be appropriate for local government and other organizations and institutions using volunteers. For example, the professional staff member of a county government office who works with elected and appointed officials, or the paid director of volunteers in a hospital, may function as supervisor for the purposes of a needs assessment. Those who supervise employees or volunteers often have a unique perspective on their performance.

Continuing educators can solicit supervisor evaluations in much the same manner as for key informants, and the two processes share many of the same advantages, disadvantages, and guidelines for implementation. However, because of their familiarity with routine or even daily practice, supervisors are likely to have more specific observations about the learning needs of those reporting to or working with them. Unlike key informants, supervisors are in a position to observe individual performance and therefore can provide information useful in identifying individual as well as group needs.

Supervisor evaluations have several advantages. By suggesting that educational needs exist, supervisors are likely to create an atmosphere of receptivity to the techniques and ideas developed in response to those needs, through educational activities. Supervisors who understand the context and problems of daily practice are frequently able to describe practitioners' educational needs accurately. This perspective can help continuing educators offer information in a manner that enables learners to apply it in their work setting. Supervisors also may be particularly alert to the distinction between discrepancies that can be addressed successfully through educational activities and those that can be addressed only by other means, such as changes in organizational procedures. A disadvantage of supervisor evaluations is the potential for personal relationships and opinions of others to color the views expressed.

A supervisor evaluation often can be the first step in identifying individual learning needs. The results of this evaluation can guide further exploration, such as collecting information from the individual, examining results of the individual's work, or reviewing the individual's education and employment record. For example, the head of an architectural firm might suggest that an individual architect appears to need additional education in cost estimating (data obtained through a supervisor evaluation). A review of the architect's recent projects may indicate that he or she did indeed substantially underestimate building costs for several of them (data obtained through examination of individual's work). Discussion with the individual may indicate an understanding that cost estimating is an area of some uncertainty (collection of information from the individual), and the person's employment history may show that until recently cost estimating was not an area handled routinely (review of education and employment records).

Supervisor evaluations can also help identify group needs. However, continuing educators must be careful to combine only comparable data when aggregating data collected from a number of supervisors. Supervisors from similar practice settings serving similar clients are more likely to generate comparable data than supervisors from varied settings. School principals' comments on the educational needs of teachers may be quite different, depending on the urban or rural nature of the schools they represent, for example, and the needs of dietitians working in nursing homes may be substantially different from those of their colleagues in other institutional settings. In aggregating data, stratification of supervisor evaluations according to the experience and, where applicable, educational levels of those they are asked to evaluate also helps ensure comparability. Aggregated data from supervisor evaluations can be used successfully in much the same manner as data obtained from key informants.

The process for assessing needs through supervisors' evaluations—the methods of identifying participants, posing questions, and so forth—can be much the same as that described in the earlier passage about key informants. The questions asked, however, will focus on supervisors' perceptions of the target population's strengths and educational needs as demonstrated by their performance. The manager of a hotel might be asked a series of questions about employees' customer service orientation as demonstrated by their interaction with hotel guests, for example, or a county administrator might be expected to provide information on appointed officials' understanding of the role and organization of local government. A second means of assessing needs through supervisor evaluation can involve reference to regularly conducted performance appraisals. One advantage of using completed performance appraisals is that no additional data collection is required. Disadvantages here may come from inconsistency between appraisals, lack of comparable data, and the need for strict confidentiality.

Summary

The methods described in this chapter obtain general information about continuing education needs. Continuing educators with little needs assessment experience and limited resources will find that these methods will enable them to identify content areas that merit further consideration, get an idea of the potential viability of proposed activities, and gather information about scheduling and delivery preferences. However, these methods neither measure educational needs in relation to objective performance criteria nor provide in-depth data about the needs perceived. Thus, the methods described in this chapter are most useful when only a broad perspective is desired or as a first step in a comprehensive needs assessment strategy. When implemented with careful planning, attention to detail, and adherence to the guidelines specified, these methods can yield data of considerable value.

Chapter Six

Surveys

When people think of needs assessment, they most often think of surveys. There are two basic types of surveys, written questionnaires and oral interviews. Well-designed and carefully implemented surveys of both types can provide a wealth of information on people's continuing education interests, problems, perceptions, and preferences. Survey format and length can be tailored to the topic, quantity and type of information needed, and to the interest level of the respondents. Surveys allow the continuing educator to reach audiences that may be geographically dispersed or unavailable for other forms of needs assessment. Frequently, surveys permit assessment of more respondents than would be possible through other methods. They can directly involve those who are potential program participants in the needs assessment process, building interest and a sense of ownership. In addition, surveys can serve a marketing function, reminding respondents of the continuing education provider, increasing their awareness of the services available through that provider, and alerting them to the possibility of new and expanded programming. However, surveys that are perceived as an annoyance can have quite the opposite effect.

Perhaps the biggest problem with surveys is that everyone believes that he or she can conduct one with little or no knowledge or experience of survey methodology. A poorly conducted survey is worse than no survey at all, for it will yield bad data, possibly leading to bad decisions. It may cause respondents to have expectations that the continuing educator cannot meet, or at worst, result in embarrassment to the continuing educator's organization or institution. Survey design is an intricate process that includes several facets—such as population identification and sampling, format, question design—and there are a myriad of details related to the data collection process itself. These issues need not be difficult to address, but their careful planning and execution do require some information, guidance, and perhaps consultation with an individual experienced in designing and conducting surveys.

Although different formats and procedures must be used for questionnaires and interviews, they share a number of characteristics. As noted in Chapter Four, selection of the population to be assessed and (unless the entire population is to be surveyed) drawing the sample of it are critical steps. One of the strengths of surveys is that continuing educators can use data collected from a relatively small sample to represent an entire, large population. However, this is true only if the population has been accurately defined and the sample carefully drawn. For surveys of either a sample or a total population, adequate response rates are critical to interpretation of the data collected. Although scholars have not reached a consensus regarding the definition of "adequate" survey response rates, confidence is well placed in surveys with response rates above 70 percent, unless the demographic data collected indicate that a particular segment of the population is severely underrepresented. (For example, if 20 percent of the population is known to have less than a high school education, and only 3 percent of respondents indicate that education level, persons with less than a high school education can be considered to be underrepresented.) Response rates of from 50 to 70 percent may be considered good, but the lower the response rate, the more important it is to determine that those responding do indeed possess the pertinent demographic characteristics to represent the total population. Surveys with response rates below 50 percent can produce highly useful information, but whether a sample or the total population was surveyed, they cannot be assumed to represent the total target population.

Confidentiality and anonymity are important considerations in designing a survey. People who may shy away from surveys often are willing to participate if assured that no one will know of their responses.

If survey participants are told that their responses will remain confidential, their identities will be known only to those conducting the needs assessment. Factors that could reveal their identity are not associated with their responses in any discussion or reporting of data, and their individual responses are not revealed to anyone beyond the individual speaking with them (in the case of an interview) and those analyzing the data. Interviewers, data analysts, and clerical personnel who have access to the data must understand the importance of confidentiality and be committed to respecting it for all data. A commitment to confidentiality may preclude the possibility of reporting correlations between demographic characteristics and other responses if such reporting has the potential to reveal a respondent's identity. For example, if only three first-line administrators are included in a survey of employees' educational needs, the findings should not be reported by such factors as position held or length of service, because such reporting could identify one or more of the three individuals and destroy confidentiality.

Anonymity means that respondents' identities are not in any way revealed to anyone, even those conducting the needs assessment. Complete anonymity for respondents is possible only with questionnaires, because any interview participant is identified during the interview process. However, continuing educators can maintain the anonymity of the interview data by separating the identify of the person interviewed from the data before analysis. When a questionnaire carries with it the promise of anonymity, no information that would reveal a respondent's identity is requested and no identifying marks are placed on the questionnaire. As with confidentiality, continuing educators must take care not to report anonymous data by using descriptors that could reveal an individual's identity.

Whether questionnaires or interviews are used, surveys require fairly extensive planning. In addition to careful design of the survey instrument, detailed procedures usually are also necessary to motivate the people contacted to participate in the survey so that an acceptable response rate will be achieved. The first contact with potential participants includes a brief description of the project they are being asked to participate in and a statement regarding their participation's importance to the success of that project. By integrating planning for data analysis in the early stages of the survey development process, the continuing educator can structure data collection to produce information in the most desirable format.

Pilot testing of all surveys is important to ensure that the questions asked are clear and the response options are comprehensive and appropriate. When the continuing educator or needs assessment team is satisfied that the survey instrument is as good as they can make it, they identify a small group of people who are comparable to the population that will be asked to participate in the needs assessment. (This group can include members of the population to be assessed, but any individuals who participate in the pilot test cannot participate in the actual assessment. Prior exposure to the survey instrument could bias their responses.) The continuing educator asks those identified as potential pilot test respondents to participate in a pilot test of the survey instrument, explaining the purpose and process of the test. Those agreeing to serve in this capacity complete the questionnaire or are interviewed as if they were participating in an actual survey. The continuing educator or assessment team reviews their responses to determine whether the directions and questions were clear and unambiguous and yielded the type of information sought. After completing the survey, pilot test participants are asked for their observations. They may be asked if they found responding easy or difficult, if they found directions and questions clear, if they found the tone of the survey instrument appropriate, and if they have any other observations.

Considerations specific to questionnaires or to interviews are discussed in separate sections of this chapter devoted to each of those survey methods. One major area common to both types of surveys, however, is development of questions.

Development of Questions

Questions are designed to elicit the information that has been deemed necessary or desirable. Each question has to be clearly understood by those who read or hear it. It must be carefully constructed to eliminate the possibility of respondents' misinterpretation, to avoid prejudicing respondents' answers, and to be as free as possible of value-laden words and phrases. In developing questions, the continuing educator or assessment team members may find it helpful to begin with a list of the information they are seeking, the broad questions that need answers. The decisions that have been made about what to assess (as discussed in Chapter Three) will guide the construction of this list, and in turn the list will serve as the basis for developing specific questions. Although it may be tempting to expand the list of information sought as the survey instrument is developed, this temptation is best resisted. Time, questionnaire space, and other constraints require educators to limit the scope of any survey. One practical criterion for inclusion of a question in a survey is the likelihood that the continuing educator will make decisions or take actions based on the response to it. If the information that may be obtained would be interesting but the continuing educator has no intention of taking any action as a result, the question should be excluded.

Questions can be close-ended, where a finite number of response options are offered, or open-ended, where respondents are asked to supply their own responses. The use of close-ended responses is preferable when the continuing educator either has a good understanding of possible responses, and hence does not risk missing potentially important information, or wants to limit the range of responses. Open-ended questions permit respondents to introduce new ideas. Thus, they can provide information the continuing educator may not have considered. Close-ended questions result in more easily tabulated data, because all possible responses are defined, but they limit possible responses to those identified by the people designing the instrument.

People's frequent disinclination to write at any length is a consideration in choosing open- or close-ended formats for questionnaires. Because many people are reluctant to write more than a few words in response to a question, it is advisable to limit the number of open-ended questions in written questionnaires and to call for short responses, unless the target group members are known to be favorably disposed toward writing. Responses to open-ended questions most often are categorized before data analysis, adding another step to the analysis procedure.

Questions utilizing attitudinal scales for response options constitute one type of close-ended question. The most commonly used attitudinal scale is the Likert scale (Crowl, 1986). Likert scales present a series of response options and respondents select the one that most closely indicates the strength of their attitude or opinion. For example, respondents may be asked to indicate if they "strongly agree," "agree," "do not agree or disagree," "disagree," or "strongly disagree" with a statement. Likert scales can be used for single items in a survey instrument but most often they are used for a series of items. When using a Likert scale for a series of items, the instrument designer generally states half of the items in positive terms and half in negative terms to avoid biasing responses. (A positive item might read, "Our work environment supports and encourages diversity," whereas a negative item would state, "Our work environment is hostile to women and members of underrepresented populations.")

It is possible to have some of the benefits of both open- and close-ended questions by making the last close-ended response one that invites respondents to list any other options. In this way, respondents who have additional ideas can introduce them. Such a response option might be worded as follows:

___ OTHER: Please specify _____

If this alternative is used, the data analysis will review the options listed by respondents. When several similar options are listed, they are combined to form one or more categories that are added to the data analysis.

Collection of some demographic data, such as gender, ethnicity, age, occupation, and education, is almost always desirable. There are two reasons for this. First, demographic data permit comparison of respondents' characteristics with those of the total population included in the survey or from which the sample was drawn, allowing the continuing educator to determine whether respondents are representative of that population. Second, demographic data can be correlated with other data to identify any relationships between individual characteristics and other findings. For marketing purposes, for example, a continuing educator may find it helpful to know which segments of the population indicated certain needs or cited specific program scheduling preferences. Because people may be reluctant to answer questions about themselves, demographic questions usually appear toward the end of a survey. At this point, respondents have enough time invested in completing the interview or questionnaire that they are likely to cooperate even if they find these questions mildly annoying or disagreeable. Tactful demographic questions encourage response. Particularly when faced with sensitive questions, such as those regarding age and income, respondents may be more amenable to close-ended questions, which require only indication of an appropriate category (for example, age 41–50, income $30,000–$49,000), than to open-ended questions, which require respondents to originate a more precise answer.

Depending on the nature and sensitivity of the survey topic, demographic questions may be preceded by a brief statement reminding respondents of survey confidentiality or anonymity, even though this subject will have been addressed in the cover letter. This statement also can include two or three brief sentences explaining why answers to those questions are important. The following is an example of a statement that could be used to introduce a series of demographic questions: "So that we can fully understand the information collected in this survey, we need to know about the people who have answered our questions. For this reason, our final questions are about you. Please remember that your responses will be anonymous, since the questionnaire contains absolutely no identification of you as the respondent."

In concluding both questionnaires and interviews, continuing educators may find it useful to offer respondents an open-ended opportunity to make additional comments on the survey topic. "What other comments or suggestions do you have regarding [the topic]?" is an example. This kind of concluding question can accomplish two things. First, the continuing educator may gain valuable information that otherwise would have been lost because it was not addressed earlier. Second, it offers respondents an opportunity to relate their thoughts, ideas, praise, or complaints, often resulting in their feeling positively about their opportunity to contribute or to air concerns.

Some general guidelines can be helpful in designing questions for either questionnaires or interviews.

Be succinct. Long questions discourage full reading or listening and increase opportunities for miscomprehension. Some people may jump to the conclusion that long questions will require more time than they are willing to give and refuse to participate in the survey. If a sentence is needed to provide explanation or context for a question, it too should be brief.

Set a positive tone. Stating questions in positive rather than negative terms whenever possible helps establish a constructive attitude for a survey instrument. (As discussed earlier, Likert scales are an exception to this guideline.) Another aspect of the tone is its degree of formality. To some extent, the survey audience will dictate the level of formality. For many audiences the survey instrument can seem informal and friendly, but all surveys should retain a businesslike, respectful quality. Conveying a positive tone is not to be confused with prejudicing respondents' answers. A positive tone can be quite neutral with regard to survey content.

Use proper language and grammar. Grammatical errors, slang, jargon, sexist language, and colloquialisms have no place in a survey instrument. Simple sentence structure and straightforward vocabulary facilitate participants' comprehension of questions.

Request one piece of information at a time. Except for questions involving matrices (described in the next section), requiring only one piece of information with each question helps avoid confusion and produces clear data. Questions that address two or more issues simultaneously may result in data that cannot be interpreted specifically enough to guide action. For example, responses to the question, "How satisfactory did you find the instructors and facilities for previous programs?" could not be accurately interpreted with any specificity. A "somewhat satisfactory" response could mean either that the instructor or the facility was highly satisfactory and the other highly unsatisfactory, or that both were mediocre. A less specific question, such as "How satisfactory did you find previous programs?" would create similar problems. Such questions should be divided into two separate items, one inquiring about the instructor and the other about the facilities.

Use branching questions when bifurcation is necessary. When different close-ended responses to a question will lead respondents to different follow-up or next questions, branching questions can direct them properly. Clear directions are particularly important when using branching questions because the possibility of confusion is substantial. If only one of the possible responses to a question is followed up by further probing on the topic, respondents giving that response should be directed to or asked one question, and other respondents should be directed to another. The following is an example:

Q–10 Have you participated in any workshops on public speaking?

```
r----------- 1        YES
|
|           2        NO (If NO, go to Q–12)
|
L----------- Q–11     (If YES) In how many such workshops have
                      you participated? _____
```

Q–12

Survey designers can use branching questions to ensure that respondents are not asked to answer a question that ignores or contradicts their previous response. For example, if respondents indicate that they have not previously participated in activities offered by the institution, branching questions can direct them past a question asking about the activities they participated in.

Offer clear response options. When close-ended questions are offered, the clarity of the response options is important. Overlapping options—a series of options in which two or more suggested responses could describe a respondent's selection equally well—are appropriate when multiple responses are sought and respondents are instructed to select as many options as apply. If respondents are likely to have difficulty choosing between options but are supposed to select only one, they may be given specific criteria such as "Please circle the number of the response option that *best* reflects your own interests."

Using a matrix format, the survey designer sometimes can ask more than one question simultaneously while allowing for separate responses to each. This format is appropriate when continuing educators want to ask two or more questions about the same items. For example, they may wish to ask respondents about the importance of each of a list of topics, the relevance of those topics to their work, and their interest in additional education on each of them. A statement indicating the issues about which the respondents are to provide information introduces a matrix format. In the case of the example, the statement would ask respondents to indicate the importance, relevance, and their interest in each of a series of topics. With the matrix, it is necessary to ask respondents to consider each topic only once. The matrix is used to record responses, as in the following example.

We are interested in (1) how important each of the following topics is to you, (2) how relevant it is to your work, and (3) how interested you are in further education on that topic. Using the following scale, please circle the letter of your response to indicate the level of each topic's importance to you, its relevance to your work, and your interest in further education on that topic.

H=HIGH LEVEL
M=MODERATE LEVEL
L=LOW LEVEL

	Importance	Relevance	Interest
Topic A	H M L	H M L	H M L
Topic B	H M L	H M L	H M L
Topic C	H M L	H M L	H M L

The matrix format saves time and lessens the boredom and repetitiveness that occur when respondents must work their way through the same list several times. When the matrix format is included in interviews, each of the response options must be repeated for the first two items, but they usually need not be repeated thereafter.

In sum, development of questions requires common sense, diligence, and pilot testing. As questions are being developed, their review by knowledgeable persons not involved in the instrument design can provide a good test of their clarity.

Questionnaires

Questionnaires may be the preferred needs assessment method when the goal is to reach a large population or sample to obtain specific information and when finances dictate that expenses not rise above a moderate level. Questionnaires can be distributed through the mail; on site to groups that have been convened for the needs assessment or for another primary purpose; or through newspapers, journals, and other media. Because questionnaires do not permit following up on respondents' answers with probing questions, they are most appropriate when the parameters of an issue have been defined rather than when issues need to be explored. Basic costs associated with questionnaires include photocopying, postage (including return postage) for mail questionnaires, and data analysis. Postage costs are eliminated if questionnaires are distributed on site or in the media, but advertising costs may be incurred with the latter. Because the considerations involved in media questionnaires differ substantially from those for other types of questionnaires, they are described separately at the conclusion of this section.

Preparation of Materials

Careful preparation of the questionnaire and accompanying cover letter is important to ensure a good response rate. Many of the details discussed here may appear trivial, but all are important to the overall appearance and tone of the questionnaire.

Cover Letter. A succinct cover letter, preferably no longer than four or five short paragraphs, offers the continuing educator the opportunity to explain why the questionnaire was sent and to motivate the recipient to complete and return it. The letter's influence is increased when it comes from the person associated with the project who has the position, name recognition, or other characteristics most likely to be viewed favorably by recipients. That individual uses his or her letterhead, and if at all feasible each letter carries that person's original signature. An acceptable substitute for the original signature is duplication of the signature, preferably in blue ink on a letter otherwise printed with black ink. Whenever possible, the letter is individually addressed, and the salutation refers to the recipient by his or her correct title (for example, Mr., Mrs., Ms., Dr.). When the marital status of a female recipient is unknown or irrelevant, Ms. is appropriate. If the individual's gender cannot be determined from the given name, M. may be used. Only if the person signing the letter personally knows the individual should the recipient's first name be used.

The first paragraph of the cover letter begins by telling recipients why they are being contacted. A phrase citing their relevant characteristic (for example, "As a zoning board member,") can be followed by a phrase tying that identification to the purpose of the questionnaire (for example, "you have gained experience that can be valuable to us in developing educational programs for local government officials"). In this manner, the introductory sentence is constructed to start recipients thinking that they have special characteristics that will enable them to make a worthwhile contribution to a stated goal. The remaining sentence or two in the first paragraph clarifies the purpose of the project. Subsequent paragraphs can explain why the project has been undertaken and provide general information on the questionnaire, such as the length of time required to complete it and the date by which it should be returned. As appropriate, the letter discusses anonymity or confidentiality issues. The closing paragraph encourages recipients to respond, invites them to call either the person signing the letter or another designated person with any questions, and thanks them in advance for their participation.

Questionnaire. The questions asked, as described earlier in this chapter, are the most important feature of any questionnaire. However, format, introductory information, instructions, transition statements, and conclusion also are important parts of questionnaires. Adequate attention to these details, although sometimes tedious, can make a difference in both the clarity of the instrument and the response rate it generates.

Format. The format merits consideration because the questionnaire's appearance is a factor in convincing recipients to respond to it. If resources permit, questionnaires of more than one page should be presented in booklet form rather than as a series of pages stapled together (Dillman, 1978, p. 121).

Booklets can be made, for example, by duplicating standard 8.5" × 11" pages onto 11" × 17" paper, then folding it in the middle to form an 8.5" × 11" booklet. Booklets of smaller dimensions, such as 6" × 9", may be perceived as more attractive, less cumbersome, and easier for respondents to handle, but duplication costs usually are higher. In addition, if they are to be mailed they require special envelopes, which add significantly to the project cost. Paper that is slightly heavier than standard duplication paper, in white or off-white, has a businesslike, higher-quality appearance. Black or dark blue ink is recommended, but another dark color also may be used. The questionnaire booklet may have a cover, particularly if the questionnaire is lengthy. Page layout and format is consistent in numbering, indentation, punctuation, spacing, capitalization, type size and style, and display of response options. Adequate space should be provided for responses.

Introduction. The questionnaire begins with a title on the cover or at the top of the first page. Although there is a cover letter, a brief introduction appears on the questionnaire itself, following the title, perhaps in boldface or in type that is slightly larger than that used for the body of the questionnaire. This introduction may seem redundant, since it includes some of the material contained in the cover letter, but if the questionnaire becomes separated from the cover letter the recipient will still recognize its purpose. In one or two sentences, the introduction explains the general purpose of the questionnaire from the respondent's perspective. The following is an example: "Your responses to this questionnaire will enable us to understand better the educational needs of practicing veterinarians. This information will guide our decisions regarding future educational programming."

If a questionnaire deals with a proposed educational activity, a brief description of that activity also might be appropriate. Such a description immediately follows the introduction, and often is set off in a box. It provides information on proposed content, format, delivery method, prerequisites, credit, and pricing, as relevant.

General Instructions. Directions for completing the questionnaire appear next, often also in boldface or slightly larger type than the body. Directions are clear, concise, and polite, rather than authoritarian, in tone. If most questions call for selection of a numbered response option, for example, the general instructions may simply state, "Please circle the number of your response to each question, unless otherwise instructed." Any question for which instructions may deviate even slightly from those given requires additional directions that can be placed in parentheses at the end of the question, as in the following examples.

- What factors are most important in your selection of an educational activity? (Please circle numbers of *all* responses that apply.)

- How interested are you in each of the following potential seminar topics? (For *each* topic listed, please circle the number indicating your level of interest.)

- What topics not listed would be of interest to you? (Please list these topics in the space below.)

<u>Transitional Statements.</u> Longer questionnaires may be made more inviting when divided into sections, with each section introduced by a transitional statement. Transitional statements also are useful in moving respondents from one topic to another, or in explaining why certain topics are included in the questionnaire. Again, boldface or slightly larger type often is used to set off transitional statements. These statements usually address the content directly following them, as these examples suggest.

- The first questions concern your perceptions of current issues within the field of life insurance.

- The next section of this questionnaire is about potential continuing education program topics that may be of interest to you and other insurance agents.

- Information about the people responding to this questionnaire will help us better understand the information we collect. For this reason, the last questions ask for information about you and your insurance practice.

<u>Conclusion.</u> The instrument ends by thanking participants for completing the instrument and instructing them how to return the completed questionnaires. It is always advisable to include such instructions. Questionnaires sometime become separated from the envelopes provided for their return, and even when questionnaires are collected on site, directions for returning them may be misunderstood.

Questionnaire Distribution and Return

The best way to handle questionnaires distributed through the mail is to enclose the cover letter, questionnaire, and a postage-paid return envelope in a mailing envelope large enough to accommodate all three pieces. Well in advance of preparing the mailing, the continuing educator can assemble sample packages and weigh them to determine the postage required for both the initial mailing and the return of the completed questionnaire. In mailing questionnaires and accompanying materials to potential respondents, the cover letter and questionnaire are folded together in thirds so that the salutation on the cover letter is on top of the folded packet, the return envelope is inserted in the fold, and the resultant package is placed in the large mailing envelope (Dillman, 1978, p. 181). This method requires that the mailing envelope be slightly larger than the return envelope. A standard 4⅛" × 9½" (number 10) mailing envelope with a 3⅞" × 8⅞" (number 9) return envelope, works well for questionnaires and cover letters that are 8½" × 11" and can be folded in thirds. Typing recipients' addresses directly onto the mailing envelopes avoids use of address labels and gives each envelope a personalized appearance. The return envelope is addressed to the individual signing the cover letter, and also bears that individual's return address.

Postage stamps, rather than a postage meter, enhance the personalized appearance of both envelopes. Concerning the return envelope, some believe that recipients are reluctant to dispose of a return envelope bearing a stamp, thus using one increases the likelihood of their completing and returning the questionnaire. The alternative to affixing stamps to return envelopes is to use envelopes that indicate that postage will be paid by the addressee, in this case the person to whom the questionnaire is being returned. This option is less attractive to recipients because it appears more impersonal. In addition, because of the extra postage charged for guaranteed postage payment, higher per-item postal costs may be incurred. If the response rate is much over 50 percent, the cost of this option will exceed that of supplying postage stamps for all return envelopes mailed out. However, using postage-paid return envelopes is less labor-intensive than putting a stamp on every return envelope. Providing no return postage at all is not a viable option in mail surveys. After all the investment of time, duplication, and initial mailing costs, to jeopardize the return rate substantially by eliminating this relatively minor expense is a false economy.

A procedure similar to that described above, absent the postage, may be followed when questionnaires are distributed in other ways—through an employment site, for example—and the questionnaires will be collected at a later time. Providing envelopes increases a sense of confidentiality, because an individual's questionnaire may pass through at least one set of hands on its way both to and from the recipient. Instructions for the return of questionnaires distributed in this manner usually specify that they be turned in at a specific, convenient location by a certain date, usually within a week's time.

Envelopes are not necessary for questionnaires distributed to and collected from an assembled group, and the information contained in a cover letter may be presented orally. When distributing questionnaires to assembled groups, allowing time for immediate completion and collection will result in a far higher response rate than asking those present to complete and return the questionnaires after leaving the site.

Time Factors

Convenience is the primary factor in determining when a questionnaire will be distributed to an on-site group; it will be distributed when the group is convened. If the group is convened frequently, other factors such as the complexity of their agenda and the number of people expected to be present will contribute to the choice of a date. Questionnaires generally are distributed to organizational groups, such as a group of employees of a particular business, at the organization's convenience.

However, several factors enter into selection of a distribution date for mail questionnaires. The time period between Thanksgiving and the end of the calendar year is not good for sending mail questionnaires. People are busier than usual at this time of year, and the large amount of seasonal mail increases the likelihood that a questionnaire will be laid aside or misplaced. Similarly, because many people take vacations during the summer, response returns may be slow during June, July, and August. In contrast, January and September are particularly good times for mailing questionnaires because both months signal a return to activity patterns for a large portion of the population.

Regardless of when a questionnaire is distributed, a response deadline should be specified. Many people will put a questionnaire aside unless given a deadline. Unless questionnaires are returned promptly, data analysis is postponed, changing conditions may cause the data to become outdated, and the project for which the questionnaire was developed will be delayed. It is possible to control the return of questionnaires distributed on site or within organizations. For mail questionnaires, a response period of two to three weeks usually allows sufficient time for most recipients to complete and return the instruments. Because a few responses may straggle in a week or so after a deadline based on this time frame, scheduling initiation of data analysis for four weeks after questionnaire distribution is sensible. A slightly longer time frame may be advisable if questionnaires are mailed to distant locations, where up to a week of mail time may be required.

Follow-Up Measures

Unless questionnaires are distributed, completed, and collected on the spot, use of follow-up measures is advised to obtain a good response rate. Key to determining which follow-up measures to use is deciding whether to code the questionnaires or the return envelopes so that those responding—and hence those not responding—can be identified. The advantage of coding is that it makes it possible to focus follow-up efforts on nonrespondents. The disadvantages are that it adds another step to the preparation process and it weakens or eliminates the shield of anonymity that is important to some respondents for some surveys. If the envelope, rather than the questionnaire, carries the identifying code, it is possible to separate the envelopes from the questionnaires upon receipt, thus preserving respondents' anonymity. By explaining this procedure in the cover letter, the continuing educator can advise recipients that their anonymity will indeed be protected. In those relatively few cases where respondents do not use the envelope provided, the code is lost. If no return envelopes are used, or if the decision is made to code the questionnaires themselves, anonymity is not possible. Unless confidentiality is not an issue it too should be addressed in the cover letter accompanying coded questionnaires.

Follow-up efforts usually begin a week to ten days after questionnaires have been distributed. Several follow-up methods are available, and more than one can be used in a survey for which a high response rate is critical or for which some urging of respondents is needed. During the first week or so following questionnaire distribution, many responses will be in the mail, making it virtually impossible to distinguish respondents from those who have not yet responded. Thus, whether questionnaire materials have been coded or not, a good first step is mailing a postcard to all recipients about a week after questionnaire distribution (Dillman, 1978, p. 183–84). For those who may have put the questionnaire aside, this communication serves as a reminder and emphasizes the questionnaire's importance. The postcard message is similar to that shown in the following example:

> Last week we mailed you a questionnaire asking about your
> interest in a number of educational programs for people dealing
> with the public.
> If you have completed and returned that questionnaire, thank
> you for helping us identify future program topics.
> If you have not yet sent your completed questionnaire to us,
> we would very much appreciate your doing so by [specify date].
> Since our survey includes only a small number of people, your

response is important to us. If you have misplaced your questionnaire, please contact us at [telephone number] and we shall be
pleased to send you another.
Thank you.
[signature of individual signing original cover letter]

Postal regulations specify that standard postcards may be no
larger than 4" × 6". Cards of this size, printed on brightly colored
card stock, are more likely to catch recipients' attention than are
standard-size white postcards. Reduced-size type may be necessary
to fit the message on these cards. Follow-up postcards are individually addressed in the same manner as the initial mailing.

This first follow-up is intended to serve as a reminder, not to
overcome resistance to completing the questionnaire (Dillman,
1978, p. 184). However, further follow-up efforts aim to convince
recipients to become respondents. A second follow-up measure usually is a letter sent two weeks after the questionnaire, explaining in
greater detail why it is important that the recipient take the short
time required to complete and return the questionnaire. If questionnaire materials have not been coded, this letter also must
include a message thanking those who have already returned completed questionnaires. This letter too is individually addressed and
signed by the same person who has signed all previous correspondence. This second follow-up measure generally is the last one
taken in surveys for which coding has not been used.

When survey materials have been coded, a third follow-up step
may be taken three weeks after questionnaire distribution, by which
time the identity of nonrespondents is known. Each nonrespon-
dent is sent a duplicate questionnaire and return envelope, accompanied by a new cover letter that notes that the recipient may not
have received or may have misplaced the initial mailing, or may
not have recognized the importance of his or her response. Because
his or her response is so important to the success of the study,
another questionnaire and return envelope are now being enclosed,

and the individual is asked to complete and return the question-naire within the week to ensure its arrival in time for data analysis. It is important to get the right tone in this letter, because the intent is to encourage cooperation, not to make recipients feel that they are being criticized or scolded. Emphasis is on the importance of the recipient's response, not on the recipient's failure to respond to the earlier mailing. Again, the letter and envelope are individually addressed, and the letter is signed by the person who signed all ear-lier messages.

A final follow-up step available is to call nonrespondents and obtain their responses through a telephone interview. This step involves considerable time and expense, and is used only when, four weeks after initial questionnaire distribution, obtaining additional responses is crucial. A situation may be defined as crucial if the response rate is substantially lower than expected, if all responses are needed, or if certain segments of the population surveyed are underrepresented among the respondents. If at all feasible, the per-son who has signed the preceding correspondence places the call. If this is not possible, the caller identifies himself by name, indicat-ing that the call is on behalf of the person who signed the previous correspondence. The caller then explains that the individual's responses to the questions asked are critical to the success of the study and asks if the person might take just a few minutes to answer those questions over the telephone. The caller then asks the ques-tions and records the responses. The tone of the call is professional, friendly, and cordial, and at no time is the recipient made to feel negligent for failing to return the questionnaire.

Media Questionnaires

Questionnaires distributed through the media serve a different pur-pose and require different materials and procedures than other ques-tionnaires. Except in the case of national publications with high advertising rates, media questionnaires provide a relatively inexpensive way of reaching members of the target group defined by the readership of a publication.

People responding to questionnaires appearing in local newspapers, journals, magazines, or other media are entirely self-selected. Most often they have strong feelings about the topic or substantial interest in the issue addressed, whereas those not responding lack emphatic opinions or have little concern about the topic. Responses can be useful in determining if a substantial number of people are interested in a particular educational program, for example. However, data generated by media questionnaires cannot be expected to reflect the total population of which respondents are a part, and findings from this type of questionnaire cannot be interpreted as applying to anyone other than those actually responding. Perhaps the best use of media questionnaires for continuing educators is in determining whether the level of interest in a particular topic, program, delivery method, or educational service is sufficient to warrant its further consideration.

In a media questionnaire, the purposes of both the cover letter and the questionnaire must be addressed in one block of space. Cover letter content is condensed to state succinctly the issue or concern and explain the importance of the reader's response. The considerations in developing questions described earlier also apply to media questionnaires, but the number of questions included must be kept quite low, usually eight or fewer. This constraint is imposed not only because the advertising expense of a longer questionnaire will be greater but also because more questions will discourage reader responses. A statement at the bottom of the block of space thanks the reader for responding and provides the address to which the questionnaire is to be sent or the telephone number at which responses will be received. Particularly in a weekly or monthly publication, which people may read over time, it is important to specify a response deadline. A deadline is less important in a daily publication because most people will read it on the day of publication and either respond immediately or not respond at all. It is helpful to set off the entire questionnaire block with a border, in order to draw attention to it. Type size should be varied to emphasize the topic of the questionnaire, which is often phrased as a question to the reader. Because of their brevity, media questionnaires usually require only simple data analysis. It often is a matter of basic frequency counts and can be accomplished by hand tallies.

Interviews

Interviews are a good alternative to questionnaires as a needs assessment method. If proper procedures are followed, few people refuse to be interviewed. For this reason, response rates for interviews almost always substantially exceed those for mail questionnaires. Thus, although the costs of interviews per respondent are usually greater than they are with questionnaires, expenses can be kept down by using a smaller sample as long as the sample is carefully constructed to be representative of the total population. With a high (over 80 percent) response rate from even a small representative sample, a continuing educator can safely make generalizations to the total population from the data collected. Basic expenses associated with interviews are for duplication of materials, postage for the advance letter, interviewers, telephone or travel expenses as applicable, and data analysis.

Interviews can be conducted either in person (face to face) or by telephone. Face-to-face interviews have the advantage of facilitating interviewers' establishment of rapport with respondents, often with the result that respondents give longer, more detailed answers and hence provide more information than through a telephone interview. Sensitive issues may be dealt with most successfully through face-to-face interviews, when nonverbal communication can be used to advantage. Although the data collection purpose of an interview should not be diminished, in some cases face-to-face interviews also provide secondary marketing opportunities. Interviewer and respondent may engage in additional conversation, enabling the interviewer to inform the respondent about, for example, available continuing education services. Travel costs (including interviewers' travel time) can be a major drawback to face-to-face interviews. Even if the interviews take place within a limited geographic area, these expenses almost always are considerably greater than telephone charges for even long-distance telephone interviews. Thus telephone interviews are less expensive and can be equally satisfactory for many types of needs assessment.

Computerized systems for directly entering telephone interview responses into a database greatly facilitate data entry and analysis. A continuing educator interested in using interviews for needs assessment but without access to such a system may contract with a survey research group that has these facilities. The procedures followed when using a computerized system vary from those outlined in the following paragraphs primarily in the way collected data are recorded.

Preparation of Materials

Preparation for the advance letter and interview protocol parallel in many ways those for preparation of materials for questionnaires. Like the cover letter accompanying a questionnaire, the advance letter is designed to appeal to recipients and encourage their participation. However, the interview protocol is prepared to eliminate any ambiguity and provide maximum clarification for the interviewer.

Advance Letter. Following the general content and format guidelines for questionnaire cover letters described earlier, a brief advance letter is sent to advise potential respondents that they will be contacted for an interview by a representative of the person signing the letter. The letter indicates that the recipient will be called and asked either to schedule an interview to be conducted in person at a future date or to take a few minutes to participate in a telephone interview. The week of the anticipated call is specified (for example, "During the week of October 2 . . . "), and the purpose of the interview and importance of the respondent's participation are stated. One benefit of sending an advance letter, even when a follow-up telephone call will be made to schedule a face-to-face interview, is that it affords the recipient an opportunity to identify suitable interview dates and times. If another person keeps the recipient's calendar, an advance letter allows the recipient to communicate scheduling preferences to that person, eliminating the need for call-backs and facilitating scheduling. A second, and important, benefit of the advance letter is that it legitimizes the project, increasing the likelihood of a positive response.

Interview Protocol. An interview protocol, or script, is necessary to ensure appropriate and clear posing of questions, and consistency of interviews. Interview protocols are prepared in much the same manner as questionnaires, with the considerations about phrasing and introductory and transitional statements quite similar. Brief, simple, and easily understood sentences are used. Except when data are entered directly into a computerized system, recording responses on the same document from which the interviewer is reading is easiest and most accurate. For this reason, a separate protocol is necessary for each interview. Like questionnaires, interview protocols include sufficient space for fully recording all responses.

An important difference between questionnaires and interview protocols is that the latter, although remaining quite businesslike, must have a comfortable, conversational tone. The tone is established in the script. If the scripted words do not seem natural as they are spoken, the interview will seem stilted and awkward. Thus, reading the interview protocol aloud as it is developed can help ensure both clarity and a conversational tone.

An interview protocol comprises a cover sheet, an introduction, the body of the interview, and a conclusion. These portions of the protocol all are written out as part of the script, so that all interviewers repeat the same things to all respondents. This consistency is important to the consistency of the data collected.

Cover Sheet. Each interview protocol begins with a cover sheet that provides spaces for the respondent's name, telephone number, address for a face-to-face interview, and any other pertinent information of which the interviewer should be aware. This information is filled in before the interview begins for each person who will be contacted. Also included are spaces in which to record the times and dates of (1) the initial call, (2) the suggested call-back if the first call was incomplete, and (3) the interview itself. Finally, a space is provided for the name of the interviewer, so that this individual can be contacted if any questions (such as those caused by illegible handwriting) arise. For purposes of anonymity and confidentiality, the cover sheet can be separated from the remainder of the interview protocol before data analysis.

Introduction. The introduction to the protocol begins with verification of the length of time and the purpose of the interview. In the case of a telephone interview for which an appointment has not been made, after a one- or two-sentence reference to the advance letter, respondents are asked if it is convenient for them to be interviewed now or if they would prefer to be called back. If the latter, agreement is reached on a time and date, and this information is recorded on the cover page.

Body. The body of the protocol parallels that of a questionnaire. Response options for close-ended questions are provided and are read by the interviewer. As with a questionnaire, directions for follow-up, or branching, questions should be clear. Questions using a matrix format and other complex questions may not be appropriate for telephone interviews if the quantity or detail of the information to be repeated is difficult to communicate orally. However, often such questions can be carefully structured for clarity and used in telephone interviews. For face-to-face interviews it is possible to put the necessary information on a card that the respondent will be shown as matrix or other complex questions are asked. Interviewers may be instructed to probe for greater detail in response to some open-ended questions. Transition statements are provided to enhance the flow of the interview from one topic to another.

Conclusion. The protocol ends by providing an opportunity for the interviewer to invite respondents to share any further comments on the topic, and to thank them for their time. If a follow-up report is to be issued or if programming will be developed as a result of the survey, the protocol may call for the interviewer to offer to share that information with the respondent when it becomes available.

Interviewer Selection and Preparation

Interviewers can come from a variety of backgrounds. They should be pleasant, articulate, and for face-to-face interviews, have a businesslike appearance. Continuing educators should choose people with appropriate experience, knowledge, and maturity to interview respondents holding positions of some prestige, seniority, or sophistication, particularly in face-to-face interviews. Regardless of their backgrounds, interviewers require some training. Interviewer training has two components, general preparation and preparation for the specific project.

General Preparation. Experienced interviewers do not need general preparation, but people with little or no experience conducting interviews similar to those planned for the needs assessment will require some basic training. This training focuses on the broad concepts involved in interviewing rather than on the specific project for which interviews are to be conducted. It includes an explanation of the role of the interviewer as a data collection agent, and emphasizes the need for neutrality, courtesy, and accurate communication. The following instructions form the nucleus of general interviewer training.

- Be courteous at all times, without exception.
- Be careful not to influence or react to respondents' answers to questions either verbally or, in face-to-face interviews, with facial expression or body language.
- Follow the interview protocol exactly. Probe for additional responses only if directed to do so by the protocol.
- Speak slowly and clearly, using appropriate facial and verbal expressions.
- Focus your full attention on the respondent throughout the interview.
- Record all responses thoroughly, accurately, and legibly, using the words of the respondent.
- Call or arrive promptly for scheduled interview appointments.
- Avoid any comments that could be perceived as judgments, even if they are positive in nature, such as "good" or "right."
- Do not attempt to answer respondents' questions unless you are certain that you have accurate information. Rather, record any questions on a separate sheet of paper, along with the respondent's name, address, and telephone number, and assure the person that someone will contact him or her with the answer. Give this written record of each question to the person in charge of interviewing for the needs assessment.

Specific Preparation. Both experienced and new interviewers can benefit from training specific to the project. A large portion of this preparation will focus on the context of the survey, including descriptions of the sponsoring organization, the purpose, and the anticipated use of the data collected. The person training the interviewer will explain any vocabulary or background information unique to the survey content or the respondents. Interviewers need to be familiar with the entire data collection process, including advance letters, so that they can answer any questions that come up and understand any references to other aspects of the process. Finally, a detailed review of the interview protocol itself is a critical component of interviewers' specific training. Encouraging, if not requiring, interviewers to read the protocol aloud several times will help ensure their familiarity with it. Role-playing the interview before actually conducting the first one offers interviewers an opportunity to identify and work through any difficult portions.

Scheduling Interviews

When a brief telephone interview is desired and respondents are likely to be available at the time the call is made, an appointment often is not necessary. The advance letter is sufficient to advise respondents that they will be contacted for an interview. If the person to be interviewed is known to have a busy schedule, the interview will take more than five minutes, or a face-to-face interview is intended, the advance letter is followed by a telephone call to schedule an appointment for the interview. The caller refers to the advance letter, explains that this is the call to schedule the interview, indicates the time frame within which interviews will be conducted, and asks for or suggests specific dates and times. If appointments are made some time in advance, a reminder postcard or letter might be sent to the interviewee a week or two before the actual interview to confirm the date and time. Interviews are scheduled at the respondents' convenience because they are giving their time to help the continuing educator. It is important to schedule adequate time for the interview itself; some participants may talk at greater length than others. For face-to-face interviews, travel time built into the interviewer's schedule should include a cushion to accommodate traffic or other delays. In addition, it is wise to allow time for interviewers to review their notes immediately following each interview, while the conversation is still fresh in their minds, to ensure that the notes are readable, clear, and comprehensive.

If a potential respondent indicates reluctance or refusal to be interviewed, the caller may gently review the importance of the interview but should not press the issue. It is better to lose a respondent than to risk angering or offending the individual, and anyone not easily persuaded is unlikely to be a cooperative respondent anyway. When respondents refuse to schedule interviews, the caller thanks them for considering the matter and politely terminates the conversation.

Conducting the Interview

Many aspects of the interview itself are covered in the previous discussion of materials, interviewers, and scheduling. Obviously, the interviewer's primary purpose is to collect information. However, the interview is an interaction between two people, and like all personal interactions, it can and should be a pleasant experience. Because the interviewer's role is to guide this interaction, the interviewer bears responsibility for the quality of the experience. In keeping with the principles of total quality management (Deming, 1986), respondents should be treated as continuing education clients or customers. The interviewer should convey a sense of commitment to serving the respondent and those for whom the needs assessment will result in educational programming. In some ways the interviewer's relationship with the respondent is similar to the flight attendant's relationship with a passenger. The flight attendant's primary function is to ensure passenger safety, but this function is cloaked within that of providing passengers with a positive experience. Similarly, while collecting data, interviewers should provide respondents with a pleasant experience that will cause them to think well of the continuing education provider the interviewer represents. In order to accomplish these dual tasks, interviewers may find it necessary to mask their own feelings or opinions and occasionally ignore an unpleasant or even rude remark. The interviewer is unfailingly polite.

Good communication skills are valuable in conducting interviews. In face-to-face interviews, a firm handshake upon entering, pleasant facial expression, and regular eye contact help engage the respondent. Good posture conveys respect for the respondent and a positive attitude toward the interview process. The telephone interviewer cannot rely on such aids to establish the rapport but can use voice intonations to express warmth and friendliness that the respondent will find encouraging.

As indicated earlier, the interviewer's strict adherence to the script is essential to the success of the survey. If the respondent asks questions during the interview, the interviewer might indicate a willingness to address those questions as soon as the interview itself has ended, making a note to return to that point after completing the interview protocol. The interviewer provides answers when in possession of the necessary information. When interviewers are unable to answer questions, they state that they either will obtain the necessary information and get it to the respondent or will have someone else who can, do so—and they do what they have promised without fail.

Brief introductory comments may be appropriate, particularly in a face-to-face interview. After these few words, the interviewer shows respect for the respondent's busy schedule and preserves the integrity of the interview protocol by moving directly to the start of the interview. If the respondent appears eager to continue discussion after the interview has been concluded, the interviewer may talk briefly and informally. Such discussion often provides an opportunity for the respondent to ask questions about the continuing education provider that the interviewer represents.

Summary

The attention to detail that is emphasized here may seem unnecessary, overwhelming, or both. In fact, this discussion was but an overview of the subject. Additional information and directions for survey design and procedures are contained in a number of books entirely devoted to the topic (for example, Dillman, 1978; Bradburn and Sudman,1979; Sudman and Bradburn, 1983). If a continuing educator's project merits a survey, it merits one that is well done. If the data collected are to provide a sound basis for decision making, the continuing educator must take whatever steps are necessary to generate accurate data and obtain a good response rate. Taken individually, moreover, the details associated with surveys are neither overwhelming nor unmanageable.

Motivating people to respond also is a key factor in conducting successful surveys. No survey can be conducted without the support of the participants. The continuing educator may be able to encourage participation through use of the techniques suggested in this chapter. The groups that potential participants belong to, such as professional associations or employee groups, also may be able to motivate their members to cooperate in completing surveys.

Because survey respondents are doing continuing educators a favor by participating in their surveys, any questionable comments, rudeness, or other less-than-perfect behavior on their part should be overlooked. These people often are past or potential continuing education clients, and they deserve to be treated like the customers they are. The interviewer should approach each respondent with a service orientation, conveying the feeling that the continuing educator's primary concern is to serve that person.

Chapter Seven

Assessing Performance

Much continuing education, and almost all continuing professional education, has as its ultimate goal the improved performance of some activity or work-related task. If continuing education is to affect ongoing behavior or practice, eventually it must identify and address those aspects of individuals' activities that can benefit from change. The needs assessment methods described in Chapters Five and Six are valuable in identifying knowledge gaps and perceived needs. Methods that collect data from people who are knowledgeable about the daily activities of target populations and familiar with the ways in which they perform often also yield excellent data on skills and abilities. However, they do not assess either actual or simulated performance. Ideally, continuing educators, professional associations, government and regulatory agencies, employers, and others seeking to improve a target group's performance would assess actual or simulated performance to identify discrepancies that can be addressed through education. Because assessment of performance almost always is more complex and more costly than other needs assessment (Keil, 1981), it generally is used for sizable or critical projects. For example, the continuing educator undertaking a long-range project to provide an ongoing educational program might well use performance assessment to identify key areas in which education is needed. These same measures would be impractical for a short-term project or for isolated educational activities with limited target audiences.

As Thornton (1992) noted, because performance assessment is

an evolving field, with new methods, procedures, and applications being introduced on a regular basis, assessment of actual or simulated performance may be less objective than other types of assessment. Much performance assessment is based on observation, in itself a subjective activity. This concern merits attention early in the assessment planning process, for relying on only subjective data for the development of continuing education activities would be foolhardy. The potentially subjective nature of performance assessment can be overcome by establishment of clear, specific criteria to divide an observation into small, discrete segments and guide data collection and recording. Properly conducted, performance assessment gives the most complete picture of practice-oriented educational needs. However, it also can be the most difficult and costly type of assessment, and perhaps the one with the greatest potential for misuse and misinterpretation. Most performance assessment requires considerable expertise.

Review of Products of Performance

Systematic review of the records, documents, or other products of performance or professional practice usually is the simplest and least costly method for assessing either an individual's or a group's actual performance and identifying areas that may warrant change. This method is appropriately applied when the performance of the target individual or group results in records, documents, or other products that can be analyzed objectively according to a set of predetermined standards. Because it is dependent on some type of regularly generated product, this method is used most frequently to assess professionals' and other workers' needs. However, it can be used successfully to identify the needs of any individuals or groups generating a product that lends itself to the type of analysis described here. For example, assessment of their recent paintings could be used to identify discrepancies pointing to the areas in which leisure painters need education.

The products reviewed may be tangible items, such as patient care plans or completed financial audits, or they may be outcomes, such as the relationship between initial cost estimates for advertising campaigns and the actual costs of the campaigns. Whether tangible or intangible, these products are reviewed systematically to determine the extent to which they meet specified criteria, and to identify related or consistent errors, failures, omissions, or results. Most often it is not the products themselves that point to educational needs, but the processes followed and decisions made in generating the products. Thus, review of products may involve multiple steps. For example, the continuing educator wishing to determine architects' educational needs in cost estimating may first look only at whether the architects' estimates for projects are consistent with contractors' bids for those projects. If the bids generally are within the predicted range, cost estimating may not be an area of educational need, and the topic may be dropped. However, if the bids received for a substantial number of projects are well in excess of the architects' estimates, further exploration of the topic is indicated. A review of the architects' cost-estimating documents may determine the points at which errors were made. For example, was enough research done on costs of materials? Were time estimates realistic? Did the architects recognize the steps needed to conform to local building codes? Answers to these and similar questions often will point to specific areas of educational need.

Other examples of potential application of this needs assessment method may be helpful in clarifying the ways in which review of products can help identification of educational needs.

- A quick review of the numbers of decisions overturned can identify judges whose decisions are overturned with some regularity. Further exploration of the cases resulting in overturned decisions may reveal the specific discrepancies, such as lack of familiarity with particular legislation or ethical issues. Educational needs can be derived from this information.

- A review of prescriptions written can provide information on physicians' prescribing patterns. They may be using inappropriate or outmoded drugs, failing to adhere to correct dosages, or ignoring important drug interactions, all behaviors that may reflect educational needs.

- Dietary plans prepared for patients with specific disease states can shed light on several aspects of dietitians' performance. If the plans do not meet accepted standards, further interpretation of the manner in which they were developed may be needed to identify discrepancies that indicate educational needs, such as lack of understanding of patients' conditions, insufficient familiarity with the nutritional content or contraindications of certain foods, or failure to consider food appeal.

Before a firm decision is made to use review of products to assess needs, a continuing educator must clarify the goal and objectives of the needs assessment and decide whether the available products will provide the information necessary to reach them. Sometimes performance products appear appropriate to the goal of a needs assessment but upon further reflection are found to be irrelevant to the more specific objectives for the type of information sought. For example, the continuing educator wishing to learn about real estate appraisers' educational needs may expect to gather some pertinent information from appraisal documents. However, if the specific objective is to learn about this population's communication skills, review of the documents will not help.

Once continuing educators or an assessment team have identified the target population and decided to use review of products for needs assessment, they usually inform the people being assessed of plans to review their products. Their cooperation will probably be required in order to access the products for review. In some cases the assessees may be asked to assist in selection of the sample products. This involvement can enhance the assessees' commitment to the endeavor and their interest in participating in the resulting educational activities. If appropriate, the continuing educator can give them criteria to use in choosing their sample products. They may be asked to pick five of their best and five of their worst products, for instance, or to select products concerned with a certain topic or issue. Although asking assessees to provide their own samples may be perceived as enabling them to bias sample selection to emphasize personal strengths, true discrepancies in the area assessed will become apparent regardless of the samples selected.

Whether a continuing educator uses review of products for individual or group assessment, several factors merit consideration when specifying the products for review. First, only products that can be expected to contain the information needed to address the goal and objectives of the assessment will be useful. The information gained through their review may be only a first step, but it should be enough to enable the assessors to narrow the focus of their quest for additional information. Second, choice of readily accessible products will facilitate the assessment process. If the products are difficult to obtain or special permission is required to review them, their use may impede progress or delay the assessment. Third, products that are easily understood by those responsible for the review process are the most desirable. Although the assessors reviewing products will require some training, products that do not require a high level of expertise or extensive training to be understood are easiest to review. Fourth, in assessing individuals for comparison purposes or in conducting a group assessment, the products reviewed must be comparable. If nurses' preparation of patient care plans are to be reviewed, for example, a group of care plans for patients with similar conditions in comparable institutional settings will produce the most meaningful and reliable data.

Once the continuing educator has identified the products to be reviewed and set the standards that define educational need (as discussed in Chapter Four), she or he is ready to establish criteria for conducting the review. This means identifying aspects of the product that will indicate acceptable performance and whenever possible, quantifying them. One or more people familiar with the content area play an active role in identifying the factors that will be reflected in judging whether a product is acceptable or indicative of one or more discrepancies between actual and desired states. This information is translated into a checklist of factors to be considered in the review. Such a checklist ensures that all pertinent points are covered and promotes consistency among reviewers if more than one is used. The checklist also can be used to record data as the review is conducted. For example, items that might be included in a checklist for review of routine correspondence prepared by secretaries are as follows:

- Letter is formatted properly.
- Address and salutation are correct.
- Letter makes reference to earlier communication.
- Message of letter accurately reflects organizational policy.
- Letter provides name, address, and telephone number of person to be contacted for further discussion.
- Letter has a positive, client-oriented tone.

By using this checklist to review samples of letters, assessors can identify discrepancies in the secretaries' preparation of routine correspondence. Following the review of the products, such as the letters, assessors aggregate the data collected and analyze them to identify trends. The nature of the product reviewed will determine the form and formality of data analysis and the number of cases considered. Often the type and amount of data do not require computerized statistical analysis but can be thoroughly and properly reviewed manually. Discussion of the data with content experts is helpful, if not always essential, to its correct interpretation. Those with expertise in the field also can suggest steps to pursue potential educational needs uncovered by the product review.

As in other types of needs assessment, confidentiality regarding the individuals being assessed is critical. However, a second type of confidentiality, that regarding the products being reviewed, also may be required. Review of a counselor's records or of financial statements for a building project, for example, may give the assessor access to confidential information. In such cases, the assessee should protect the anonymity of the patients, clients, or other individuals or organizations by eliminating names and other identifying information before the documents are reviewed.

Performance Observation

Another method for assessing performance is observation, collecting data on individuals' behaviors in their practice settings according to specific, predefined criteria. Continuing educators can assess either individual or group needs in this manner. Performance observation has two advantages over the performance simulations, which are described later in this chapter. First, it allows for assessment of actual performance rather than simulated, and often artificial, situations. Second, it eliminates the need for assessees to leave their work sites. One disadvantage of actual performance observation is that unlike simulations, no two performance situations are exactly alike. They vary according to several factors, including the context, people involved, and specific conditions. Because of these differences, the continuing educator striving to gather group data or to compare individuals may find it more difficult to get comparable data from actual performance observation than from performance simulations.

Performance observation may sound deceptively simple. But in order to obtain reliable data it requires establishment of detailed criteria, development of a checklist or observation form that permits recording of all data pertinent to those criteria, and well-trained observers. If the performance to be assessed is videotaped, it is necessary to factor additional arrangements and costs into the assessment plan. Costs for videotaping are not inconsequential. Arrangements for videotaping involve equipment and technical personnel, and accommodating them in the practice setting. Frequently it also is necessary to obtain written permission to videotape those who will be included in the interaction.

As with all other forms of needs assessment, performance assessment to identify educational needs should not be confused with that to determine competence. Criteria used to establish competence must be more comprehensive than those used to define educational need. These two purposes of performance assessment need not be mutually exclusive, however. For example, many school administrators routinely observe teachers in their classrooms. In the cases of new teachers or those about whom questions have been raised, determination of competence may be the primary purpose of the observation. Once competence has been ascertained, a secondary purpose may be to identify areas in which further education may be beneficial.

Performance observation can be live, with the observer rating the selected behaviors in the performance setting, or it can be accomplished by videotaping certain performance situations for later assessment by one or more raters who were not present for on-site observation. Videotapes produced for this purpose need not be of professional quality, but they do have to be accurate and complete representations of what took place. The videographers will benefit from advice about any special actions or behaviors they should capture, such as facial expressions or body language.

Both live observations and videotaping have their advantages and disadvantages. Either will add another person to the performance setting, a perhaps uncomfortable reminder that the assessee is being observed. Videotaping permits more than one observer, or rater, to view the performance segment. Even if multiple raters are not used for all participants in a group assessment project, for example, some cases can be selected at random to check interrater reliability. Another advantage of videotaping is that it permits raters to review certain portions of performance segments if they have questions or are unclear about what took place. However, in many settings videotaping can be even more obtrusive than an observer, and it represents an additional expense. For continuing educators working with employers who wish to have employees assessed, one variation on videotaping includes use of an in-house coordinator to capture the selected performance segment on videotape. The continuing educator then sends the videotape to external, commercial performance assessment experts who have been hired to score it. This procedure eliminates the need to train or hire people with specialized scoring competencies for just one project (Development Dimensions International, n.d., a).

With performance observation, as with all other forms of needs assessment, continuing educators must make decisions regarding the areas to be assessed. Thus the first step in preparing for performance observation is identification of the dimensions, or aspects of performance, to be assessed. Any performance situation will include numerous dimensions, all potentially valid subjects for a needs assessment. However, it is difficult, if not impossible, to assess all dimensions of a performance situation simultaneously. A focus on three or four major dimensions will be manageable and, if handled properly, will yield enough data on which to base decisions about educational activities. For example, in assessing a clinical dietitian's work with a diabetic patient, the focus might be on instructional skills for teaching the patient about appropriate diet, application of knowledge about the patient's disease state, integration of sound nutritional concepts, and interpersonal skills in working with other professionals (for example, the nurse, physical therapist, or physician) in caring for the patient. Representatives of the target population or people familiar with the broad area to be assessed can make substantial contributions to selection of the specific dimensions of performance to be assessed. Focus on performance abilities or dimensions of performance, rather than on knowledge or skills, takes full advantage of the potential of performance observation. As discussed in Chapters Five and Six, knowledge and skills can be assessed by less costly methods.

Whether using live observations or videotaping, in most settings it is difficult to observe performance unobtrusively. This is particularly true for settings in which only a few people are usually present, such as hospital rooms. It is less problematical in well-populated settings like factory floors, libraries, and well-attended public meetings. Minimizing the intrusion is important if the performance observation is to attain a realistic picture of routine practice. Observers or videographers should position themselves where they can have a clear view without drawing attention to their presence, and they should avoid movement, noise, or motion that would attract notice. If practitioners truly are focused on what they are doing, they soon will forget they are being observed. In cases involving clients or patients, they also may become so involved in the tasks being performed that their awareness of the observation dwindles or disappears. However, they may need some preparation for the intrusion represented by the observation, and even with this consideration, may behave somewhat differently than they otherwise would.

As with other forms of needs assessment, it is essential to establish both standards of performance and clear, uniform criteria to be used in assessing whether those standards have been met. This is particularly true with performance observations because many aspects of the situation will compete for an observer's attention. Without specific criteria to focus on, performance observations become a series of random observations of little or no value. People knowledgeable about the dimensions to be assessed are important members of the needs assessment team when it is establishing suitable standards and criteria, because both of these must reflect not only good performance but also the realities of the performance setting.

Standards

The goals of the continuing educator, employer, professional association, or other individual or group for whom the needs assessment is being conducted guide the establishment of standards. As discussed in Chapter Three, needs can be assessed according to standards ranging from the minimum acceptable level to levels of excellence. If the goal is to provide educational activities for people who may not have reached a basic level of practice, the assessment team sets standards that reflect this. Likewise, if enhancement of current practice is the target, the standards set are for excellence.

Criteria

Once the standard is chosen, criteria are specified to describe what should be done, how it should be done, and what, if anything, the visible result of meeting that standard should be. These criteria are incorporated in a checklist to form the basis for the observation and later for the data analysis. For example, a checklist for observation of a journalist's interviewing ability might include the following criteria, in the format shown.

To what extent did the journalist demonstrate each of the following criteria?

	COMPLETELY	SOME	NOT AT ALL
Has done some homework; demonstrates knowledge of the subject	1	2	3
Has an agreeable manner and establishes rapport through positive comments, eye contact, facial expression, and body language	1	2	3

Shows interest in the information given through questions, facial expression, and body language	1	2	3
Gets key words spelled and defined	1	2	3
Asks pertinent questions	1	2	3
Is a good listener; asks open-ended questions, periodically paraphrases or summarizes	1	2	3

The observer uses a form incorporating this checklist during the observation, recording data as the performance segment progresses. Because of people's natural tendency to forget details, waiting to record data until after observing a performance segment is never a good idea.

Observer training is an important component of performance observation. As with interviewer training, observer training can be of two types—general and specific. In their general training, observers must learn the importance of confidentiality. For live observations, they are taught to be unobtrusive, not to converse with others, and not to communicate through body language. All observers receive specific training to understand and adhere to those items included in the checklist provided and to record all data accurately and completely. Their training specific to a particular observation site or dimensions to be assessed includes a thorough review of the criteria to be used and the key indicators of those criteria for which they are to observe.

Based on the dimensions selected for assessment, the assessment team identifies and confirms one or more observation sites, and makes arrangements for the actual observation. Visits to these sites ahead of time eliminate any last-minute surprises about the physical setting and layout and, particularly if the observations are to be videotaped, permit any necessary planning. The team makes plans with observers or videotapers and people at the site who are respon-sible for scheduling. The individuals who will be observed must be notified and informed consent confirmation obtained from them. If observations are to be videotaped, additional written consent from those with whom the assessee will interact, including clients or patients, may be required. Videotapes made for assessment pur-poses usually are erased or destroyed after the assessment has been completed. This fact or any planned deviation from this practice should be noted in any written agreement.

Performance Simulations

Often it is feasible neither to review products of performance nor to observe performance itself, yet some measure of the implemen-tation of knowledge, skills, and performance abilities is desired. Continuing educators may be able to use performance simulations, artificially created scenarios that imitate real performance, as these measures. Performance simulations have a major advantage over actual performance observations in that they present an opportu-nity to assess all participants in virtually identical situations. Sim-ulations can be carefully controlled for consistency, with the same problems, tasks, contexts, and other factors presented to all assessees; in contrast, no two actual performances will provide exactly the same situations. In assessing physical therapists, for example, different patients respond differently and the problems they present to each assessee vary somewhat despite all efforts to maintain uniformity. These variations affect the physical therapists' performance so that data collected from observation of several per-formances are not comparable. However, in a performance simula-tion actors and actresses portraying patients can respond according to a prescribed script or pattern, thus presenting all physical thera-pists being assessed with the same situation.

Performance simulations also are usually expensive activities. Although it is possible to conduct a simple survey or focus group, for example, with limited experience and expense, the same cannot be said of most types of performance simulations. If they are to be accurate portrayals of real situations, their development usually is a complex, complicated process for which considerable resources and expertise are needed. Each performance simulation is unique, requiring the same type of specialized development that goes into writing a short story or a television script. Attention to the physical setting, use of professional actors and actresses, videotaping and other recording, and preparation of materials are among the factors that can increase costs of performance simulation beyond the reach of many continuing educators much of the time.

Given the resources involved in their creation and implementation, do performance simulations have a place in the continuing educator's needs assessment portfolio? The answer is a qualified yes, based on two factors. First, as noted in the following descriptions of simulation exercises, with careful planning continuing educators can create and use some individual simulations without abundant resources. Second, it is primarily large organizations that are able to develop and use performance simulations. For example, large employers who are serious about the continuing education of their workers over several years may recognize the long-term economy of using performance simulations to identify areas of actual practice in which discrepancies exist. The continuing educator can help such employers identify a range of educational needs to be addressed through a continuing education curriculum rather than provide a series of unrelated educational activities that may or may not affect performance. This approach most often is used with employees at relatively high levels in an organization because they represent the greatest human resources investment.

Because of the uniqueness of each performance simulation, it is not feasible to provide generic step-by-step guidelines that can be applied routinely. Thus the purpose of this discussion is to provide a brief overview of the nature and potential applications of performance simulations as an introduction of the topic to interested readers. Those wishing to pursue use of performance simulations will want to seek additional, specialized information and assistance for development of appropriate exercises and of the criteria with which to assess participants' performances in those exercises (Moses and Byham, 1977; Keil, 1981; Thornton and Byham, 1982; Thornton, 1992).

Performance simulations can take many forms. Ideally a needs assessment team will design them to employ whatever format can best represent the situation being replicated, but most often available resources also are a factor in the format selection. Live interactions, case studies, in-basket exercises, trigger films, and structured interviews are among the formats continuing educators can choose from. These examples do not represent an exhaustive list, however. Any activity that positions the assessee to perform certain tasks or roles in a lifelike situation and lends itself to establishment of documentable standards for assessing that performance may be used.

Live Interactions

In live interactions, assessees role-play an activity, practice segment, or other performance as if it were a real-life situation. In fact, many effective simulated live interactions are based on situations that actually have occurred. The continuing educator usually employs actors to portray the other people involved in the simulation, such as patients, clients, co-workers, employees, or supervisors. The actors are trained to be consistent in their interactions with all assessees, and not to respond to any of them in idiosyncratic ways. As with performance observations, an assessor can observe the simulation and conduct the assessment as it is taking place, or the simulation can be videotaped for later observation and assessment. To give assessees an understanding of the simulation and their expected role in it, immediately before the role playing the assessor gives them background information and a description of the practice scenario. Pertinent documents, such as patient charts, audit reports, or correspondence may be included in these materials. The assessor establishes a time frame for review of the materials and for the role-play itself. At the conclusion of the interaction, the assessee is advised that the exercise has been completed and is thanked for participating. Feedback is given after data analysis has been completed either in written form or orally with written back-up materials.

Live interactions can be fairly brief and quite simple, or they can be longer, more complex scenarios. An example of a simple interaction is one that involved the assessee and one other person, with few written background materials. The assessee was cast in the role of an accountant who was to gather information from a client in order to prepare a tax return. The interaction was short and focused on a single issue. Another situation, in which the assessee played the role of a nurse preparing a patient and his family for his death, is an example of a complex interaction. The assessee reviewed the patient's medical records and reports from several allied health professionals before entering the role-play, and spent considerable time interacting with those portraying the patient and three family members. Whether the interaction is simple or complex, assessees often enter live interaction exercises feeling somewhat awkward about performing in this context. However, most often they rise to the occasion and find the experience a positive one.

Case Studies

Case studies are written exercises that offer another option for performance simulations. They provide assessees with an opportunity to indicate how they would handle a specific situation and to demonstrate their ability to make the judgments and decisions necessary to apply theory to practice. Like live interactions, case studies can be based on actual situations, or they can be fictitious scenarios created specifically for assessment purposes. Although assessees may not be able to follow through with many of the tasks, procedures, and other physical, on-site actions highlighted in the case study, in many situations case studies can be designed to include actions such as preparation of written or oral materials. A case study for financial planners, for example, could include actual portfolio preparation exercises. Case studies are prepared in narrative form and frequently include background information, records, correspondence, and other materials to be reviewed by the assessees. For example, a case study for physicians may include a patient's laboratory reports, X rays, and other medical records, as well as transcriptions of interviews with the patient and information from other health care providers. The assessee reviews all materials according to the directions given, and responds to the questions asked. Frequently the assessee reviews some materials and responds to some questions, and then is directed to review additional information before moving on to another set of questions. Responses to a case study may be written or entered into a computer, or for group assessment they may be discussed in small groups.

In-Basket Exercises

Assessments of management performance and other desk-based roles lend themselves particularly well to in-basket exercises. This type of performance simulation gets its name from the in-basket usually found on office workers' or managers' desks, collecting mail and other items to be read and acted upon. Assessees are presented with the contents of a hypothetical in-basket containing a variety of written documents and asked to work their way through the materials, handling each as they deem appropriate. The collections of memoranda, letters, reports, and other communications may present different types of problems. A management assessment might include items dealing with personnel, financial, time management, politics, and organizational matters, for example. Items usually are to be taken in sequence, with the assessee responding to each in turn. Often the assessee is not permitted to return to earlier items, an order that is imposed to force assessees to deal with the consequences of their earlier actions.

Trigger Films

Like case studies, trigger films present a real or fictitious situation as the context for assessing participants. Trigger films show a series of incidents in brief segments, with the film stopping between segments. At each interval, assessees are asked to respond to questions about the scenario they have just witnessed. They may be asked to evaluate performances in the film, indicate what they would do next, or respond to other questions that can provide information on their perceptions regarding the proper handling of the situation presented.

Structured Interviews

Structured interviews can be used to assess participants' relevant characteristics and the ways in which they would perform in specific situations. Assessees are presented with vignettes and then asked how they would handle the scenario described. The vignettes may portray actual or simulated situations, and are prepared in much the same way as case studies or trigger films, but with less detail. Protocols for structured interviews are developed much like protocols for other types of interviews, with the addition of specific criteria for assessing the responses received.

Other Considerations

Two factors are particularly important in designing performance simulation exercises. First, close adherence to realism not only makes the simulations believable but also, and more importantly, eliminates potential distractions caused by features that would not occur in an actual situation. For this reason, attention to detail is important. Carefully prepared settings for live interactions help assessees forget their nervousness and help them to feel as if they are indeed in a real situation, for example. Inclusion of tangential information in a case study enhances the reality of the scenario. Second, specific criteria for assessing responses to the exercises are absolutely critical if meaningful data are to be derived from performance simulations. Development of these criteria as the exercises are developed can facilitate both processes (Keil, 1981; Thornton, 1992).

Assessment Centers

Although performance assessment exercises can be used individually, often they are incorporated in assessment centers, frequently with the addition of other needs assessment and descriptive instruments. The assessment center concept originated in the early 1940s as a response to the Office of Strategic Services' need for a uniform screening process for potential members (MacKinnon, 1991). Assessment centers, which provide "a means for measuring human potential," usually are one to three days in length and include a variety of exercises (Development Dimensions International, n.d., b). Rather than focusing on specific skills, assessment centers seek to assess "the 'man as a whole,' the general structure of his being, and his strengths and weaknesses for rather generally described environments and situations" (MacKinnon, 1991, p. 2).

An important advantage of this more comprehensive approach is that it provides an assessment of individuals' preparedness for a number of related roles rather than for one specific set of tasks. Thus assessment centers can provide a broad, long-range assessment that identifies individuals' educational needs for large portions of their careers, not just for their current roles. Assessment centers can measure a number of dimensions pertinent to the content area under consideration, and may include such things as motivation, leadership, instructional skills, communications skills, and ability to handle details. Individual exercises almost always measure several dimensions, and specific factors may be assessed in two or more different exercises. The primary objective of assessment centers is to observe as many aspects as possible of assessees' "behavior in situations which simulate as realistically as feasible the kinds of situations they would be likely to encounter" (MacKinnon, 1991, p. 4).

Historically, assessment centers have been used to "predict the likelihood of [individuals'] success in a given job" (Development Dimensions International, n.d., b). Their use has been expanded considerably, however, from selection of personnel (particularly managers) to include counseling and development, as well as needs assessment (Moses, 1977). Those working closely with assessment center methodology have recognized that even when used for personnel selection, assessment centers also have "aided in the selection, promotion, and development of individuals" (Development Dimensions International, n.d., b). Thus, even when the primary focus of an assessment center is selection of individuals for hiring or promotion, assessment results can and often do indicate areas that should be targeted for development or further education.

Because development and conduct of assessment centers is costly, time consuming, and dependent on considerable expertise, their use by continuing educators has been limited. In some cases the high cost can be offset by assessing only a small, carefully drawn random sample of the population to be studied. However, because development of assessment center exercises usually accounts for most of the expense associated with this form of needs assessment, limiting the number of participants may not be sufficient to make assessment centers financially feasible for most continuing educators.

Assessment center concepts were used in the Continuing Professional Education Development Project conducted at The Pennsylvania State University. In that case, the national scope of the project justified development of modified assessment centers for five professions (accounting, architecture, clinical dietetics, clinical psychology, and nursing), and it was financially feasible because of funding from the W. K. Kellogg Foundation and the participating state and national professional associations. The assessment centers were a full day in length, but most were conducted over two days, beginning at noon one day and concluding with lunch on the second day. The assessment center for each profession was quite different. The entire assessment center for architects was based on one case study, for example, whereas the nurses' assessment center included live simulations, a trigger film, and a case study. Assessment center exercises were developed by teams including continuing educators, faculty members in relevant academic disciplines, and professional association and practitioner representatives. Specialists in performance assessment were called upon to advise and consult as needed. Educational programs were developed and delivered as a result of these assessments (Office of Continuing Professional Education, 1985).

Summary

Performance assessment is the most sophisticated and difficult form of needs assessment, but it also offers the greatest opportunity for identifying practice-oriented educational needs. Continuing educators should not enter into it lightly, but neither should they automatically discard the possibility. Particularly for the continuing educator with a long-term commitment to serve a particular profession, industry, or employer, performance assessment can be a valuable and a feasible tool. The continuing educator not in a position to devote substantial resources to performance assessment may wish to incorporate some of the concepts underlying performance assessment in other forms of needs assessment. Simplified and abbreviated case studies can be used in surveys, for example. Thus, whether the continuing educator has an opportunity to carry out a performance assessment or not, knowledge of the methodology can be useful.

Chapter Eight

Needs Assessment as Part of Program Planning

Careful assessment of educational needs "is the first step in developing [educational] interventions that are relevant" (Sleezer, 1992, p. 34). Because assessment results are imprecise, by themselves they rarely point with certainty toward specific action. Properly used, however, they can and should provide guidance for an entire range of decisions related to the audience, content, format, and delivery of continuing education activities. Proper use implies development, implementation, and interpretation of needs assessment in the context of the larger program planning process. Continuing educators should plan needs assessments and review the data they collect with an eye toward matching the data to their strengths, resources, and mission. For example, if a continuing educator has access to a faculty member with a field of expertise or to equipment for delivery of education via satellite, it would be appropriate to use needs assessment to collect information relative to those strengths. Following the assessment, the continuing educator should review the data to identify opportunities to build on the strengths. The characteristics and preferences of the target population also provide continuing educators with an important framework in which to consider needs assessment data. In the final analysis, no matter how great the need for an educational activity may be, people are not easily persuaded to participate in it if it is not compatible with their scheduling needs, learning styles, and interests.

Too often considerable thought and care are devoted to development of the needs assessment process itself, but little attention is paid to what happens once the data are collected. Data analysis, or the compilation into meaningful information, is the first step in handling the data. Analysis can range from simple summaries of comments offered by focus groups to computerized statistical analyses of information collected in a survey. Whatever its form, data analysis is an integral part of any needs assessment, and as such merits inclusion in the needs assessment planning process. As a needs assessment activity is developed, methods and procedures for analyzing the data to be collected are outlined, with plans made for their timely implementation. Involving the persons who will have responsibility for data analysis in the early stages of planning the needs assessment helps ensure that the data will be generated in the best form for efficient, effective analysis.

Interpreting Needs Assessment Data

After data have been analyzed and recorded in well-organized and easily comprehended summary form, interpretation is necessary to translate them into a useful form for continuing education activities. When conducting a group assessment, a key first step is identification of the unit of interpretation. All data may be considered as a single group, or they may be stratified into subgroups according to demographic or other population characteristics. Geographic location, experience, and educational level of the respondents are examples of stratification criteria. Rarely, if ever, can continuing educators view individual data in isolation as part of the program planning process, for practicality dictates that educational activities be developed for groups, not individuals. Thus, for program planning purposes continuing educators most often aggregate even individual data to some extent. The participants in individual assessments should be given their own assessment results for their use in their own educational planning, but this does not interfere with the subsequent aggregation of the data for interpretation for program planning.

Needs assessment data will provide information that points to knowledge, skill, or performance ability discrepancies. Through careful interpretation continuing educators can integrate the data with relevant information from other sources and translate the resultant information into a description of educational needs. As they examine each deficiency identified through assessment, they will want to consider the content and format of education needed to address it. Also as part of data interpretation they will review the special characteristics, learning styles, and limitations of the target population. Each of these considerations can affect the feasibility of developing educational programming to address specific needs, and can determine the types and characteristics of activities that will be appropriate. Focus, a collective approach, reliance on multiple indicators, avoidance of data glut, adaptation for limitations, and use of data for new or expanded endeavors are factors that contribute to successful data interpretation. Each is dependent on the accuracy of the data analysis that precedes the interpretation of the data.

Focused Interpretation

A successful needs assessment exercise will have a fairly narrow focus, for as noted earlier, it is not feasible to pursue a broad variety of issues in a single assessment. Even with a narrow focus, however, most needs assessments will yield more potential ideas than the continuing educator possibly can consider at one time (Knox, 1986). Just as it is wise to limit the breadth of an assessment exercise, it is important to limit the scope of a proposed educational activity. An attempt to incorporate too much into any program almost always results in superficial treatment of topics, diminished quality, or both, with the result that limited learning occurs. For this reason, when interpreting needs assessment data continuing educators find it helpful to center the discussion of results either on a single, broad area or on a constellation of related discrepancies, content areas, or constituencies. Other areas uncovered in the needs assessment need not be discarded but can be saved for consideration at a later time.

This narrowing of focus is recommended with a caveat. There may be exceptions if a series of related needs or of different constituencies with similar needs have been identified in the needs assessment, or when comprehensive needs assessment strategies result in a plethora of data and educational programming ideas. In such cases, development of a series of activities usually is indicated. Most often continuing educators divide this wealth of information into manageable segments to be addressed over a specified time period, so that they are not confronted with more information and opportunities than they realistically can handle simultaneously. If an initial review of the data indicates this potential, data interpretation begins within the broader framework of outlining the series. Once this step has been accomplished, the focus returns to interpreting the data for one educational activity at a time.

Collective Approach to Data Review

The interrelatedness of data is important, because discrete pieces of data are readily misunderstood. Taken individually, even those isolated pieces of data that are obtained from carefully structured assessment exercises and then accurately analyzed cannot automatically be accepted as reliable indicators of needs. Viewing groups of data simultaneously leads to a clearer, more comprehensive understanding of educational needs than can be obtained by considering the same data separately. For example, an assessment of architects indicated that they needed further education in the area of cost control, but it also revealed that they had little interest in this topic and greatest interest in the creative areas of their work, such as design (Staff, 1985). Thus it could have been a mistake to plan and market a continuing education program based only on the data indicating that cost control was an area of educational need; it was important to recognize that the target audience was not aware of cost control as a need and that action was needed to heighten that awareness and then develop the program to appeal to architects' creative leanings.

Because market research is an important adjunct to needs assessment, it also is useful to view data on both needs and interests in the context of a target population's scheduling preferences and the likelihood of their participating in certain activities. Continuing educators can collect information on these factors as part of a needs assessment so that activities can be tailored accordingly. For example, nurses may need to learn more about techniques for dealing with mentally impaired patients, and may recognize that need—even be eager to pursue it. However, if the hospital cannot spare these nurses from duty on the hospital floor for more than an hour at a time, they will be unable to attend a day-long workshop on the topic.

Reliance on Multiple Indicators

Just as continuing educators would be unwise to rely on single data points, they should not expect one needs assessment exercise to provide all the data they require to develop an educational activity. Viewing needs assessment data in combination with information available from other sources is critical to optimum use of the data. For example, an inventory of existing continuing education activities similar to those under consideration, including information regarding the success of those activities in attracting participants, can help continuing educators determine if existing activities already are meeting the identified need or if additional programming is warranted. Information about access to the academic expertise needed to teach a proposed program and information about available resources for design, development, and delivery are also potentially useful indicators.

Other relevant information concerns the target audience. The learning patterns of target group members often indicate the likelihood of their actually participating in new educational activities. If they have pursued continuing education in the recent past, for example, they are more likely to do so in the future (Aslanian, 1985a). The population to be served may be seeking academic credit, Continuing Education Units, or approved sponsorship for employer reimbursement or credit toward some form of credential. Continuing educators should be aware of, consider, and plan for these preferences early in the program development process. Information on these and other characteristics of the target population is available from a number of sources.

Avoidance of Data Glut

It is also important to separate relevant information from that with little bearing on the decisions at hand and to know when enough data have been considered. Certainly it is important to have enough data to make informed decisions, but at some point the continuing educator must be willing to declare that the study period is over. One can be overwhelmed by the quantity of information, conflicting indicators, and the need to check just one more piece of information, until "analysis paralysis" sets in and prevents forward movement. If the quantity of data becomes too sizable to manage, the continuing educator may have carried data collection activities too far. A clear summary of a reasonable amount of available data can facilitate decision making—too much data can obstruct the process.

Adaptation for Limitations

Expectations that all data must be perfect and point in the same direction are sure to impede the use of needs assessment data to develop educational activities. As noted in earlier chapters, needs assessment can be conducted in many ways and at many levels. Although more sophisticated assessments may yield more extensive data, the continuing educator can also have confidence in the information collected through simple methods, as long as they are executed properly. However, even when executed with the greatest rigor, needs assessment may be an imperfect process. All assessments have real value only if continuing educators interpret their results in light of the limitations imposed by the methods used. For example, a continuing educator conducted a focus group with local bank presidents, asking them to discuss their employees' needs to learn certain banking procedures. From that assessment it was possible to learn whether there were enough community people with an educational need that could be addressed by a workshop on those procedures. Yet the data collected said nothing about the likelihood of those deemed in need of the education recognizing that need in themselves, nor was the information collected generalizable to bank employees in other locations. However, because the local bank presidents were willing to send their employees to a program on the topic it was likely the minimum number of participants would enroll, and this was all the information that was needed for an initial offering. As a next step, the continuing educator wishing to offer the program to other audiences could collect additional data on employee interest in this topic and on comparable needs in other communities.

Use of Data for New or Expanded Endeavors

Even needs assessment findings that indicate no substantial discrepancies in the assessees' current activities can have educational implications. Such findings can be used to identify areas in which additional learning could help members of the target population progress from basic competence to higher levels of achievement, or move in new directions or into areas of greater responsibility. This aspect of needs assessment frequently is overlooked, but it is critical. The work of Development Dimensions International (Byham, 1980) offers a good example of ways in which needs assessment methods can be used to select individuals for additional responsibilities. The principles reflected in this group's work can be applied to identification of areas in which individuals must improve if they are to enhance their current performance or handle new responsibilities successfully. Interpretation of needs assessment data in this manner requires establishment of standards specific to the stated purpose. For example, standards established to determine achievement of minimal competence will not be sufficient to identify areas in which people need additional work to achieve excellence.

Reporting Data

Organizations, institutions, and individuals frequently approach identification of needs with dread, fearing that it will uncover deficiencies that will show them in a bad light. Thus they may be apprehensive about the needs assessment process and reluctant to participate in it. Yet needs assessment findings can lead to positive action: the creation of educational activities that meet learning needs. The needs assessment report is a vehicle to emphasize that opportunity.

A needs assessment report can be either written or oral, or both. It usually is advisable to have at least some form of written report so that a permanent record of the needs assessment is created and a reference for future consultation remains. A written report in summary form can be disseminated widely, with more detailed information made available to those who request it. An oral report of needs assessment findings allows a continuing educator to clarify any questions that arise and permits exchange of ideas among the interested parties in attendance. In either written or oral form, succinct reports are most successful in attracting and holding people's interest. By inviting response and comments, both written and oral reports can involve others in the overall process and build their commitment to implementation of the needs assessment findings.

The content of a needs assessment report can vary depending

on its audience. Different audiences might require somewhat different reports, or presentation of the same information from different perspectives. The basic information to be covered most often will include the following:

- Background: What factors led to examination of this topic?
- Standards: What is the minimum level below which it is considered that a need exists?
- Needs identified: What are the assessed levels compared with the established standards, and what is the extent of the needs?
- Reasons for the discrepancy: What factors in addition to educational needs might be responsible for the discrepancies between the assessed levels and the established standards?
- Remedies: What educational interventions might address the discrepancies identified?
- Implications: What are the educational, political, environmental, or other ramifications of the needs assessment findings for the organization or institution?
- Proposed action plan: What steps might be taken in response to the needs assessment results?

Once this information is presented, people will want to respond. Whether the report is oral or written, it should include an easy mechanism for all interested parties to offer their own interpretations and solutions.

The formality of a needs assessment report is determined by the scope of the assessment and the audience for the report. A small assessment being reported to a group of colleagues can be informal, whereas a larger effort presented to organization executives might require some formality. Informality is not to be confused with sloppiness, however. Accuracy of data, thoroughness, attention to detail, proper grammar, and respect for the project are always essential.

When the needs assessment report is presented without negativism or a punitive tone, it can help overcome misperception and fear. It is possible to state almost any identified need in positive terms, presenting it as an opportunity rather than a threat, so that individuals being assessed (and their employers, if relevant) will not react defensively. The following is an example: "Your middle-level managers have good communication skills, and their technical knowledge is outstanding. Education regarding basic leadership skills would enable them to increase their effectiveness in motivating other workers."

When a continuing educator conducts a needs assessment for an employer, professional association, or other organization or institution, it usually is with the understanding that the results will be reported to the organization's leaders, the human resources or education director, or others who are responsible for incorporating the results into an educational plan. Usually, these people had a role in deciding that the assessment would be conducted and served either as needs assessment team members or in an advisory capacity. They will anticipate a report of the needs assessment and most likely will have formed some tentative ideas regarding its use.

As discussed in Chapter Four, individual assessment results most often are reported as group data when they are shared with other interested parties. Aggregating the data gives the organization that initiated the assessment the information it needs to develop appropriate educational activities and also protects the anonymity of individual participants. However, individual data sometimes are reported to the organization for other reasons. Organizations may use needs assessment findings to help improve individual performance. For example, needs assessment data can be a very positive component of a performance appraisal. Any supervisor who takes the appraisal process seriously will want to give even the strongest employees suggestions for their continued growth. Needs assessment data can provide objective information about areas in which employees can learn new things or improve existing knowledge, skills, or performance abilities. Working together, supervisor and employee can use this information to begin identifying steps to enhance the employee's current performance or prepare for new opportunities.

When continuing educators plan to report individual data at the organizational level, they advise participants that the assessment results will be distributed in this manner, and therefore will not be anonymous, before they enter into the assessment. Information on the eventual use of their assessment data (for example, for design of an individualized professional development plan) also is shared. If these steps are not taken, the assessment may be viewed as punitive rather than positive and participants may feel that assessment is something that has been done to rather than for them. Such a situation could produce unwilling participants and even defeat the purpose of the assessment, which is to help individuals gain the knowledge, skills, and performance abilities they need to function more effectively.

Because "most adults have a pattern for the way they approach learning, and understanding that pattern will help them discover how they process information" (Dagavarian, 1990, p. 13), continuing educators can construct needs assessment reports to help recipients understand the pattern and how it fits into the larger context of the target group's related activities. Thus a continuing educator might present a report with an explanation of how the areas included in the assessment were selected; their relevance to the profession, work, or other interests of the target population; and their implications for individuals' learning plans. If needs assessment data are based on a sample, the report should include an explanation of the method and rationale for using that sample and any limitations imposed by the sample.

Needs assessment data must look valid as well as be valid. For this reason the continuing educator includes an explanation of any findings in the assessment report that appear to lack face validity. For example, a needs assessment finding that social workers' interviewing skills are weak, when they regularly collect information from clients, might appear doubtful. It may make the finding appear more plausible to explain that people usually assume that they perform routine tasks well, when in fact they often tend to neglect learning more about routine work in favor of acquiring new information and skills.

People who have participated in either individualized or group needs assessments expect to receive some feedback. From the continuing educator's perspective, informing participants of the needs identified increases the likelihood of their participation in the educational activities developed to address those needs. Such feedback also will "give them a sense of accomplishment . . . enable them to feel that they contributed to tangible results" (Queeney, 1992, p. 3.13). This information enhances individuals' understanding of their group, whether it is their profession, work unit, alumni association, or other occupational, social, or interest group. Feedback can help participants recognize the importance of some type of needs assessment in planning their own lifelong learning.

By providing information on available educational activities to address the needs identified, the needs assessment sponsor can make it easy for recipients to take positive action. For example, feedback provided to architects and dietitians as a result of their participation in self-assessment exercises not only identifies their strengths but also, in citing the discrepancies identified, lists educational opportunities to address them, pointing participants toward a positive course of action (Klevans, Smutz, Shuman, and Bershad, 1992; Klevans, Pollack, Smutz, and Vance, 1991).

Not all needs assessment findings can be translated into educational interventions. Some identified discrepancies will point to problems in the work setting, lack of adequate facilities or materials, organizational problems, or other factors that the continuing educator cannot directly affect. Often the continuing educator can relay such findings to the individuals or organizations in positions to take appropriate action in response to them. In other cases, the data may point directly toward educational needs, but an adequate number of appropriate educational activities may already exist, precluding the need for further programming. However, in most cases the continuing educator will have focused needs assessment on those areas that are amenable to educational intervention, and those in which adequate programming, in both quality and quantity, does not exist.

Translating Needs into Educational Activities

Between the moment that conducting a needs assessment is first considered and the evaluation of the completed educational activity that resulted from it, a variety of skills will be needed. In order to bring together all of these skills, continuing educators will find it helpful to think of the entire process, including needs assessment, as a team effort. When possible, they will assemble a program development group. If a needs assessment team is formed, it can be viewed as a unit of this group. Needs assessment team members can be members of the program development group as well, but most often the needs assessment team is represented in the group by one or two individuals. Program development group members may be actively involved with the process from beginning to end or move closer to it and further from it as their expertise is more or less crucial to individual phases. In addition to people responsible for needs assessment, the program development group can include experts in delivery methods, the proposed content area, instructional design, marketing, and evaluation. Some individuals may have expertise in several of these areas. Throughout the program development process, the continuing educator serves as the catalyst, bringing all team members together to focus on each phase of their activity.

The first step in translating needs assessment findings into educational activities consists of converting those findings into learning objectives to guide development of educational activities that will address the discrepancies identified. Learning objectives are the "programmatic pivot" (Brookfield, 1986, p. 211) for development of any continuing education activity, providing the foundation and purpose on which the program or activity will be built. They clearly and succinctly state the desired outcomes of each educational activity to be developed, outlining what participants can expect to gain from that activity. Statements of learning objectives are most effective when they use action verbs that indicate what learners will be able to do as a result of the educational activity. (For example, "Participants will *use* the computer to access information from all the libraries on the network.") Learning objectives serve to focus the content and may suggest format and delivery methods, selection of materials, and evaluation procedures as well (Knox, 1986).

Because most continuing education participants are adults, a flexibility that accommodates their diversity and range of experiences is important in continuing education programming. Thus while the "concept of purpose" provided by learning objectives is critical to the continuing education program development process, "general purposes need not always be translated into sets of closely specified objectives" (Brookfield, 1986, p. 214). Good learning objectives offer direction but leave some room for adaptation and interpretation. Learning objectives evolve primarily in the early stages of planning but can be refined as an activity is developed (Knox, 1986).

The needs assessment data on which learning objectives are based may indicate a need for additional knowledge or for enhancement of participants' skills or performance abilities. Thus learning objectives can range from acquisition of basic learning to higher level performance-based objectives such as analyzing, synthesizing, and applying concepts. Learning objectives for knowledge-based activities can be offered in straightforward terms citing the new information to be mastered. For example, a learning objective for a program for accountants might be, "Participants will understand new state tax laws relating to earned income." If new or improved skills or performance abilities are the goal, learning objectives are likely to be stated in behavioral terms. In such cases, the objectives indicate that upon completion of the program, participants will demonstrate particular skills or perform at a certain level. Again using accountants as the example, an objective in this case might be, "Participants will be able to apply new state tax laws relating to earned income in assisting clients with their financial planning."

Behavioral learning objectives have substantial implications for design and evaluation of educational activities. If the goal is to change behaviors, which is necessary if skills are to be mastered or performance changed, the educational activity has to deliver more than information. This can be accomplished by incorporating into design of the program such activities as simulations and role playing, to "practice" the desired skills or performance abilities. Similarly, evaluation of this type of educational activity includes some measure of participants' changed behavior.

The educational objectives and the type of learning—knowledge, skills, or performance abilities—needed to address them define the content and often the format of the educational activity that will be developed.

If the needs assessment also yielded information on the target population's preferences regarding, for example, delivery mode or scheduling, this information is integrated into the planning process. If information on these preferences is not available from the needs assessment, representatives of the target population may be able to provide it. For example, lawyers may report that because time spent in a seminar represents lost opportunity to earn money they prefer educational activities they can pursue on their own. Senior citizens may prefer daytime scheduling. Continuing educators should give consideration to all of these factors in determining the type of educational activity they will offer. If they do not, the likelihood of program success is substantially diminished.

Once continuing educators have decided on the type of educational activity to be developed, they rely on guidelines, expertise, and experience in designing, developing, and delivering it. Often continuing educators or their organizations have special equipment or capabilities to utilize specific delivery methods, such as compressed video, interactive videodisks, or televised instruction. In such cases, exploiting these capabilities clearly is desirable when it is appropriate to the program being planned, but it is not educationally sound to fit the content and learning needs to a delivery method that would be inappropriate. The content and the potential audience's learning style and needs are the basis for selection of a delivery method. Thus continuing educators may have to seek assistance with forms of delivery that are less familiar to them, especially as new technology continues to expand the possibilities for educational programming.

Because no continuing educators have expertise in all content areas, they usually identify an individual with expertise in the content area to be addressed to work with them on development of any educational activity. Frequently they invite one or more members of the target population to collaborate with the content expert to ensure that the material being developed will be relevant to their application of it. This approach is particularly helpful when a faculty member with little recent practical experience serves as the content expert. Working with the needs assessment data, the content experts outline the instructional content, select the level at which it will be taught (for example, basic or more advanced), and specify the topics to be covered and material to be included. Considering whether the activity is to address discrepancies in knowledge, skills, or performance abilities, and with regard for the facilities and capabilities available to the continuing educator, the content expert helps determine an appropriate format and delivery mode for the educational activity. Within the framework of the target group's learning preferences, as discussed earlier, those involved in program planning select both the format and delivery mode to transfer knowledge, skills, or performance abilities to participants in a manner that will optimize the likelihood of igniting and maintaining their interest. They also give careful attention to selecting format and delivery modes that permit the most effective learning experience for the content to be addressed. Although knowledge can be delivered through self-study methods, for example, performance abilities often can be taught only in small-group, interactive sessions.

As continuing educators and those working with them make decisions about content, format, and delivery mode, they give consideration to the need for instructional personnel and materials. The content expert may become involved in these issues or serve as instructor, should one be needed, or others may be found for these functions. The program planners may identify existing materials and secure permission for their use, or decide that new materials—ranging from course manuals to videotapes to self-study documents and practice exercises—are required. They also make decisions regarding the audiences for whom materials are needed. For example, if a workshop, seminar, or conference is to be developed for delivery in numerous locations, an instructor's manual, in addition to participant materials, might be appropriate to ensure uniformity among several local presenters.

Throughout this process, frequent reference to the needs assessment data helps maintain a focus on meeting the identified needs of potential participants in a manner that is compatible with their preferences. Without periodic referral to the data collected, it is easy for the program development process to take on a life of its own, leading the continuing educator away from the original purpose of the activity.

Marketing Activities on the Basis of Needs

The continuing educator should make sure that a marketing plan is developed as any program is being designed. Programs developed in response to needs assessments are no exception. The first step in marketing a needs assessment–based activity is to reach the people who are likely to have the discrepancies identified and hence an educational need for the program. The second step is to convince them that they will benefit from the program and should enroll. For all but the most trendy, attractive educational activities, a marketing strategy is necessary to meet these objectives.

By working with the program planning team, the person responsible for marketing a continuing education program has an opportunity to contribute ideas as the activity evolves. When involved from the start, a marketing person often can include some market research questions in the assessment itself to provide information on which to base a marketing plan. Someone with a marketing perspective also can contribute suggestions about available mailing lists for target populations; socioeconomic, demographic, and other factors that might affect the proposed activity; and even such simple things as the choice of words to make a program title sound attractive. Because areas of educational need do not always coincide with the content areas in which a particular group of adults is most interested, early inclusion of a marketing perspective is particularly important for activities based on needs assessment results. A special marketing strategy is often needed to interest target audiences in educational activities that are designed to meet their needs rather than simply to respond to current trends or provide an enjoyable experience. An understanding of the derivation of an educational activity, including its needs assessment basis, can be helpful in designing the marketing strategy. In order to gain that understanding, the person responsible for program marketing should be involved in the total program planning process, from needs assessment on.

The fact that the educational activity has been developed on the basis of an identified need can be a powerful marketing tool. Through marketing, the continuing educator can inform potential participants that the program has been designed to provide them with knowledge, skills, or performance abilities for which people like them have demonstrated a need. This approach is most effective when the message is presented in a positive way, rather than creating the impression that the people who need to participate have less-than-desirable abilities. Tying the need into the target population's known interests is one way to cast the needs in positive terms. Messages can avoid negative language and stress the manner in which the anticipated outcomes of participation in the educational activity will address the need. This kind of approach is illustrated in the following examples:

- Like other freelance writers, you may have difficulty finding appropriate outlets for your work. This independent study course will provide the information you need to identify and approach potential publishers.
- Adult students give college faculty members high marks for their knowledge and experience but observe that their teaching could benefit from more interactive discussion. Ways to involve students in the learning process will be highlighted in "Enlivening Your Lectures: A Workshop for Teachers of Adults."

Because only a critical mass of participants can justify the investment needed to develop and deliver educational activities, it is only logical that such activities are more likely to be developed in response to group, rather than individual, needs. Unfortunately, individuals usually need help understanding that they do indeed have the same needs as others with similar professional, personal, or other interests. For this reason, an important part of marketing is helping individuals relate to the needs that have been identified through assessment of their peers or colleagues. It is useful to explain that an assessment of people with whom they share characteristics has identified a discrepancy, and that they too may wish to build their strengths in that area. The following excerpt from a program description is an example of such an approach: "In assessing the educational needs of secondary school English teachers, we have learned that teaching creative writing is the area in which they are least strong. Because you teach English to secondary school students, you also may find it beneficial to improve your skills in this area."

Often continuing educators will find it helpful to use information about potential participants' interests and preferences to develop a strategy for making information about identified educational needs attractive to them. Local elected officials, found to have needs related to their performance abilities to work as a team, may find an educational program on teamwork unappealing. However, they may be swayed by reference to research on the relationship of teamwork to effective performance. Because they are concerned about voters' images of them, they may respond well to a marketing strategy that suggests that the educational activity will make them more effective public servants, enabling them to win voter respect. Clinical psychologists, who enjoy informal interaction and discussion with their peers, might find a seminar on diversity more appealing when it is presented as an opportunity for discussion of the topic rather than simply as a seminar, even though the two descriptions are of the same program.

Building on the target audience's concerns and addressing them in program promotion is another strategy that enables the continuing educator to relate needs-based educational activities to potential participants. Threats of dire consequences are not desirable (and may even border on the unethical) in marketing educational programs, but straightforward, positive descriptions of ways in which educational activities can help prevent negative consequences can be motivational. Health care professionals faced with mounting quantities of medical waste may become interested in learning new ways to handle it if they realize that new regulations dictate that their current procedures may put their practice in jeopardy. Chemists with little interest in programs on laboratory safety may have their interest piqued upon learning that most injury-producing laboratory accidents result from lack of knowledge of proper safety procedures.

Data on potential participants also can influence the choice of vehicle used to promote an activity. Too often continuing educators rely on standard brochures mailed in large quantities to loosely defined groups of people to convey their message. The result frequently is a response rate of well under 5 percent (often only 1 or 2 percent). Building and maintaining well-defined mailing lists for populations served can help avoid such inefficiency but may not be enough. Particularly when marketing educational activities developed for target populations with identified needs, continuing educators can devise a strategy to reach effectively the appropriate people while screening out others. For example, brochures may be sent to a carefully built mailing list, but there also may be advertisements in professional publications or hobby magazines, personal letters to individuals, direct communication from an organization to which potential participants belong, or some other form of marketing approach that has been tailored to the group for which needs have been identified.

Summary

A needs assessment and the data it generates have little meaning or utility when looked at in isolation. They are valuable only when considered as part of the comprehensive program planning process. Needs assessment provides a first step in this process, the information to guide the continuing educator in defining the content and target population for educational activities; in determining when, where, and how those activities should be delivered; and in choosing the most effective way of promoting them. Complete, accurate interpretation and reporting of needs assessment data are critical to their full exploitation and use.

For their successful adoption the receptivity of the continuing educator, employer, professional association, and others to the needs assessment findings is at least as important as correct interpretation and reporting of the data. Needs assessments may confirm previously articulated ideas, but they also can generate findings that are in direct opposition to the beliefs of educators or the organizations concerned. People are disappointed when needs assessment data indicate that a faculty member's research findings are not pertinent to a group's educational needs, or that a target population will not accept a program delivered via satellite. The continuing educator who has long advocated a line of programming to a population may be embarrassed by needs assessment data indicating a dearth of need in the area. These problems are minimized, although not eliminated, when continuing educators undertake needs assessments with an open mind and a genuine interest in obtaining data that can be used to guide program development activities. These goals must take priority over personal agendas or beliefs. Following the directions suggested by needs assessment may require the continuing educator to develop and deliver programs on topics not previously considered, to populations not on the list of those to be served, using methods and faculty not normally chosen. Flexibility and adaptability to accommodate needs assessment findings in this manner are essential to their effective incorporation into the program planning process.

Chapter Nine

Continuous Assessment: Evaluating Program Effectiveness

All continuing education activities are submitted to some type of evaluation, although much of it may be informal (Knox, 1985). Participants express opinions to their colleagues, and if they feel strongly enough about an activity they voice praise or criticism by calling or writing the instructor or the provider. They may "vote with their feet" by failing to complete an activity or to enroll in subsequent activities delivered by a provider or instructor whose previous program they found unsatisfactory. Continuing educators may become aware of these informal evaluations, particularly if they ask new program participants about their reasons for enrolling or past participants about why they have not returned for further activities. Casual conversations may reveal program participants' perspectives on an educational activity. This kind of feedback represents informal evaluation and can be useful to the continuing educator.

Many circumstances call for a more formal evaluation. Programs that will be offered several times often merit an evaluation so that they can be continually improved. Continuing educators serving certain audiences over time may wish to use program evaluation to demonstrate the value of their programs. Credentialing requirements, conditions of funding, and a desire to document performance outcomes also may lead to or even dictate an evaluation. However, just as every proposed educational activity does not merit a needs assessment, every educational activity does not need a formal evaluation. If the activity will not be repeated, or if it was intended simply to provide an enjoyable or enriching experience, the benefits to be derived from evaluating its effectiveness may be minimal or nonexistent (although an evaluation of participants' satisfaction with it may be useful for future programs). If an educational activity is not sufficiently intensive to have a marked impact on participants' knowledge, skills, or performance abilities, an evaluation of its effectiveness is probably not worthwhile (Knox, 1985, p. 69), because minor changes will scarcely be discerned and if documented, may be too small to be attributable to the educational intervention. Conversely, if the educational activity addresses an area in which participants have had no previous experience, great changes can be expected and an evaluation again will not be needed to determine the program's impact. For example, a program to teach physical therapists to use newly developed equipment clearly will have an effect, providing information that participants previously had no access to. However, if the program were to be offered again, a continuing educator might find it worthwhile to evaluate the ways in which participants use the new equipment, to identify opportunities for program improvement.

The key factor in deciding whether to conduct an evaluation is its potential impact on future programming. Program evaluation is of value only when the resultant data will be of use to the continuing educator. Without a commitment to using evaluation results in future program planning, the continuing educator is likely to waste resources on evaluation that could better be used in other ways. At the same time, evaluation of a specific activity should not be ruled out because the continuing educator perceives evaluation as something that can be easily eliminated. Sadly, this is exactly what often happens. It is very easy to declare that one cannot afford the time or other resources to conduct an evaluation. Yet for programs of substantial size, importance, or longevity, the continuing educator often cannot afford *not* to conduct an evaluation.

Evaluation frequently focuses only on determining whether participants liked the activity, instructor, and facilities. Although this information is useful to continuing educators, it tells them nothing about the educational benefits or quality of an activity. Continuing educators who are truly eager to provide activities that enable participants to strengthen their knowledge, skills, or performance abilities evaluate the extent to which a continuing education activity has met the needs it was designed to address and accomplished its educational goals. Such an evaluation most often is summative—that is, conducted after that educational activity has been completed—and can be used to determine whether participation in the activity made a difference. Were participants' knowledge, skills, or performance abilities improved or enhanced in some way? This type of evaluation of an activity's impact on educational needs goes well beyond the common program evaluation. More than a measure of satisfaction with an educational activity, it is a measure of program quality.

Evaluation of the extent to which an educational activity has met the needs it was designed to meet is a critical yet often ignored link in the program development chain. Needs assessment provides the continuing educator with a sound basis for making decisions about program audience, content, format, level, delivery, and other factors, but needs assessment and the resultant program development and delivery do not represent a complete process. Not until the program's effectiveness in responding to assessed needs has been evaluated is the process complete. Evaluation data are fed back into the program development process, beginning with the next needs assessment. These data may have application beyond the single activity to which they are related, for they can be useful in planning other activities. For example, information on the effectiveness of particular teaching and delivery methods can be shared with program developers, instructional designers, and faculty members working on future programs. Knowing whether the content level was appropriate to the audience can be valuable in developing future educational activities for that audience.

Evaluations that document program success in meeting needs

are the most satisfying, but those that indicate program shortcomings may be the most valuable. A program that does not address the educational needs it aimed to requires reexamination before damage is done to the credibility of the continuing educator and any supporting agency. Program evaluation can yield valuable insights into the complex relationship between assessed needs and the educational activities intended to respond to those needs.

Evaluation of program effectiveness in addressing assessed needs measures the value added by the educational activity in one of two ways, and both involve pretest and posttest comparisons:

- If the individuals who participated in the educational activity are the same individuals who participated in the needs assessment, the evaluation focuses on measuring changes in their strengths and weaknesses between the time of the assessment and completion of the educational activity.

- If the participants in the educational activity are different from those assessed earlier but have key relevant characteristics in common with them, the evaluation measures differences between the group that participated in the needs assessment and the group that completed the educational activity. Measurement of a control group of comparable individuals who did not participate in the educational activity, although not essential, can strengthen such an evaluation.

In either situation, the evaluation will seek to determine whether the initially identified needs are less acute after program participation. For example, some time ago a needs assessment revealed that physical plant supervisors were not attending to preventive maintenance activities in schools and other public buildings. In response to this need, continuing educators developed a seminar to highlight the types of preventive maintenance needed and the advantages of developing and implementing a routine maintenance schedule. One year later an evaluation, including audits of building records (for example, energy usage) revealed that systems maintenance had improved substantially. Although other factors also may have had an impact, the seminar appeared to have been effective in addressing the need that had been identified. The greater the extent to which individual or group needs are reduced following participation in the educational activity, the more justifiable the claim that the educational activity has been effective in addressing those needs.

Together, needs assessment and program evaluation provide an ongoing link in the program development process. Needs assessment represents initiation of a program development cycle, and evaluation marks its conclusion. Evaluation can enable continuing educators to modify future programs so that they more closely meet participants' needs, thus commencing the next cycle. The areas in which evaluation indicates improvement may require no further assessment, but those in which evaluation indicates that needs remain might be targeted for closer scrutiny in a future needs assessment. In this manner the evaluation is formative; that is, it provides information to influence the course of future activities. This kind of evaluation functions in much the same way as a needs assessment does: just as continuing educators use needs assessment data to guide program development and delivery, they can use information gleaned from evaluations to plan future educational activities.

Even when an educational activity is developed without a needs assessment, its impact can be evaluated on the basis of the objectives it was designed to meet. Continuing educators can use pretests and posttests to determine participants' levels of knowledge, skills, or performance abilities at the start and at the conclusion of educational activities. Alternatively, evaluation strategies designed to measure other factors, such as quality of instruction, satisfaction with scheduling, facilities, and program administration, and enjoyment of the activity, can incorporate questions or activities to collect information on the extent to which the educational activity has had an impact.

Like needs assessment, evaluation should not be seen as an examination. In neither case is the individual's performance the issue under consideration. It is the educational activity that is being evaluated, a message that should be communicated clearly to all evaluation participants. They are being asked to contribute to understanding the educational activity's success in meeting its intended purpose, and there will be no judgment of their own knowledge, skills, or performance abilities. Evaluation exercises that give participants an opportunity to demonstrate what they have learned in a positive way have relevance for them and feel less like an examination. For example, although open-ended questions are more difficult to score than close-ended questions, they allow participants to emphasize what they have learned and they do not carry the stigma of right and wrong. Involving participants as partners in the evaluation by soliciting their suggestions in an open manner also contributes to a positive experience and engenders the cooperation necessary for successful evaluation.

Although evaluation of program effectiveness is not commonly and regularly used by continuing educators, "this kind of direct assessment has been going on for quite some time and is not particularly new. Evaluation tools such as live performance, products, teacher judgment, and school grades have a long history in education" (Cizek, 1991, p. 695). The demand for accountability in continuing education has increased steadily since the 1970s, and with it the need for sound evaluation. Continuing educators who ignore the importance of program evaluation or mask its absence by evaluating other things (for example, satisfaction with location, meals) are shortchanging the educational process. They may as well not conduct needs assessments, for they have no idea of their level of success in addressing the needs they identify.

Continuing education participants and the organizations and institutions that support their participation understandably want to know if their time, money, and other resources are being well spent. Organizations considering mandating continuing education for practice of certain professions often raise questions about whether participation in an educational activity makes a difference in participants' knowledge, skills, or performance abilities. These interested parties would like precise, quantifiable data to document the value, but such data are not easily produced. Although the impact of continuing education has been debated extensively (Cervero, 1988; Nowlen, 1988, pp. 4–8, 232), the relative dearth of information on the topic is evidence of the difficult nature of this type of evaluation. Evaluation of an educational activity's effectiveness is a form of outcome evaluation, and perhaps the most challenging form of educational evaluation. It is far easier to evaluate faculty performance, usually measured by self-, peer, or student perceptions, or a program's operational success, which usually is based on such easily measured factors as number of enrollees and income generation. At the other extreme, proving a direct cause-and-effect relationship between participation in an educational activity and diminished need or discrepancy can be most challenging. Changes that do occur often may be attributed to multiple factors, not the least of which is increased awareness brought about by the needs assessment and evaluation procedures. Rather than striving to document that an educational activity is completely responsible for reducing discrepancies, a more realistic evaluation goal may be to determine whether the educational activity contributed to the reduction.

Considerations in Developing an Evaluation Strategy

According to Hutchings and Marchese, any type of "assessment is best understood as a set of questions" (1990, p. 12). Before continuing educators can consider the components of an evaluation strategy, they have to make decisions about the questions the evaluation will answer. If, as emphasized here, the focus will be on the educational activity's effectiveness in addressing identified needs, the range of considerations is narrowed, but other decisions remain to be made. Is the objective to learn about the extent to which knowledge, skills, and performance abilities have been acquired, or is it to determine whether what was learned has been applied in regular activities? Defining the focus and purpose of the evaluation in terms of the questions it is to answer is the first step in developing an evaluation. A clear statement of these dimensions increases the likelihood of achieving willing, if not enthusiastic, participation in the process, and facilitates meaningful application of the evaluation results.

Like needs assessment, evaluation of program effectiveness should synthesize a variety of components if it is to measure assimilation of knowledge in usable form (Elman and Lynton, 1985). Ideally, an evaluation includes all aspects of the program that are relevant to the needs assessment, but such a comprehensive evaluation may not be realistic. Decisions may have to be made regarding which aspects of the needs assessment are most critical and hence most important to evaluate. Whenever possible, continuing educators should strive to include some objective, quantifiable measure of knowledge, skills, and performance abilities, because data presented in numerical terms are easy to understand and summarize, and can present a clear and compelling picture of an educational activity's strengths and weaknesses. Subjective data, including comments from participants, provide interesting and worthwhile vignettes and their collection creates a positive context for participants to stress what they know, but such data do not readily facilitate tight, numerical analysis. A combination of both objective and subjective data is ideal, although not always feasible.

Determining the scope—or scale and complexity—of the evaluation is a key factor in developing an evaluation strategy. Like a needs assessment, an evaluation "can be conducted on almost any scale" (Knox, 1985, p. 63), ranging from informal conversations to multifaceted strategies. A strong factor in determining the scope of an evaluation is the magnitude and importance of the educational activity, and the extent to which it will be repeated or serve as the basis for future programming. In general, activities that are intended to serve large audiences and have greater potential to be offered repeatedly merit evaluations of broader scope than do smaller programs that have limited audiences and less likelihood of repetition.

A second key factor in establishing the scope of an evaluation is the extent to which the findings will be used in future decision making. If the decisions to be made involve considerable risk and if other information that might be used to guide decision making is limited or unavailable, an evaluation that is broad in scope may be advisable. Available resources may be a limiting factor in planning an evaluation, but conversely, it makes no sense to expand the scope of an evaluation simply to use all available resources.

As suggested earlier, evaluation should be "embedded in the cycle of program development" (Cervero, 1988, p. 133) as a measure to promote continuous improvement. From the time a needs assessment is completed, evaluation plans are included in the design and development of an educational activity. The factors to be considered in choosing needs assessment methods, discussed earlier, also apply in the selection of evaluation methods. Because needs assessment and evaluation of program effectiveness measure participants' knowledge, skills, or performance abilities in similar fashion, the methods most commonly used for needs assessment also are appropriate for evaluating educational activities' success. Working with the program development team, the continuing educator selects methods that are suited to the type of learning being measured, the resources available, the assessed needs and learning objectives of the educational activity, and the audience. One or more methods may be incorporated in an evaluation strategy.

The types of learning to be measured are related to the knowledge, skills, or performance abilities that individuals were expected to gain or improve as a result of participation. Knowledge measurement is fairly straightforward and can be accomplished easily through use of paper and pencil tests and other common exercises that determine participants' information levels. Skills evaluation requires examination of participants' methods of using and manipulating knowledge, and usually involves demonstrations of knowledge application such as a bookkeeper's record keeping or a nurse's use of a new piece of equipment. Evaluating performance abilities incorporates the factors necessary for knowledge and skills evaluation, and it also includes measurement of the judgment, attitudes, and behaviors displayed in the practical application of knowledge and skills. Hence this evaluation is the most complex, costly, and difficult type, and the one that requires the greatest expertise to be successfully designed and implemented. Review of a dietitian's teaching of diabetic patients or a teacher's use of cooperative learning techniques are examples of evaluation of performance abilities.

As in needs assessment, reality dictates that continuing educators consider resources in selecting the methods they will incorporate in an evaluation strategy. They must be sure that all the necessary resources are available before beginning. Some of the methods most effective in evaluation of performance abilities, such as direct observation and live simulations, are costly. Use of these methods, which often have the potential for producing the most comprehensive results, may be tempting. However, unless the resources are available for proper implementation, other evaluation methods should be selected. Properly used, less resource-intensive methods can also provide valuable feedback, although it may be less sophisticated, thorough, or conclusive. However, good basic data are far more valuable than detailed data that are less accurate because they were collected in questionable ways. As with needs assessment, the most important consideration in conducting an evaluation is that no matter what method is selected, it be implemented carefully and thoroughly. It is far easier to explain the limitations of an evaluation method than the potential inaccuracies of poor data.

The questions to be addressed by an evaluation are based on the program's learning objectives, which in turn were derived from the needs assessment data. The continuing educator has no means of determining whether educational objectives that cannot be measured through evaluation were met. For this reason such objectives may be unacceptable, and the conscientious continuing educator may insist on objectives that are stated so that success in meeting them can be monitored. The learning objectives of the educational activity to be evaluated may differ somewhat from the needs identified through assessment. An assessment can identify a number of needs, only some of which may be addressed by a single educational activity, and the educational objectives may represent modifications of those needs. (Other learning objectives for an educational activity may bear no relationship to the needs assessment but may have been incorporated for other purposes.) However, any needs that are to be addressed by the educational activity should be reflected in the learning objectives for that activity. Thus, both the needs assessment results and the related learning objectives are considered in determining the items to be addressed through program evaluation. Without this link to the program development process, evaluation results can say nothing about an educational activity's success in addressing participants' needs. The questions spring from the desired outcomes, emphasizing the "direction in which change ought to take place" (Elman and Lynton, 1985).

Program evaluation designed to determine the extent to which needs identified through assessment have been met emphasizes changes that occur as a result of completing an educational activity. As such it most often is summative rather than formative. However, particularly if the educational activity extends through several sessions, formative evaluation may be appropriate to obtain an indication of the extent to which participants are learning as intended. If a formative evaluation indicates that needs are not being adequately addressed, it may be possible to introduce changes in either program content or the manner in which it is being conveyed, as suggested by the evaluation results, during the remainder of the activity.

Because evaluation relies on participants' willingness to cooperate, evaluation is most successful when the methods selected are appropriate and appealing to the audience. Enjoyable, brief exercises that allow participants to demonstrate their strengths, are neither too elementary nor too sophisticated for the group, and are nonthreatening are likely to generate a willingness to complete the process.

Choosing and Applying Evaluation Methods

The needs assessment tools discussed earlier in this book will not be reviewed in this chapter because their adaptation to evaluation is straightforward and in most cases, similar to their use for needs assessment. However, some methods have particular strengths, weaknesses, or characteristics when used for evaluation of program effectiveness. Some special considerations regarding the use of questionnaires, interviews, and focus groups, self-reporting measures, consensus-rendering techniques, practice observations, simulations, critical incident technique, and computerized evaluation methods are summarized here.

Questionnaires, Interviews, and Focus Groups

People who have completed an educational activity may have good recall of certain information but little or no understanding of what it means or how it is to be applied. They may easily provide the objective information when asked direct questions, but such recall says little about their ability to understand or employ the information memorized. The continuing educator seeking to measure comprehension of educational content through use of questionnaires, interviews, or focus groups has to structure questions to require processing, as well as recall, of information if this measurement is to be effective. For example, rather than simply asking people who participated in a photography workshop to list the common film sensitivity numbers (or speeds), the continuing educator might ask them to indicate the criteria for using each film speed. Union members completing a seminar on negotiation strategies could be asked to select appropriate responses for specified situations, which offers an opportunity to apply, rather than simply recall, information.

Self-Reporting Measures

Activities such as keeping charts, diaries, checklists, self-reporting inventories, and rating forms allow participants in an evaluation to become active partners in the evaluation process through self-monitoring. Having completed the educational activity, they will have a heightened awareness of the factors included in the evaluation, allowing them to be sensitive to those items they are asked to report. Because of this increased awareness, self-reporting measures often are better used in evaluation than in needs assessment. Self-reporting activities are most successful if clear directions, well-designed forms for recording information, and an adequate range of response options are provided. Asking participants in a golf class to report their scores is a simple example of an evaluation using self-reporting. Participants in a course on sales techniques could be asked to report their sales totals before, during, and after completing the course.

Consensus-Rendering Techniques

Evaluation methods that bring groups of participants together offer an opportunity to simulate that aspect of applying knowledge that forces an individual to operate cooperatively with peers or colleagues. These methods are particularly appropriate for evaluation of programs that focus on knowledge, skills, and performance abilities used in settings that require interaction and communication. Consensus-rendering techniques include leaderless discussions, charette (that is, keeping all group members together until they are able to reach consensus), juries, and conferences. Delphi techniques also fall in this category. Although they lack the face-to-face interaction of the other methods, they require participants to adapt to others' preferences and judgment. The following is an example of consensus rendering: At the conclusion of a program on nondirective interviewing methods, participating counselors were divided into small groups and asked to identify the three greatest strengths and the three greatest weaknesses of the program.

Practice Observation

Direct observation of participants' application of what they have learned in their everyday activities, if done properly, is an excellent means of evaluating educational activity effectiveness. However, the knowledge, skills, or performance abilities to be considered must lend themselves to measurement in an objective manner. Criteria are established for the observation, with specific factors identified in checklist form. For example, if a workshop on cooperative learning is to be evaluated, participants may be observed working with students in the classroom, teaching a lesson that calls for use of these techniques. The observer is provided with a list of behaviors (for example, discusses benefits of cooperation with students; monitors students to ensure that everyone is an active learner) that the participant is expected to demonstrate and a rating scale with which to record the extent to which those behaviors are observable.

Simulations

Evaluation exercises that simulate everyday situations in which participants might apply what they have learned can provide information similar to that obtained from practice observation. For example, nurses participating in a workshop on interacting with patient families viewed a videotape of a nurse talking with the family of a dying patient and responded to questions about how the nurse handled the situation. Simulations can be pencil-and-paper exercises (such as case studies), role-playing, or a prerecorded activity (such as the videotape cited in the example of the nurses). All of these simulations can be considerably less cumbersome to implement than actual practice observation. As with practice observation, objective criteria are necessary to evaluate adequately the extent to which the knowledge, skills, and performance abilities covered in the educational activity are applied.

Critical Incident Technique

The critical incident technique is an additional method that can be used for evaluation. This technique is not suitable for needs assessment because it requires consideration of the learning that took place in an educational activity. However, when continuing educators use it to evaluate an educational activity, it can point to strengths that have been developed or to remaining discrepancies that indicate further educational need.

In the critical incident technique, participants are asked to describe one or more situations, or incidents, in which they applied something learned from the educational activity. If they were taught a new skill, they might be asked to describe a situation in which they used that skill. In evaluating each participant's response, consideration is given first to whether they were able to describe a situation in which the specified skill was used, and then to the appropriateness and correctness of the way in which they applied it. Critical incident questions can be quite general, simply asking respondents to describe a situation in which they used something learned from the educational activity. However, more detailed, and hence more useful, information can be obtained from more focused questions that ask for a description of a situation in which participants used specific knowledge, skills, or performance abilities addressed by the educational activity. For example, participants in a word processing class might be asked to describe a situation in which they used a graphics package rather than simply to describe a situation in which they used something learned from the class. Each critical incident question requires respondents to write a few sentences, a paragraph, or more, which can be a deterrent to completion of the evaluation. For this reason, the method is not a good choice for use with groups of people who consider writing a chore or do not feel comfortable writing. It also is advisable to limit an evaluation to one or two questions of this nature.

Computerized Evaluation Methods

As use of technology for continuing education delivery increases, computerized evaluation methods embedded in continuing education programs can be expected to gain popularity. For those continuing education programs that are delivered via computer or for which participants communicate with the instructor or each other electronically, both formative and summative evaluations can be integrated into the educational activity. The continuing educator can insert evaluation questions or exercises directly into the software program at any point. Participants record their answers directly into the computer, from which they can be accessed, compiled, analyzed, and reported to provide the continuing educator with information on the extent to which the educational activity is having an impact. This process streamlines data analysis and reporting, reducing data handling costs and permitting the continuing educator to implement evaluation findings almost immediately. Undoubtedly opportunities for simplified, direct evaluation and data analysis, interpretation, reporting, and application to educational activities will increase as use of this kind of technology becomes more widespread.

Other Considerations

Evaluation exercises that are the same as those used for the needs assessment permit comparison of pre- and postassessment scores.

This can be an excellent means of evaluating program effectiveness. Identical questions can be asked or assessment activities can be repeated. However, if the individuals who participated in the needs assessment also participate in the evaluation, it is possible that they will remember these questions or activities. This familiarity could lead to evaluation data that reflect memorization of acceptable responses rather than whatever learning has taken place. Creating evaluation questions or exercises that differ in detail from but are comparable to those used for the needs assessment avoid this problem yet can obtain information that is directly comparable. Use of pre- and posttests also can be useful at the start and conclusion of an educational activity if program participants are not the same people who participated in the needs assessment. Pretest findings can be compared with the needs assessment data to determine the extent to which program participants' needs mirror those identified through the assessment. The continuing educator can also compare data from the pre- and posttests to determine the extent to which participants' knowledge, skills, or performance abilities were improved by the educational activity.

It is possible to declare an educational activity successful in addressing needs if the evaluation indicates any reduction—even a slight one—in those needs. However, given the impreciseness of both needs assessment and evaluation measures, it is difficult to defend such a statement unless the small changes appear as a trend over time. A more realistic and justifiable approach is to establish criteria to define an educational activity's success in addressing needs. Just as standards are established for needs assessment to determine at which point a need exists, standards in evaluation specify the point at which an educational activity can be considered to have satisfactorily addressed the needs it was intended to address. As with needs assessment, these standards can be based on an established average, or norm, or on specified criteria to be met, including improvement in the knowledge, skills, or performance abilities identified as areas of discrepancy in the needs assessment. In each case, the level of attainment considered indicative of success is critical to interpreting the data collected and should be established before the evaluation. If improvement is the standard to be used, the amount of improvement desired or expected should be defined. For example, does the ability to respond correctly to three more questions in the evaluation than in the needs assessment mean program success in addressing needs, or must a greater number of questions be answered correctly?

In addition to measuring what was learned and applied, the continuing educator interested in learning about program effectiveness can ask participants about which aspects of the educational activity they found to be beneficial, about why they have or have not applied what they learned, and if they have suggestions for future programming. This information can be collected in either close-ended questions, with response options provided, or open-ended questions, in which participants are asked to put their suggestions in their own words. Close-ended questions are more easily quantified and analyzed, but open-ended questions provide a broader range of information and responses to them often can be coded and thus easily quantified.

Special Considerations

The differences between using the instruments and procedures described in Chapters Five, Six, and Seven for needs assessment and using them for program evaluation are minimal but merit some consideration. The basic procedures are the same for each method, but the ways in which the methods are administered (that is, selection of participants, location, timing) may vary slightly.

All enrollees in an educational activity may participate in the evaluation, or if the group is quite large or the evaluation procedure complicated or costly, a sample of the total group can be used. In the latter case, those included in the sample should be representative of the total population of participants in all pertinent characteristics (for example, prior knowledge and experience, educational level) so that their responses to the evaluation can be generalized to the total population they represent.

As mentioned earlier in this chapter, most continuing education program evaluations are summative in nature; that is, they are conducted after the educational activity has been completed. The insights gained from summative evaluations can be used to revise the educational activity before offering it again and also may prove helpful for other programs. Furthermore, summative evaluation results enable the continuing educator and others to document the extent to which they were effective in addressing the needs identified through assessment. If positive, this information can be useful in validating their activities and in demonstrating the value of the needs assessment and program development process to individuals, employers, professional associations, and other clients. For decades a controversy has raged over the question of whether continuing education can or does affect daily activities and practice; any information showing a relationship between educational participation and diminished discrepancies is worthy of wide dissemination.

Summative evaluation may be immediate, conducted at the conclusion of an educational activity, or it may be a follow-up, carried out some weeks or months after the activity has been completed. Both time frames have advantages and disadvantages, and each lends itself to a somewhat different type of evaluation. Ideally, an evaluation is conducted at the activity's conclusion to obtain participants' immediate impressions, and a follow-up evaluation is conducted to gather information on the longer-term impact of the activity. However, not all educational activities merit such an extensive evaluation strategy.

Immediate Evaluation

Evaluation conducted at the conclusion of an educational activity provides immediate feedback and if handled on-site or incorporated in final activities, it generates a strong response rate. When all participants are in one location (for example, seminars, workshops, other on-site programs) a high level of participation is virtually assured since the continuing educator essentially has a captive audience. Even for distance education activities, participants are more likely to complete an evaluation exercise that is incorporated into the activity than a similar one that is to be completed at a later date. For those activities carrying some type of credit or credential, such as a Continuing Education Unit or credit toward mandatory continuing education, completion of the evaluation may be a condition for granting of that credit, thus offering a strong motivation.

Evaluations conducted at the conclusion of a seminar, workshop, or other location-specific program are distributed before the program is wrapped up. The continuing educator builds sufficient time into the program for their completion and collects them before the participants leave. Because response rates drop considerably when participants take evaluations with them for completion at home or in the office, the program time devoted to evaluation is well spent. Furthermore, on-site evaluations permit use of a wider range of evaluation strategies, such as focus groups, demonstrations of skills, and methods incorporating technical equipment, whereas evaluations completed away from the activity site usually are limited to paper and pencil questionnaires and exercises.

Immediate evaluation has advantages beyond the response rate. Specific details of an educational activity are fresh in participants' minds. These details, ranging from a confusing example to a particularly good explanation of a new concept, can lead to program improvements and should not be lost. Because of the currency of the experience and the enthusiasm the activity may have spawned, participants may provide more information, and more detailed information, in an immediate evaluation than in an evaluation at a later date. If any serious deficiencies or areas of strong interest are identified, the continuing educator may find it possible to send participants additional information while these issues are fresh in their minds. Similarly, if any glaring misconceptions have emerged, they can be corrected by a prompt follow-up communication.

Lack of time for participants to reflect on and apply what they have learned from the educational activity is the biggest drawback to conducting evaluations at the conclusion of a program. Only time can tell if participants will retain the information imparted or if they will absorb and apply what they have learned. However, in addition to the previously noted drawbacks to delaying evaluation, intervening factors (such as changes in a work setting, additional education, new experiences) may have effects that cannot easily be separated from the effects of the educational activity, making it unclear whether the changes observed later are the result of the educational activity or of other influences.

If a continuing educator decides to conduct an immediate evaluation, it is possible to at least partially compensate for the brief time participants have for reflection. Questions that lead them to identify ways in which they will apply what they have learned force them to think beyond the simple acquisition of information to its use in their routine activities. "What two things that you have learned in this seminar do you expect to be most useful to you?" and "Please give an example of a situation in which you expect to use the technique presented in this workshop" are examples of such questions. Questions of this type require people to make connections between the material covered in the continuing education activity and its use, and to articulate its potential applications in their work, leisure, family, or community activities.

Follow-Up Evaluation

As already noted, evaluations conducted some time after the program's conclusion provide an opportunity for the continuing educator to determine the extent to which an educational activity resulted in ongoing enhancements or changes in knowledge, skills, or performance abilities. These evaluations, which ideally measure the impact of an educational activity on participants' practices and behaviors, usually are more complex and costly than immediate evaluations. Measurement of impact simply is more difficult than measurement of knowledge, skills, and performance abilities acquired, because most impact evaluation involves consideration of ways in which the material learned is being applied.

Continuing educators usually conduct follow-up evaluations from three to six months after the activity. The timing will depend on the type of learning that was expected to take place and its intended use. For example, if the educational activity focused on skills intended for daily use, three months would allow adequate time for participants to either incorporate those skills in their routine activities or discard them. In contrast, if the educational content was intended for only occasional use, six months might be required in order to allow sufficient time. As the time between completion of the educational activity and the evaluation increases, the likelihood of other factors affecting the evaluation results increases. Because these other factors, such as additional education or new procedures, can have an impact on the areas being evaluated, attributing changes to the educational activity becomes less defensible. For this reason and because participants' recollection of the educational activity itself will become less clear with time, few evaluations of individual educational activities should occur more than six months after the activity itself.

Because participants' responses to a follow-up evaluation are rooted in their work, home, or community settings, data collected are less controlled, and hence less uniform and comparable, than data collected at the conclusion of an educational activity. Follow-up data most often are collected through self-reports, observation, or review of records or other products of practice (Cervero, 1988, p. 142). A clear causal relationship between the educational activity and the knowledge, skills, or performance abilities evaluated is not readily established, not only because of the subjectiveness of the data but also because of the potential influence of intervening factors. Still, follow-up evaluation can provide some information on the lasting effects of an educational activity and for this reason it is valuable.

At the conclusion of an educational activity for which a follow-up evaluation will be conducted, participants should be advised that they will be contacted for this purpose and that their cooperation is essential if the continuing educator is to serve them and their colleagues well. Because the rate of response to evaluations often decreases markedly after completion of the educational activity, it may be desirable to encourage responses. If participants are asked to respond to a questionnaire or evaluation instrument by mail, electronic mail, or other means that requires some action on their part, the continuing educator should follow the suggestions for increasing response rates detailed in Chapter Six. Because response rates are higher for telephone or face-to-face interviews, these methods merit consideration if they are appropriate to the type of evaluation needed.

Interpreting and Reporting Evaluation Results

As with other types of educational program evaluation, the results of an evaluation of an educational activity's effectiveness in meeting assessed needs can be used in several ways. The data collected can be used for program improvement, identifying ways in which the educational activity can be enhanced to meet even more effectively the needs it was designed to address. From the evaluation the continuing educator may learn that some content areas should be covered in greater detail, whereas others should be incorporated into other activities. The evaluation may indicate that certain formats, delivery modes, teaching styles, or other aspects of the activity are ineffective in helping participants learn. This information can be used to improve existing activities and in future program planning. If the evaluation shows that the educational activity does indeed address the assessed needs successfully, it can be used to justify the activity to those who have supported participants' enrollment, for example, and to promote it to other audiences.

A properly designed evaluation instrument will result in data that can be reported and interpreted easily and in a straightforward manner. The purpose of an evaluation report is to communicate information clearly, not to dazzle the audience. Clear and accurate reporting facilitates meaningful interpretation of the data for continuing educators' use in decision making about the educational activity being evaluated and about future programming. Ambiguous information is likely to be misunderstood. Continuing educators should interpret data in the context of the type of evaluation conducted, including the methodology, population or sample characteristics, and timing. They should note any limitations of the method used or its application, making adjustments for them as appropriate. Acknowledgment of the evaluation's limitations will avoid misinterpretation or overly strong reliance on partial or weak data, and in the long run it may protect the continuing educator from accusations of false claims. Isolating the effects of the program from external factors unrelated to the educational activity also is important, although difficult. These external factors may include "changes in procedures, processes, and technology . . . experience and maturity of [participants]" (American Society for Training and Development, 1986, p. 6), and other learning experiences. It is a good idea to be objective and to quantify data whenever possible. Examples of data that can be understood and applied readily are descriptions of specific pieces of information that program participants were given or specific tasks that had been beyond their reach but that they learned to perform.

Because evaluation results facilitate and support informed decision making, they will be of interest to several groups. For the continuing educator, of course, evaluation data will provide information to be used in future program planning. Improvements in the existing program, marketing strategies, and new programming ideas can arise from evaluation data. Enrollees in the educational activity, particularly but not exclusively those who participated in the evaluation, will be eager to learn of the program's success in meeting its objectives. From the evaluation data they may gain insights into ways in which they can continue or reinforce the learning that occurred. And the employers and other individuals or organizations who supported participants in the educational activity will want to know what their resources bought them to enhance their accountability. Evaluation data that indicate an educational activity's success in meeting identified needs can help all of these parties justify the decisions they made with regard to the educational activity. The information also can help people make informed decisions about future use of continuing education, choose from among available opportunities, recognize strengths, gaps, or discrepancies in the continuing education that they are either delivering or finding available to them, and address personal or organizational missions and goals.

Evaluation results sometimes will be negative. It is tempting but totally unproductive to push such results aside. Although such findings can be extremely disappointing, they often are among the most instructive results. They should not be seen as a sign of failure but rather as a series of constructive criticisms that can be used to improve the activity evaluated and to guide future program design, development, and delivery. Negative results are less overwhelming and more manageable when separated into individual components, to be examined one by one for the suggestions for improvement they can yield. A list of positive steps to be taken should emerge from such an examination.

Summary

Evaluation of continuing education activities can be a fairly simple examination of operational factors, such as the financial success of the endeavor or participants' satisfaction with the amenities (for example, the site, meals) surrounding the event. However, continuing educators and their colleagues who are truly concerned about the quality of the education they provide welcome evaluation as an opportunity to learn about the effectiveness and the impact of that education. This can highlight the things they are doing well and identify ways to improve performance. In this sense, evaluation can be considered as a needs assessment for the continuing educator, pointing out the strengths and weaknesses of the finished product, the educational activity. However, evaluation viewed in this manner is valid only if it is entered into with an open mind and a commitment to ongoing improvement.

This perspective is intensified when evaluation is applied to educational activities that have been designed specifically to address educational needs. The continuing educator responsible for these activities has made a commitment to providing education that addresses identified discrepancies, creating the expectation that those discrepancies will be diminished by participation in the educational activities offered. This is a difficult assignment, one with which the continuing educator may not realize overwhelming success for some time. Evaluation not only offers the opportunity to measure progress toward this goal but also has the potential to provide information that can bring its attainment closer.

Any conscientious continuing educator wants the information that evaluation offers. The continuing educator who seeks to improve knowledge, skills, and performance abilities through appropriate continuing education recognizes evaluation as a key factor in doing so.

Chapter Ten

Institutionalizing Needs Assessment for Continuing Education

When integrated into the program planning process, needs assessment can help continuing educators design, develop, and deliver educational activities that will serve individual learners, employers, and society while also meeting the continuing educator's own organizational goals. Although careful assessments do not ensure the instructional and financial success of all activities, they increase the likelihood of such success. However, needs assessment does not stand alone. It is more than a useful tool for continuing educators. In reality, it is related to power and to institutional and organizational politics, both within higher education and in the organizations represented by continuing education clients. Continuing education itself is part of a larger organization or institution that is "a major, if not *the* major, determinant of continuing educators' understanding of effective practice" (Cervero, 1988, p. 75). That organization has many operational and political agendas, among them the development and delivery of educational activities to fulfill a strategic plan, further a mission, reward faculty members, court potential benefactors, enhance the institutional image, or serve target populations. Within the context of such political and ethical dimensions, continuing educators can use needs assessment data to support both individual and organizational agendas. Conversely, continuing educators might find that the most comprehensive, thoroughly derived needs assessment data are cast aside if they conflict with the prevailing political climate or if another agenda has priority. Despite all the logic that might be brought to bear on a decision, "a very high priority target audience need may go unaddressed because colleagues have other commitments and interests, or because the need does not align well with [institutional] priorities" (Gilmore, Campbell, and Becker, 1989, p. 14). Ultimately, regardless of how appropriate an educational activity may seem, continuing educators cannot be successful if that activity is not compatible with their organizational and institutional goals (Cervero, 1988, p. 93). Similar circumstances govern acceptance of needs assessment data by those organizations (for example, businesses, health care agencies and institutions) the continuing educators strive to serve. Despite all efforts to create an atmosphere that is open to needs assessment findings, some data may not be acknowledged because they do not fit into an organization's larger agenda.

Multiple constituent groups can exist both within and outside of the continuing educator's institution. These groups might include other administrators, faculty members, and units within the institution; learners; employers of learners; and society in general. Whose interests should be served by needs assessment? What is the continuing educator's responsibility regarding the use of needs assessment data? Honest appraisal of these questions before conducting a needs assessment is the key to ensuring that the results will be used effectively and with integrity. Most successfully implemented needs assessments begin with an openness to all possible purposes, then focus on the particular purposes that are perceived as compatible with the constituents to be served, the political climate, and the continuing educator's strategic plan and mission. Thus, in addition to considering available resources and other factors as discussed in earlier chapters, the continuing educator striving to make needs assessment an integral part of the planning process also takes into account the politics of the situation, the people who have a problem they want solved, and the best ways of communicating with those people (Rossett, 1987, p. 226).

Questions about who will or will not want the needs assessment, who should be kept informed of the findings, and who will welcome the findings should remain in the forefront of the continuing educator's thinking. Often continuing educators can anticipate the concerns and agendas of various potential stakeholders and integrate them as a needs assessment is developed. They can prepare the needs assessment report and the evaluation of the resultant educational activities to address those factors.

Following the course suggested by needs assessment can lead to market identification and definition. Because continuing education units frequently are market driven and have financial accountability as a top priority, they may be tempted to adapt needs assessment as a market indicator. For example, in the name of fulfilling needs, continuing educators "can easily disguise subtle and perhaps unconscious manipulation . . . whereby cost-benefit or system-maintenance or the educator's personal preference becomes the sole criterion for the sponsorship of educational programs" (Monette, 1977, p. 124). The opportunity to seek information on what will sell is a powerful draw; furthermore, following needs assessment to a market is not necessarily a bad thing. However, when exploiting the market becomes the dominant basis for programming decisions, the compatibility of the approach with the political, ethical, and educational climate merits examination. It is frequently more justifiable and desirable to try to achieve a balance between the agendas. Any needs assessment can address more than one agenda, and it is possible to be attentive to several or even all relevant agendas while identifying one as the primary focus. When continuing educators routinely include needs assessment in the program development process, they find that it is possible to emphasize one agenda in one needs assessment and others in other assessments.

Application of Needs Assessment Data

Needs assessment does not end with completion of the data collection, analysis, interpretation, and report that result in identification of needs, it ends with integration of needs assessment data into the decision-making processes that guide program planning (McKillip, 1987). Continuing educators and their colleagues can discuss application of needs assessment data in conjunction with the report of assessment described in Chapter Eight, or they can do so in a separate context. In either case, discussion of the use of needs assessment findings goes beyond interpreting and reporting the findings to making recommendations and convincing the appropriate people and organizations that specific actions should be taken. This type of discussion offers continuing educators opportunities to demonstrate the usefulness of the data collected and the value of the educational activities they are able to develop and deliver as a result of needs assessment. The continuing educator undertaking a needs assessment generally assumes that the data gathered will be utilized to make decisions about educational activities, but in reality this is dependent on acceptance of the value of the data and the process through which they were obtained as well as on the institutional climate. Key decision makers' recognition of needs assessment as an integral part of the larger continuing education program design, development, and delivery process is an essential step in providing educational activities that can affect performance and practice. Frequently the importance of needs assessment is not established, and as a result, needs assessment data are not fully used and the potential value of the process is not appreciated. When this happens, continuing educators may encounter a lack of confidence in their abilities to provide meaningful educational activities.

Effective communication by the continuing educator and others with direct responsibility for conducting a needs assessment can help alleviate this problem. Continual communication throughout the needs assessment process is ideal, but because of time, distance, and opportunities for interaction it often is not feasible. Those with decision-making power and responsibility are the primary audience for any discussion of the application of needs assessment findings, and they may be within the continuing education unit, elsewhere in the educational institution, or in the managerial structure of external clients such as employers or professional associations. Communication with them should take place in a forum that is small enough to permit open exchange of ideas, and in which the levels and interests of participants are sufficiently similar to encourage a common dialogue. Continuing educators may best serve additional people with known interest in the topic by providing different types of presentations, oral or written. For those potentially interested parties furthest from the decision making, the continuing educator can distribute a simple summary sheet with an invitation to request more information if it is desired.

Like most people, key decision makers have greatest receptivity to information when it is presented in a manner compatible with their backgrounds, interests, and expectations. Information about needs assessment processes and data is no exception. By becoming familiar with the decision makers' perspective, continuing educators may be able to tailor their presentations to their audience and anticipate and be prepared for possible problem areas and controversies. They can discuss implications of the assessment and its application in a manner that emphasizes the benefits of basing decisions on the assessment findings, benefits that would be lacking had the assessment not been conducted.

Discussion of the use of needs assessment data is needed for several reasons, primarily to encourage decision makers to support the design, development, and delivery of continuing education activities based on documented needs. Discussion of needs assessment data also highlights the opportunities identified through the assessment and emphasizes the importance of data-based decision making for continuing education programming. In many cases, the data obtained will point to areas of need or interest not directly related to continuing education but important to other units or organizations. Finally, by building awareness of the use of needs assessment, continuing educators can broaden understanding of the extent of their commitment to a sound process for serving their constituents. They can help create an expectation that needs assessments will be conducted as a regular part of the continuing education program development process, and an understanding that documented needs must exist if they are to act on a faculty member's, client's, or other partner's ideas for educational activities.

Discussion of information in a simple, straightforward fashion, with important points highlighted almost in outline form, helps decision makers form consistent judgments in an efficient manner (McKillip, 1987, p. 106). Decision makers' ability to interpret data and their acceptance of findings vary with their experience, values, and political and other agendas. As already mentioned, continuing educators can present the information in the context of these factors when they are known, enabling the audience to assimilate the needs assessment results within a framework that is significant to them. Room for judgment always will exist, and indeed it should. "Judgmental, value-laden aspects of the process" cannot be avoided, but rather should be "explicit and open to negotiation and experimentation" (McKillip, 1987, p. 118).

Like the needs assessment report that precedes it, communication about the application of needs assessment can be either oral or written, or some combination of the two. However, relying entirely on written communication eliminates the opportunities afforded by discussion. Oral communication, whether face-to-face or via some form of distance linkage, provides an opportunity for interaction and questions. It also allows the continuing educator or other needs assessment spokesperson to gauge the audience's receptivity and adapt to both verbal and nonverbal responses given. Because many decisions can hinge on these discussions, they are not occasions for everyone involved to have a chance to perform but rather for the most knowledgeable, articulate, and engaging speakers available to take the stage. Speakers can be brief in their suggestions for using the needs assessment results, thereby encouraging people to ask for more information as they are drawn in by the presentation of ideas. In addition to drafting introductory remarks, the continuing educator and others promoting use of the needs assessment can prepare for this discussion by anticipating likely questions and devising possible responses. Brainstorming with others who have been involved in the needs assessment and related activities can be useful in this regard.

Written presentations permit those receiving them to review them at their convenience and their own pace, and they give the decision makers facts and figures to refer to in the future. However, there is no guarantee that they will ever be read, or even skimmed. In preparing both oral and written information, it is useful to remember that people often are busy and want to get right to the bottom line. As long as they are given an opportunity to ask questions and raise additional issues, most decision makers will appreciate succinct presentation of information.

Reporting Evaluation Results

Once needs assessment data have been used to develop an educational activity, evaluation (as discussed in Chapter Nine) can measure the data's value in guiding the design, development, and delivery of the activity. Evaluation data that indicate that the assessed needs were addressed with some degree of success allow the continuing educator to demonstrate to key decision makers that needs assessment can indeed lead to meaningful educational activities. It is important to present these factors objectively and honestly, although different aspects of the evaluation may be reported to different audiences and it is up to the continuing educator to determine what to present to each. For example, people in a position to make changes based on the evaluation should have access to all information that can help them with this task. Other audiences may be interested only in knowing, at the most general level, which factors were evaluated most highly and which were deemed in need of the most extensive improvement.

Most evaluations reflect both strengths and weaknesses in meeting the assessed needs. By discussing both the successes and failures openly with key decision makers, continuing educators can actively involve them in using the needs assessment data and thus make the needs assessment/program development process more meaningful. Offering an opportunity to suggest ways in which the needs assessment and subsequent evaluation data can further guide the redesign and delivery of the same or related educational activities can strengthen their commitment. Evaluation data can be reported in terms ranging from the activity's amelioration of measured or perceived needs to its financial statement and the number of people it served. Other ramifications, such as an activity's potential for building or enhancing partnerships, strengthening fund-raising, or highlighting faculty and institutional resources, may not have been explicit in the needs assessment but might be included in discussion of the evaluation. Discussion of a program's evaluation is unique in that it provides the continuing educator with an opportunity to demonstrate the relationship between needs assessment and program success, to show that needs were identified and met, indicating that continuing education can make a difference. It also can be used to set the stage for next steps to be taken.

Building Institutional Commitment to Needs Assessment

If needs assessment is to become an integral part of the continuing education program development process, the support of two groups is important. First, continuing educators themselves, at all levels within the continuing education unit or organization, must recognize the value of assessing needs. They must be willing to devote the time and other resources necessary to assess needs regularly, and they must be sufficiently committed to the concept to make it a routine step in their operations. Second, faculty members, administrators, clients, and other continuing education partners must be convinced of the merit of needs assessment so that they, too, are willing to allocate the resources and endure the delays that are inherent in integrating needs assessment into the program development process. All parties must do more than pay lip service to the value of needs assessment; they must be committed to the concept of identifying learners' needs in order to serve them better.

The most effective, and some would say essential, way to build this commitment is to involve people in one or more aspects of the needs assessment process. Involvement of key decision makers not only contributes to their understanding of the value of needs assessment but also gives them a sense of ownership of the process. Occasionally these people, whether from within continuing education or external to it, may have the skills, experience, interest, and time, to play a role in actually conducting the needs assessment. However, it is more likely that this kind of participation will not be feasible. Fortunately, membership on committees that help with needs assessment offers other, frequently more appropriate, opportunities for involvement.

Committees can be either ad hoc (convened for a specific event or activity) or standing (Gilmore, Campbell, and Becker, 1989, pp. 15–18). Continuing educators are most likely to form ad hoc needs assessment committees to participate in or respond to a specific assessment or series of assessments. Standing committees may take a more proactive role, requesting that needs assessments be conducted as well as offering guidance for specific assessments. With both committee types, it is important that continuing educators limit the questions asked and responsibilities given them to those on which they do not already have firm opinions, commitments, or ideas. Establishing parameters or ground rules also is critical to the smooth operation of such groups.

The size and membership of committees can vary widely. A committee should be large enough to include a diversity of perspectives but not so large that it is unwieldy, that all members cannot be heard, or that individuals lack the sense that their contributions are important. Committees ranging in size from ten to sixteen members are ideal in meeting these criteria. Committee membership can include key decision makers or those known to influence them; individuals with expertise in continuing education, program planning, higher education, or the content areas to be addressed; representatives of the target population or those who supervise or interact with them; and past continuing education participants. In addition to these qualifications, continuing educators should seek committee members with qualities such as good interpersonal, communications, and listening skills; effective leadership; motivation; a sense of priorities; and enthusiasm for the project (Black, 1983), as well as the flexibility to adapt to different goals, circumstances, and conditions. Furthermore, it may be desirable for committee membership to reflect a balance between people appointed primarily for political reasons and people appointed specifically because they bring an informed perspective on some aspect of the needs assessment or its implementation. Appointments to ad hoc committees, by the very nature of the committees, are short-term. By specifying a term for appointments to standing committees, the continuing educator ensures a mechanism for regular, orderly membership change. Learning how the needs assessment process—and often, the continuing education organization—works takes time, so continuity may be important, but sometimes a standing committee can benefit from fresh appointments (Drucker, 1990).

The primary role, or charge, of some committees may to be serve as liaisons between continuing educators and academic departments, students, or organizational clients. That of others may be to lend credibility to the needs assessment process. Each of these purposes can be valid, but each must be accompanied by a practical function for the group: the design and implementation of a needs assessment, or the interpretation and application of the needs assessment data, for example. The tasks must fit the capabilities of its members; they should not be asked to address issues about which they lack knowledge or experience. A committee's underlying purpose and its functions may be identical or they may differ. They would be the same, for example, if the charge is to establish a program development strategy based on the needs assessment results. But in another case—for example, if a committee's purpose is to involve people or legitimize the needs assessment process—tasks must be specified. In such cases the tasks may be to review the needs assessment strategy or materials, or to provide suggestions for interpreting and reporting the data collected. The tasks must be work that is really needed, and the continuing educator must be prepared to include it. Even when the committee's performance of these tasks is secondary to its purpose, they must be meaningful and completion of them should generate a sense of accomplishment among committee members.

Two types of committees commonly are used in various aspects of needs assessment. They are advisory committees, which are recommending bodies, and planning committees, which are empowered to make decisions.

Advisory Committees

As their name implies, advisory committees provide ideas, insights, and suggestions to those responsible for conducting the needs assessment. To make sure that everyone serving on an advisory committee understands that it is a recommending, rather than decision-making, body, this role should be made clear to members when they are asked to serve. Because they are not policy-making bodies, advisory committees' recommendations may be accepted or rejected. The continuing educator is under no obligation to do anything more than consider the points raised, although repeated failure to heed any of the group's suggestions will cause committee members to question the desirability of contributing their time. For this reason, continuing educators would do well to ask advisory committees to address only those issues that they truly want an opinion on and that they really have an open mind about. Discussion of issues that already have been decided benefits no one.

It is helpful to identify the areas in which advisory committee input is needed, desired, or has potential to be useful from the start and then structure the committee meetings to address them. Discussion that turns to an undesirable topic does not have to be terminated immediately, but it should not be allowed to continue at length. The advisory committee should be informed that final decisions on that topic already have been made, and it is unlikely that those decisions will be altered. At no time should continuing educators lead advisory committee members to believe that their recommendations will be considered if, in fact, there is no intention to do so. Although the continuing educator may not choose to follow an advisory committee recommendation, committee members have the right to expect that all of their suggestions will receive serious consideration unless they are advised otherwise.

Planning Committees

Planning committees have greater power than advisory committees. Under most circumstances acceptance of the planning committee's recommendations is not optional. Planning committees are policy-making bodies, and as such they become partners of the continuing educator and other staff members conducting a needs assessment (Drucker, 1990). For this reason, the charge that a continuing educator gives to a planning committee is particularly critical. A committee should be asked to address only those areas in which members are competent and adequately informed, and on which their decisions will be welcome and beneficial to the needs assessment process. Depending on the specific areas included in their charge, planning committees may take an active role in making decisions ranging from identifying sample populations and content areas for assessment to determining which educational activities should be developed on the basis of the data collected.

Working with committees can be both a blessing and a curse. Given the opportunity, their recommendations and actions can have a strong positive impact on continuing education activities. Because committee members are able to gain firsthand experience of the benefits to be derived from needs assessment, they can serve as advocates for continuing education activities and as representatives of the continuing educator's viewpoint. They can justify the course of action selected and convince others of its merit. However, by inviting others' advice or giving them a role in the needs assessment process, continuing educators relinquish some autonomy. They must be willing to accept ideas that differ from their own and to move in directions they may not have chosen. Although the extent of these concessions can be minimized by careful structuring of committees' roles and agendas, committees do need some latitude. When people are asked to serve on committees they expect to be active participants. As such, they require the flexibility to move things in the directions they deem appropriate.

An Institutional Role for Needs Assessment

Organizational and institutional leaders often use strategic planning to ensure that a college or university, business, industry, professional association, or other organization does not operate haphazardly. Strategic planning encourages formation of a clear mission, goals, and an active, rather than passive, course of action. An important feature of strategic planning is that it "looks outward and is focused on keeping the institution in step with the changing environment" (Keller, 1983, p. 145).

Needs assessment can be a useful tool in strategic planning. It can provide the solid information required for data-based decision making. Through effective, ongoing needs assessment, continuing educators can shape their programs in light of local, national, and international trends reflected in individuals' day-to-day professional and personal practices.

The extent to which such institutional benefits of continuing education needs assessment are possible is directly related to the degree to which the following conditions are met.

- Continuing educators and those working with them must be committed to quality in needs assessment and to its use in their program development process. Poorly conceived and executed needs assessments will result in poor data, leading to bad programming decisions and eventually, to an erosion of confidence in continuing education. It is better to omit a needs assessment altogether than do a shoddy job of it.

- Recognition of the value of needs assessment must extend beyond those intimately involved to those in other areas of the institutions and the organizations involved. Organizational and institutional leaders who are made aware of the benefits likely to be derived from needs assessment will support its use, but they cannot appreciate these benefits if they do not know about them.

- People involved in all facets of needs assessment and its implementation must be truth seekers, approaching needs assessment with open minds and receptivity to the new ideas it may bring. They must be willing to set aside their own interests and preferences if they conflict with the concrete data generated by needs assessment.

- The continuing education unit itself must have respect, a recognized role, and centrality within the larger organization that it is a part of. Without this position, continuing education can use needs assessment to guide its own work but will lose the opportunity to put it to its optimum use—for the organizational good.

Clearly, the last condition is the most difficult, and one with which continuing educators have struggled for several decades.

Often the continuing education or training function is viewed as less rigorous, less committed to excellence, or simply more removed from mainstream activity than other units in an organization. This situation exists not only in higher education but also in professional associations and business and industry. Needs assessment can be a route away from this marginal role assigned to continuing education. Through programming based on rigorous needs assessment, continuing educators can serve the clients that are important to their institutions and organizations. Needs assessment can help them deliver education that has an impact on professional practice and quality of life. It can help them identify the people who are eager to apply the research results coming out of their universities, and to learn of the gaps left by standard education. These uses of needs assessment reflect the kinds of goals set in the strategic plans of the organizations represented and served by continuing education. Can it be that needs assessment is continuing education's ticket to integration into its parent and client organizations?

Summary

Needs assessment can be an isolated activity for continuing educators, helping them identify the content, target audience, and optimal delivery for a specific educational activity. This limited use of needs assessment is valid, and it is likely to result in better program design, development, and delivery than otherwise might occur. However, needs assessment can do more than that. Continuing educators can use it to optimize their service to clients and to enhance the organizations and institutions they represent.

The continuing education division of a large state university approached an organization employing engineers at several locations across the United States. Through discussion with the organization's leaders, the continuing educators learned that there were no existing opportunities for the engineers to further their education. There simply were no colleges or universities with engineering programs in reasonable proximity of any of the organization's plants. The continuing educators recognized this situation as an opportunity to highlight their distance education capabilities, feature their very strong engineering college, develop innovative programming that could bring recognition to their institution, and serve a sizable (and hence possibly lucrative) audience. This potential fit well with their own organizational mission and goals, which included building a national reputation as a leader in distance education, building collaborative relationships with and showcasing outstanding faculty members, enhancing their institution's reputation for creativity and excellence, and last but not least, generating income.

The continuing educators went to the engineering college to determine the level of interest and resources available there. They learned that the college would consider offering an extended degree at least partially via distance education and that some of its faculty members within certain departments were willing to participate in such a program. The continuing education division itself had a range of distance education capabilities and a mandate to use them.

A two-pronged needs assessment was the next step. First, the continuing educators conducted a focus group, inviting managers in the target organization to share their views of the educational needs of the engineers they supervised. They also asked this group for suggestions on educational program scheduling and on potential barriers. Second, they used questionnaires to collect information from the engineers themselves, asking about their educational background, their educational goals, the types of courses they believed they needed, their interest in pursuing additional education, and their scheduling preferences. From these assessment measures the continuing educators determined that both the managers and the potential participants believed that the greatest educational need was in the area of acoustical engineering. The engineers could not leave their job sites for extended periods of time, but they could take courses during the work day. They were eager to pursue master's degrees, but they felt that they could handle no more than two courses per semester.

The continuing educators put together a project team that included representatives of the employing organization, the engineering college, and their own distance education and program development units. This team developed a strategy for offering the engineers at various organization locations an existing master's degree program that would include specific courses suggested by the needs assessment. Most courses would be transmitted by satellite, with the capability of two-way interaction. However, students would have to spend one month during each of two summers at the university in order to use laboratory facilities for some course work. A faculty member would visit their work site once each year to meet with students who were ready for an in-depth discussion of their thesis proposals.

This effort resulted in a viable program that was based on assessed needs and tailored to the unique requirements and preferences of the group that was assessed. It allowed the continuing educators to use a variety of resources, including technology and faculty members, to provide a program for which they have since received a national award. The needs assessment on which the program was based was neither costly nor complex, but it provided the information needed to guide the program design, development, and delivery.

When needs assessment is allowed to become an integral part of the continuing education program development process it has the potential to make every activity meet a defined goal, suit a purpose, or further an organizational priority. Needs assessment can enable continuing educators to excel.

References

American Society for Training and Development. *Essentials for Evaluation*. Info-line. Alexandria, Va.: American Society for Training and Development, 1986.

Apps, J. W. *The Adult Learner on Campus*. Chicago: Follett, 1981.

Arbeiter, S., Aslanian, C. B., Schmerbeck, F. A., and Brickell, H. M. *40 Million Americans in Career Transition: The Need for Information*. New York: College Entrance Examination Board, 1978.

Argyris, C., and Schön, D. A. *Theory in Practice: Increasing Professional Effectiveness*. San Francisco: Jossey-Bass, 1974.

Aslanian, C. B. "The Causes and Timing of Adult Learning." *Adults and the Changing Workplace*. Arlington, Va.: American Vocational Association, 1985a.

Aslanian, C. B. "Community Assessment Project." Presentation to Harvard University's Institute for the Management of Lifelong Education, Boston, June 14, 1985b.

Aslanian, C. B. "Back from the Future." Presentation at the National University Continuing Education Association Conference, New Orleans, Apr. 1990.

Aslanian, C. B., and Brickell, H. M. *How Americans in Transition Study for College Credit*. New York: College Entrance Examination Board, 1988.

Atwood, H. M., and Ellis, J. "The Concept of Need: An Analysis for Adult Education." *Adult Education*, 1971, *19*(7), 210–212.

Black, R. *The Best of Black Notes*. Washington, D.C.: American Symphony Orchestra League, 1983.

Boyle, P. G. *Planning Better Programs*. New York: McGraw-Hill, 1981.

Bradburn, N. M. and Sudman, S. *Improving Interview Method and Questionnaire Design*. San Francisco: Jossey-Bass, 1979.

Bradshaw, J. "The Concept of Social Need." *Ekistics*, 1974, *220*, 184–187.

Brookfield, S. D. *Understanding and Facilitating Adult Learning*. San Francisco: Jossey-Bass, 1986.

Byham, W. C. "The Assessment Center as an Aid in Management Development." *Training and Development Journal*, 1980, 34(6), 24–33.

Cervero, R. M. *Effective Continuing Education for Professionals*. San Francisco: Jossey-Bass, 1988.

Cizek, G. J. "Innovation or Enervation? Performance Assessment in Perspective." *Phi Delta Kappan*, 1991, 72(9), 695–699.

Crowl, T. K. *Fundamentals of Research: A Practical Guide for Educators and Special Educators*. Columbus, Ohio Publishing Horizons, 1986.

Dagavarian, D. A. *Proceedings of the National Institute on the Assessment of Experiential Learning*. Trenton, N.J.: Thomas Edison State College, 1990.

Daloz, L. A. *Effective Teaching and Mentoring*. San Francisco: Jossey-Bass, 1986.

Delbecq, A. L., Van de Ven, A. H., and Gustafson, D. H. *Group Techniques for Program Planning: A Guide to Nominal Group and Delphi Processes*. Glenview, Ill.: Scott, Foresman, 1975.

Deming, W. E. *Out of the Crisis*. Cambridge, Mass.: MIT Center for Advanced Engineering Study, 1986.

Development Dimensions International. *Skills Diagnostic Program*. Pittsburgh, Penn.: Development Dimensions International, n.d., a.

Development Dimensions International. *What is an Assessment Center?* Pittsburgh, Penn.: Development Dimensions International, n.d., b.

Dillman, D. A. *Mail and Telephone Surveys: The Total Design Method*. New York: Wiley, 1978.

Drucker, P. F. *Managing the Nonprofit Organization*. New York: HarperCollins, 1990.

Dubin, S. S. "Maintaining Competence Through Updating." In S. L. Willis, and S. S. Dubin (eds.), *Maintaining Professional Competence*. San Francisco: Jossey-Bass, 1990.

Elman, S. E., and Lynton, E. A. "Assessment in Professional Education." Paper presented at National Conference on Assessment in Higher Education, Columbia, S.C., Oct. 1985.

Eurich, N. P. *The Learning Industry: Education for Adult Workers*. Princeton, N.J.: The Carnegie Foundation for the Advancement of Teaching, 1990.

Fernicola, K. L. "Your Members Can Tell You a Lot." *Association Management*, May 1987, 71–73.

Flexner, A. "Is Social Work a Profession?" *School and Society*, 1915, 1, 901–911.

Freedman, L. *Quality in Continuing Education*. San Francisco: Jossey-Bass, 1987.

Gilmore, G. D., Campbell, M. D., and Becker, B. L. *Needs Assessment Strategies for Health Education and Health Promotion*. Indianapolis: Benchmark Press, 1989.

Gross, S. J. *Of Foxes and Henhouses*. Westport, Conn.: Greenwood Press, 1984.

Hagedorn, H. J. A *Manual on State Mental Health Planning*, Document 017–024–00649–1. Washington, D.C.: Superintendent of Documents, 1977.

Houle, C. O. *Continuing Learning in the Professions*. San Francisco: Jossey-Bass, 1980.

Hutchings, P., and Marchese, T. "Watching Assessment: Questions, Stories, Prospects." *Change*, 1990, *22*(5), 12–38.

Keller, G. *Academic Strategy: The Management Revolution in American Higher Education*. Baltimore, Md.: The Johns Hopkins University Press, 1983.

Kennedy, D. W., and Queeney, D. S. "Marketing Continuing Medical Education Programs." *Journal of Continuing Education in the Health Professions*, 1991, *11*, 205–214.

Keil, E. C. *Assessment Centers: A Guide for Human Resource Management*. Reading, Mass.: Addison-Wesley, 1981.

Klevans, D. R. *Developing a Needs Assessment Plan in Continuing Professional Education*. University Park, Penn.: The Pennsylvania State University, 1987.

Klevans, D. R., Pollack, L. E., Smutz, W. D., and Vance, R. "Self-Assessment, Phase II." Presented at the 74th Annual Meeting of the American Dietetic Association, Dallas, Tex., Oct. 28, 1991.

Klevans, D. R., Smutz, W. D., Shuman, S. B., and Bershad, C. "Self-Assessment: Helping Professionals Discover What They Don't Know." In H.K.M. Baskett and V. Marsick (eds.), *Professionals' Ways of Knowing: New Findings on How to Improve Professional Education*, New Directions in Continuing Education, no. 55. San Francisco: Jossey-Bass, 1992.

Knowles, M. *The Modern Practice of Adult Education*. Chicago: Follett, 1980.

Knox, A. B. "Evaluating Continuing Professional Education." In R. M. Cervero and C. L. Scanlon (eds.), *Problems and Prospects in Continuing Education*, New Directions for Continuing Education, no. 27. San Francisco: Jossey-Bass, 1985.

Knox, A. B. *Helping Adults Learn*. San Francisco: Jossey-Bass, 1986.

Krueger, R. A. *Focus Groups: A Practical Guide for Applied Research*. Newbury Park, Calif.: Sage, 1988.

Lampe, S. "Getting the Most out of Needs Assessments." *Training*, 1986, *23*(10), 101–104.

MacKinnon, D. W. "How Assessment Centers Were Started in the United States." Pittsburgh, Penn.: Development Dimensions International, Monograph #1, 1991.

Manning, P. R., Lee, P. V., Denson, T. A., and Gilman, N. J. "Determining Educational Needs in the Physician's Office." *Journal of the American Medical Association*, 1980, *244*, 1112–1115.

Merriam, S. B., and Simpson, E. L. *A Guide to Research for Educators and Trainers of Adults*. Malabar, Fla.: Robert E. Krieger, 1989.

McKillip, J. *Needs Analysis: Tools for the Human Services and Education*. Newbury Park, Calif.: Sage, 1987.

Monette, M. L. "The Concept of Educational Need: An Analysis of Selected Literature." *Adult Education*, 1977, XXVII(2), 116–127.

Moore, C. M. *Group Techniques for Idea Building*. Newbury Park, Calif.: Sage, 1987.

Moore, D. E. "Assessing the Needs of Adults for Continuing Education: A Model." In F. C. Pennington (ed.), *Assessing Educational Needs of Adults*, New Directions for Continuing Education, no. 7. San Francisco: Jossey-Bass, 1980, 91–98.

Moses, J. L. "The Assessment Center Method." In J. L. Moses and W. C. Byham (eds.), *Applying the Assessment Center Method*. New York: Pergamon Press, 1977.

Moses, J. L., and Byham, W. C. *Applying the Assessment Center Method*. New York: Pergamon Press, 1977.

Nowlen, P. M. "Origins." In A. B. Knox (ed.), *Developing, Administering, and Evaluating Adult Education*. San Francisco: Jossey-Bass, 1980.

Nowlen, P. M. *A New Approach to Continuing Education for Business and the Professions*. New York: American Council on Education and Macmillan, 1988.

Office of Continuing Professional Education. *An Overview: Continuing Professional Education Development Project*. University Park, Penn.: The Pennsylvania State University, 1985.

Opinion Research Corporation. *American Attitudes Toward Higher Education*. Princeton, N.J.: Opinion Research Corporation, 1985.

Pennington, F. C. "Needs Assessment: Concepts, Models, and Characteristics." In F. C. Pennington (ed.), *Assessing Educational Needs of Adults*, New Directions for Continuing Education, no. 7. San Francisco: Jossey-Bass, 1980, 1–14.

Queeney, D. S. "Needs Assessment." In D. E. Tallman (ed.), *Adult Education Perspectives for Judicial Education*. Athens, Ga.: The University of Georgia, 1992.

Queeney, D. S., and Smutz, W. D. "Enhancing the Performance of Professionals: The Practice Audit Model." In S. L. Willis and S. S. Dubin (eds.), *Maintaining Professional Competence*. San Francisco: Jossey-Bass, 1990.

Queeney, D. S., Smutz, W. D., and Shuman, S. B. "Mandatory Continuing Professional Education: Old Issue, New Questions." *Continuing Higher Education Review*, 1990, 54 (Winter), 11–25.

Rossett, A. *Training Needs Assessment*. Englewood Cliffs, N.J.: Educational Technology Publications, 1987.

Safman, P. "Evaluating the Assessment: Did Anything Happen After We Left?" In F. C. Pennington (ed.), *Assessing Educational Needs of Adults*, New

Directions for Continuing Education, no. 7. San Francisco: Jossey-Bass, 1980, 83–90.

Schein, E. *Professional Education*. New York: McGraw-Hill, 1973.

Shimberg, B. S. *Occupational Licensing: A Public Perspective*. Princeton, N.J.: Educational Testing Service, 1982.

Simon, R. I., Dippo, D., and Schenke, A. *Learning Work: A Critical Pedagogy of Work Education*. New York: Bergin and Garvey, 1991.

Sleezer, C. M. "Needs Assessment: Perceptives from the Literature." *Performance Improvement Quarterly*, 1992, 5(2), 34–46.

Sleezer, C. M., and Swanson, R. A. "Culture Surveys." *Management Decision*, 1992, 30(2), 22–29.

Smutz, W. D., and Queeney, D. S. "Professionals as Learners: A Strategy for Maximizing Professional Growth." In R. M. Cervero and J. F. Azzaretto (eds.), *Visions for the Future of Continuing Professional Education*. Athens, Ga.: The University of Georgia, 1990.

Staff. "Report of the Practice Audit Session for Gerontological Nursing." Unpublished report. University Park, Penn.: The Pennsylvania State University, 1984.

Staff. *Continuing Professional Education Development Project Summary: Architecture*. University Park, Penn.: The Pennsylvania State University, 1985.

Staff. *Self-Assessment Series for Dietetics Professionals: Management Module*. University Park, Penn.: The Pennsylvania State University, 1992.

Stern, M. R. "A Disorderly Market." In M. R. Stern (ed.), *Power and Conflict in Continuing Professional Education*. Belmont, Calif.: Wadsworth, 1983.

Sudman, S., and Bradburn, N. M. *Asking Questions: A Practical Guide to Questionnaire Design*. San Francisco: Jossey-Bass, 1983.

Thornton, G. C., and Byham, W. C. *Assessment Centers and Managerial Performance*. New York: Academic Press, 1982.

Thornton, G. C. *Assessment Centers in Human Resource Management*. Reading, Mass.: Addison-Wesley, 1992.

Vella, J. *Learning to Listen, Learning to Teach: The Power of Dialogue in Educating Adults*. San Francisco: Jossey-Bass, 1994.

Verduin, J. R., Jr., and Clark, T. A. *Distance Education: The Foundations of Effective Practice*. San Francisco: Jossey-Bass, 1991.

Watkins, B. T. "New Tests Expected to Bring Dramatic Changes in the Way Prospective Teachers are Assessed." *The Chronicle of Higher Education*, Nov. 9, 1988.

Wlodkowski, R. J. *Enhancing Adult Motivation to Learn*. San Francisco: Jossey-Bass, 1985.

Index

Performance assessment; Question-
naires
Needs assessment reports, 206–211; with
individual assessment, 99–100
Needs assessment strategy, 6; complexity
of, 53–54; scope of, 41–42
Needs assessment teams, 7, 111–114
Nominal group process, 129–132
Nowlen, P. M., 8, 10, 62, 119, 227
Nursing, 1, 17, 67–68

O

Objectives: learning, 212–213, 231; of
needs assessment, 27–28, 29
Observation: for evaluation, 234; of per-
formance, 110–111, 183–189
Office of Continuing Professional Educa-
tion, 13, 70, 83, 197
Office of Strategic Services, 195
Opinion Research Corporation, 8

P

Participants: with Delphi method, 133;
in focus groups, 127- 128; needs
assessment, 102–103, 104–107; in
nominal groups, 131–132; potential
program, 103–104. See also Key informants
Pennington, F. C., 3
The Pennsylvania State University:
assessment centers at, 196–197; self-
assessment projects of, 13–14, 99–100
Performance abilities: as area for assessment, 73–74, 79–81; measuring learning of, 230; and setting standards,
89–90
Performance assessment, 177–178, 197;
at assessment centers, 195–197; observation for, 110–111, 183–189; of
products, 178–183; simulations for,
189–195
Performance observation, 110–111,
183–189
Performance simulations, 189–191,
194–195; formats for, 191–194
Physicians, 21
Pilot testing, of surveys, 146
Planning: committees for, 258–259; integrating needs assessment into,
199–200, 219–220; strategic, 259; for
surveys, 146; using results of evaluation, 222; without needs assessment, 1

Pollack, L. E., 23, 96, 99, 210
Population: and scope of needs assessment, 38–39; secondary, 105; selecting, for assessment, 102–107; total,
106; underserved, 32–33. See also Participants; Target population
Practice description, 67–68
Priorities, in continuing education,
63–66
Products of performance, review of,
178–183
Program evaluation. See Evaluation
Programs: delivery mode for, 34–35;
determining content of, 14–16; development of, 225, 261–263; integrating
needs assessment into planning of,
199–200, 219–220; potential participants in, 103–104; without needs
assessment, 1. See also Educational
activities
Psychologists, 96

Q

Queeney, D. S., 14, 16, 17, 21, 62, 67, 79,
81, 83, 86, 90, 210
Questionnaires, 154–166; cover letter
with, 154–155; with Delphi method,
132, 134–135; distribution and return
of, 158–160; for evaluation, 232–233;
follow-up with, 161–164; media,
164–166; outline for, 156–158; questions for, 147–154; time factors with,
160–161
Questions: branching, 151–152; close-
ended and open-ended, 147–149; for
evaluation, 238; for focus groups,
125–126; guidelines for designing,
150–154; for immediate evaluation,
241; for key informants, 137–139;
matrix format for, 152–153; with
nominal group process, 130

R

RAND Corporation, 132
Real estate agents, 89
Records: analysis of, 110; performance
assessment of, 178–183
Reports. See Needs assessment reports;
Self-reports
Resources: and complexity, 56; for group
versus individual assessment, 98–99;
for needs assessment, 48–53, 58–59;

for performance simulations, 189–190; and selection of method, 108

Response rates: for follow-up evaluations, 243; for surveys, 144

Rossett, A., 248

S

Safman, P., 24

Samples: convenience, 106–107; for group assessment, 101–102; random, 106; for surveys, 144

Scheduling: of interviews, 172; preferences in, 16, 35–36

Schein, E., 79

Schenke, A., 109

Schmerbeck, F. A., 8

Schön, D. A., 56, 82

Scope: and complexity, 54–55, 57; of evaluation, 228–229; of needs assessment, 37–43

Secondary data, 48–49, 111

Secondary population, 105

Self-assessment, 17, 96, 99–100

Self-evaluation measures, 110

Self-reports, 117–123; for evaluation, 233; limitations of, 13–14

Shimberg, B. S., 23

Shuman, S. B., 16, 17, 99, 210

Simon, R. I., 109

Simpson, E. L., 132

Simulations, 111; for evaluation, 234–235; performance, 189–195

Skills: as area for assessment, 73–74, 77–79; measuring learning of, 230; and setting standards, 89–90

Sleezer, C. M., 27, 82, 93, 94, 199

Smutz, W. D., 14, 16, 17, 23, 67, 79, 81, 83, 96, 99, 210

Staff, 17, 68, 100, 202

Standards: and at-risk indicators, 88; deviations from, 87; and maintenance requirements, 88–89; for needs,

86–90; for performance observations, 187

Stern, M. R., 11

Sudman, S., 175

Supervisor evaluations, 139–141

Support personnel, for needs assessment, 51–52

Support services, for needs assessment, 52

Surveys, 110, 143–147, 175; questions for, 147–154. *See also* interviews; Questionnaires

Swanson, R. A., 93

T

Target population: aspects of, 43–47; for educational activities, 33–34, 102–103; and scope, 38–39; and selecting content area, 70; and selecting participants, 104–107; and setting standards, 89. *See also* Population

Task forces, 109

Tests: pilot, 146; pre- and post-, 236–237

Thornton, G. C., 177, 191, 195

Training: of interviewers, 170–172; of performance observers, 188

Trigger films, 194

V

Van de Ven, A. H., 133

Vance, R., 23, 96, 99, 210

Vella, J., 7

Verduin, J. R., Jr., 11, 16, 35

Veterinarians, 22

Videotapes, for performance observation, 184–185, 189

W

W. K. Kellogg Foundation, 197

Wants, 3–4

Wlodkowski, R. J., 8, 16

Work samples, analysis of, 110